THE IDEA OF WORLD LITERATURE

THE
IDEA
of
WORLD
LITERATURE

HISTORY & PEDAGOGICAL
PRACTICE

JOHN PIZER

LOUISIANA STATE UNIVERSITY PRESS

BATON ROUGE

Published by Louisiana State University Press
Copyright © 2006 by Louisiana State University Press
All rights reserved
Manufactured in the United States of America
First printing

DESIGNER: Michelle A. Garrod
TYPEFACE: Adobe Garamond Pro
PRINTER AND BINDER: Edwards Brothers, Inc.

LIBRARY OF CONGRESS CATALOGING-IN-PUBLICATION DATA

Pizer, John David.
　　The idea of world literature : history and pedagogical practice / John Pizer.
　　　　p. cm.
　　Includes bibliographical references and index.
　　ISBN 0-8071-3119-9 (alk. paper)
　　　1. Literature—Study and teaching. I. Title.
PN59.P55 2006
807.1—dc22

　　　　　　　　　　　　　　　　　　　　　　　　　　　　2005012469

The paper in this book meets the guidelines for permanence and durability of the Committee
on Production Guidelines for Book Longevity of the Council on Library Resources. ♾

*This book is dedicated to the memory of my father,
Dr. Marvin I. Pizer (1915–2003), a scholar
and practitioner of medicine.*

Contents

Acknowledgments

THIS BOOK CONTAINS MATERIAL from two previously published articles: "Goethe's 'World Literature' Paradigm and Contemporary Cultural Globalization," *Comparative Literature* 52 (2000): 213–27, and "Heine's Unique Relationship to Goethe's *Weltliteratur* Paradigm," *Heine-Jahrbuch* 41 (2002): 18–36. I would like to thank the editors of these two journals, George E. Rowe and Joseph A. Kruse, respectively, for their permission to reprint.

Many colleagues at Louisiana State University have been helpful and encouraging while I composed this book, but I would particularly like to thank Bainard Cowan, who helped me put together the one-year sequence in World Literature now offered at LSU. I am also obliged to Emily Batinski, Chair of the Department of Foreign Languages and Literatures at LSU, who has consistently granted me a course release each spring from my traditional German language and literature obligations so I could offer my "Introduction to Modern World Literature" classes, and to Malcolm Richardson, former Chair of the Department of English, for initially allowing me to teach the course for his department. I also want to recognize the students in my Fall 2002 and Fall 2003 "Introduction to Modern World Literature" courses, who were the initial participants in my pedagogical experiment. I would like to thank Candis LaPrade, Literary Studies Editor at LSU Press, for her strong support and consistently quick work; Derik Shelor, who did a fine job with the copy editing; and Cynthia

Williams, Manuscript Editor at LSU Press, for her helpful advice during the galley proof stage of the manuscript. Thanks are also due to Erin Breaux for her proofreading. I also appreciate the advice of many scholars and friends outside Baton Rouge, but would like particularly to acknowledge David Damrosch, Azade Seyhan, Adrian Del Caro, Gail Finney, Jeffrey Sammons, Emily Apter, and Todd Kontje, as well as the manuscript's anonymous readers. I would like to thank the College of Arts and Sciences at LSU for granting me a sabbatical leave in the spring of 2002, which greatly facilitated my work on this book. As always, I appreciate the love and support of my wife, Patricia, and daughter, Jasmin, and, in Los Angeles, my mother, Roselle Pizer, and sister, Liz Quicksilver, and her family.

Unless otherwise indicated, all translations in this book are my own.

Introduction

What Is *Weltliteratur* and Why Teach It in a World Literature in English Translation Course?

A poet, thrown into the international bouillabaisse where, if anything can be distinguished at all, it is only lumps of overboiled fish and shrimp, suddenly discovers that he sits firmly in his province, his town, his countryside, and begins to bless it.

CZESLAW MILOSZ, *Road-Side Dog*

IN A MISCELLANEOUS PIECE published in the German Comparative Literature journal *Arcadia* in 1987 and entitled "'Weltliteratur' zuerst bei Wieland" ("World Literature" First Appeared in Wieland), Hans-J. Weitz announced his discovery that Johann Wolfgang von Goethe, contrary to popular belief, was not the first author to use the term *Weltliteratur*. It was another figure associated with Weimar Classicism, Christoph Martin Wieland, who seems to have first employed the expression in handwritten notes to a previously unknown copy of his translation of Horace's letters. Included in Weitz's piece is a facsimile of the fragment of the copy containing the handwritten word "Weltliteratur." Because the copy is undated, Weitz cannot precisely determine when Wieland provided German letters its first enactment of the expression. However, Wieland died in 1813, so his handwritten note had to have preceded Goethe's first employment of the term in 1827. Most of Weitz's three-page miscellany is devoted to outlining how the discovery of the Wieland manuscript came about, the context in which the term is used, and differences between this context and that of Goethe's initial instantiation of Weltliteratur; while Wieland considers only world literature at the time of Horace, Goethe uses the term to signify a hoped-for contemporary concert of all nations, an epochal formation still in the process of being constituted.[1]

Certainly, Weitz's discovery cannot be categorized as earth-shattering. Indeed, I believe it is safe to say that many, if not most, students and even teachers of World Literature in English Translation courses in American universities and colleges will ask themselves why this bit of archival research was even published. What difference does it make if Wieland preceded Goethe in using the German term for "world literature?" Is not world literature simply the literature of the world in its entirety, the *belles lettres* of all corners of the globe, chronologically encompassing all of history, from *Gilgamesh* to cyberpunk? Certainly, "world literature" can be understood in this comprehensive sense, and a not insignificant number of scholars have undertaken the enormous task of writing its history. In his review essay "Writing Histories of World Literature," J. C. Brandt Corstius has outlined the limitations of such enterprises: they are inevitably unbalanced with respect to representing the output of individual nations, they are almost always Eurocentric, and they necessarily, if unknowingly, repeat the findings of previous scholars.[2]

Whatever its drawbacks, the present study does not propose to offer yet another history of the sort analyzed by Corstius. Instead, it will chronicle the "adventures of a concept," to borrow from the title of Martin Jay's book on "Totality" as a historically developed paradigm in the previous century.[3] As the publication of Weitz's study indicates, Weltliteratur ("world literature") is not a self-understood signifier. It denotes a concept with its own specific genealogy, its unique and circumscribed historical development, a development not heretofore comprehensively explored.[4] To be sure, much has been written on world literature as a discursive paradigm. Most of this research has been generated in Germany, and few German literary scholars would fail to immediately grasp the historical significance of Weitz's finding. A not insignificant number of English-language writers and teachers, such as Homi K. Bhabha and Sarah Lawall, have shown a keen interest in world literature as a concept as well, and I am indebted to their pioneering work in this field. The volume *No Small World: Visions and Revisions of World Literature* opens with a reference to Goethe's putative coining of the term in 1827,[5] and many teachers of World Literature in English Translation courses (to whom *No Small World* is addressed) are aware that world literature has a discrete lineage as a paradigm.

Because Wieland's use of the word Weltliteratur first became public knowledge in 1987 and, at any rate, refers only to the works of antiquity, our exploration of the term will begin in 1827, when Goethe first employed it. To be sure, as we will see, public and even scholarly awareness of Goethe's thoughts on the matter became widespread only after 1836, when the *Gespräche mit Goethe* (*Conversations with Goethe*) were published. Nevertheless, his earliest comments have consistently shaped debate and research on Weltliteratur, particularly in Germany. Given the centrality of German discussions of this expression as a discrete critical concept quite distinct from the creative literary output of the entire globe,[6] I will henceforth use the German term to designate any such self-aware critical discussions and the English "world literature" to refer to the notion as understood by the scholars critiqued by Corstius and, indeed, by most individuals, as the comprehensive signifier for all creative writing produced at all times by all peoples, even when popular and often scholarly imagination reduces its proportions to manageable dimensions through recourse to such signifiers as "great books" and "canonic literature." I will capitalize the term—"World Literature"—when referring to it as an academic subject. Traditionally, of course, such postulates have, in most instances if sometimes unconsciously, achieved this desired diminution through a tacit equation of "world literature" with the *belles lettres* of Europe and North America.

This book examines the development of Weltliteratur as a discursive concept in Germany and in its various pedagogical manifestations, as "World Literature," in the United States. In undertaking this endeavor, I am not exclusively motivated by the desire to fill a critical gap in literary history, to set a largely neglected historical record straight. What I hope to achieve is also practical, that is to say, directly related to classroom praxis in World Literature in English Translation courses. With respect to curriculum, there is no question that great strides have been made in the anthologies used in these classes. World Literature in English Translation textbooks have truly begun to represent the writing of women and ethnic minorities, as well as of authors from Asia, Africa, and Latin America.[7] While this new diversity is a welcome addition to the World Literature curriculum, I believe it must be supplemented by a metatheoretical dimension. That is to say, students in introductory World Literature courses should gain a knowledge of the history of Weltliteratur itself, an overview of the development of this paradigm from Goethe to the present day. I view my book as a means by which those who teach World Literature can obtain this knowledge. I hope such faculty will find my book useful in providing background information and teaching tips for their introductory World Literature courses.

At this point, most readers of this study will undoubtedly raise an entirely understandable objection. Given the enormous expansion of the range of material World Literature instructors are being asked to cover in this new century, how can one justify taking precious time away from actually discussing the imaginative writing itself in order to explore the Weltliteratur paradigm in its historical dimensions? To begin to answer this question, we must begin by rehearsing some of the obvious intellectual and cultural conditions informing our current age and, thereby, the perspectives of our students. The dominant catchword used to describe the contemporary human condition is "globalization," and the term used to connote the overall status of world culture under the sign of globalization is "transnationalism." Certainly, transnational literature written by bilingual and bicultural authors in the twentieth and twenty-first centuries, by writers who, from economically and/or politically induced exile, are creating contemporary works that call into question the very notion of discrete "national" literatures, is helping to redefine the very principle of world literature. That is to say, transnational literature is now considered world literature because it is thematically, culturally, and even linguistically the product of multiple cultures, and cannot be included in nationally based canons; it is not French, German, or Spanish literature. In *Writing Outside the Nation,* Azade Seyhan demonstrates that such current exilic work complexly sustains cultural memory through a dialectic literary geography which articulates life creatively experienced in the interstice between the lost homeland and the locus(es) of exile.[8] This new literary movement, which can be distinguished from traditional exilic writing in which authors attempted to efface—or at least transcend—their original motherland/fatherland contexts, is a major force today and should also be given attention in World Literature in English Translation courses.

However, there are obvious negative aspects with respect to cultural (and, for that matter, socioeconomic and political) globalization. One is its trend toward homogeneity. When American students consider the contemporary world outside their borders, or even when they venture into this external world through travel or surfing through foreign Web sites, it is only a slight exaggeration to say that what the inattentive among them see, hear, and experience is: America. This perception is generally interrupted only when acts of terror committed by foreigners take place. When such events occur, the Other emerges as a figure indeed marked by radical alterity, but precisely thereby as evocative of violence and malevolence, someone to be dreaded, despised, and feared. Such perceptions are still widespread in the wake of the atrocities committed on September 11, 2001. Otherwise, American values, American businesses, the English/American language, American popular culture, and American architecture have become so predominant, at least superficially, across most of the globe that even the American eager to experience and appreciate cultural diversity, to know the "Other" *as* other,[9] generally must make substantial efforts, such as gaining a genuine knowledge of foreign languages.[10] This is, of course, not to say that American students have more *inherent* difficulty than students in other countries in comprehending cultures other than their own. However, given what William Paulson terms "the specter of worldwide cultural homogenization in the form of American-style entertainment and consumerism,"[11] it is inevitable that the cultural filter blocking perception of what has lain, and still lies, outside this homogenization is particularly strong at its source. Even translations of foreign works do not always help American students to overcome this distorting influence caused by American linguistic and cultural dominance. Lawrence Venuti has noted that many translations of foreign works into English simply conform to American stereotypes concerning the culture of the translated language, and a vastly greater number of works are translated *from* English than *into* English, reflecting the dominance of Anglo-American culture abroad *and* at home.[12]

What does all this have to do with Weltliteratur and the teaching of Weltliteratur in World Literature in English Translation classes? Certainly, the link between world literature and complaints of dawning linguistic/cultural homogeneity are not new. Horst Steinmetz has cited Erich Auerbach's lamentations in the essay "Philologie der Weltliteratur" ("Philology and Weltliteratur," 1952) that a creeping uniformity of previously diverse "life worlds" is to be associated with the development of the litera-ture of the world at mid-twentieth century, and we will return to Auerbach's misgivings later. Steinmetz also cites Karl Vossler, who already in 1918 spoke of an impending age marked by "world literary barbarism" and caused by the predominance of trivial literature throughout civilization; this putative reversion to cultural primitivism makes it a matter of indifference whether one's verbal snippets are enunciated in German, French, or another lan-guage. Steinmetz dismisses such fears that world literature is or will be marked by monolingualism and monotony,[13] but he wrote his own article on "Weltliteratur" in 1985, before the collapse of European Communism and the concomitant rise of a globalization dominated in all its particulars by the United States. In order to understand how a historically grounded knowledge of Weltliteratur can productively counter a possible feeling of pedagogic helplessness in the face of such ever-increasing uniformity, I would like to consider the quote from Czeslaw Milosz that prefaces this introduction: "A poet, thrown into the international bouillabaisse where, if anything can be distinguished at all, it is only lumps of overboiled fish and shrimp, suddenly discovers that he sits firmly in his province, his town, his countryside, and begins to bless it." Though Milosz refers to "the specific character of Polish poetry" in a different aphorism on the same page of *Road-Side Dog*,[14] it is clear that his prescribed refuge from the culinary equivalent of Vossler's trivialized, fragmented world literary barbaric mishmash is a domain the following study will consistently refer to as the subnational. This term is almost a synonym for "regional," but I find it more broadly signifies all those sociocultural activities within a country that are more locally than nationally inflected, more reflective of tribal (in that term's expanded definition) than stateist consciousness. As such, the term is useful as a pendant to "transnational," reflective of *supra*stateist interests and domains.

It is my thesis that one can only recuperate cultural memory in transnational literature by focusing on the discrete subnational elements in works belonging to this movement; this circumstance is rendered evident through a close reading of Seyhan's own reading of Maxine Hong Kingston, Oscar Hijuelos, Eva Hoffman, Rafik Schami, and the other transnational authors who come under her critical gaze. My own reading of Schami's *Erzähler der Nacht* (*Damascus Nights*, 1989; trans. 1993) in the final chapter of this book will, I hope, illustrate this point. Even more importantly, Goethe's own Weltliteratur paradigm is rooted in a subnational-transnational dialectic informed both by his own broad critical and scientific predilections and by Germany's historical-political environment in the 1820s and 1830s, when his ruminations on Weltliteratur came into being. Scholars of Weltliteratur, even those whose focus is Goethe, rarely consider this circumstance. By making an articulation of this dialectic the consistent thread running through the course of this book, the desideratum of an awareness of Goethean Weltliteratur in World Literature in English Translation courses will become evident. For Goethe's critical and creative grounding in what Milosz refers to as the poet's "province," "town," and "countryside," and what Mikhail Bakhtin, citing Goethe, consistently refers to in his reading of this writer as "Lokalität," will allow a subnational-transnational (the latter term understood here in its broad, nonchronologically restricted sense, as universal) reading and teaching of World Literature to be suggested, a praxis designed to help such literature emerge in its genuine linguistic/cultural alterity. This focus will also help to show how and where traditional "great works"–based approaches to teaching World Literature in English Translation courses went wrong, an insight that will prove helpful to both student and teacher. With respect to the subnational-transnational (or universal) dialectic in Goethe's oeuvre, Bakhtin was probably his most insightful reader, and he will therefore constitute one of this book's major critical voices.

Regarding the reading of world literature with a feel for its linguistic diversity and alterity,[15] a major proviso must be introduced. One cannot, of course, appreciate the subtlest linguistic nuances of a work of literature read in translation, and teachers of introductory World Literature in English Translation courses populated by generally monolingual Americans must recognize this circumstance, regardless of how metatheoretically informed the pedagogical praxis grounding these courses may be. However, an understanding of Goethe's own translation theory and how it relates to his Weltliteratur paradigm will at least help to ameliorate the limitations of reading in translation, assist in providing the students an *appreciation* for linguistic diversity and alterity, and, just possibly, inspire some of them to study foreign languages. We will explore Goethe's translation theory in the following chapter, but a few remarks are in order here. Goethe's most significant pronouncements on translation are to be found in his extensive notes to the poetic cycle *West-östlicher Divan* (*The West-Eastern Divan*, 1819). The poetic portion of this work constitutes Goethe's most seminal creative engagement with Weltliteratur, an attempt to consciously mingle his European voice with the Asian voice of the fourteenth-century Persian poet Hafiz at least partly in order to bring about the "*great meeting . . . of all nations*" Weitz defined as Goethe's Weltliteratur ideal.[16] In a note entitled "Übersetzungen" (Translations), Goethe proclaims that the German comes closer to the Orient through contemporary translations, necessitating an elucidation of the three different modes of the rendering of foreign text into mother tongue. The first kind makes us broadly aware of the foreign land in a manner familiar to us ("in unserm eigenen Sinne"). Stylistically, simple prose is most suited to this mode because it neutralizes the foreign work's distinct particularities and acquaints us with what is magnificent in the foreign through the filter of our own national domesticity, without our even being aware that we are thereby being elevated (3:554).[17] We might associate this mode with the traditional telos and practice of World Literature in English Translation courses; at a certain cost, the beginning students in these courses are made to feel comfortable as they engage in what is probably their first real hermeneutic dialogue with the foreign world. The fact that the vast majority of such courses are taught in English departments by instructors and professors whose primary expertise is in Anglo- and/or American literature, or at least in literature of the English-speaking world, inevitably helps provide a filter that will ameliorate the shock of the foreign and lift the student into an exotic, unknown domain almost without his/her cognizance of this experience.

In Goethe's view, and in my own, this is not a bad thing; the first translation model/the traditional World Literature in English Translation course can lead to a positive, enriching, albeit somewhat unconscious experience. However, it is worth considering what Goethe has to say about the other translation genres. The second is termed "parodistic." Without direct explanation, Goethe introduces this mode as an epoch ("Epoche"); "a second epoch follows" the first (3:555). Goethe is implicitly indicating that a translator undergoes phases in honing his craft. Goethe's essay "Einfache Nachahmung der Natur, Manier, Stil" ("Simple Imitation of Nature, Manner, Style," 1789) also outlined a tripartite process of development, in this case for the artist. An artist must learn to simply imitate nature before he can achieve his own distinctly expressive manner, which occurs in this second stage. At the third level, "style," the artist is able to creatively capture the inner essence of the object he is representing (13:66–71). Like the artist at the level of manner, the translator in the "second epoch" does not bring out the immanent nature of the foreign object/text, but injects and brings to the fore his own personal proclivities.[18] The "parodistic" translator attempts to transport himself into the circumstances of the foreign but is really only at pains to appropriate the foreign sensibility and re-represent it with his own sensibility (3:555). According to Hans-Georg Gadamer, whose view of Weltliteratur will be discussed in chapter three, this subjective distortion is an inevitable and inherent element in the hermeneutic dialogue,[19] and making students conscious of the fact that we all bring to bear a certain preconditioned attitude toward literature formed by our own life circumstances, by our discrete existence in history, and by our national affiliation(s) is a valuable practice in teaching any literature, but especially in World Literature classes, where the average student's ignorance of the languages and cultures outside the Anglo-American domain dramatically elevates the distortions of which Gadamer speaks.

The last and "highest" phase in Goethe's translation model occurs when the translator wishes to make original and translation perfectly identical, so that the one can be validly interchanged with the other.[20] This mode generally finds resistance on the part of the reading public, for the translator who so strongly identifies with the original essentially gives up the originality ("Originialität") of his own country. Ultimately, however, this mode of translation is of greatest value to the public and its mother tongue, for the unique rhythms and meters in the foreign idiom that the translator attempts to approximate, at first so strange and unappealing to mass taste, ultimately expands the variety, the suppleness of the mother tongue (3:555–56). This phase is similar to "style" in the domain of art; in both cases, the original object/language is represented in its unique, immanent essence. Teachers of World Literature in English

Translation will not, in most cases, be acquainted with the innate linguistic and cultural nuances of the foreign works they are teaching. Thus, those who would approximate Goethe's third level of translation in the World Literature classroom will have an impossible task unless they are remarkably multilingual. However, guest lectures by experts in various foreign languages and literatures on how the discrete properties of these tongues shape the form and content of the works under consideration will be helpful here.

In 1986, the *Yearbook of Comparative and General Literature* published a translation of Ernst Elster's influential essay "Weltlitteratur und Literaturvergleichung" ("World Literature and Comparative Literature," 1901),[21] a work to which we will devote some attention in the third chapter. In his elaborate response to this essay, entitled "The Difference of Eight Decades: World Literature and the Demise of National Literatures," Claus Clüver takes issue with Elster's nationally oriented perspective. Clüver correctly notes that "national literature" can no longer be regarded as a self-understood concept, but must be seen as "a historical construct," a way of treating literary texts "in the light of a specific dominant ideology."[22] Alternative taxonomies must respond to contemporary paradigms, through which nation-based categorizations are being called into question. Clüver asserts that the decline of "national literature" as a valid taxonomic principle must bring the extinction of Comparative Literature in its train, since comparatists traditionally compare texts from a national basis: works of "German Literature" are compared to works of "French Literature," etc. Clüver treats Comparative Literature's putatively shaky status as "another symptom of the progress of *Weltliteratur*" and concludes his article as follows: "But given the new paradigm and the expanded horizons of literary studies, the mental habits fostered through what used to be called Comparative Literature should protect us from the sense of orthodoxy if not superiority displayed by some national philologists in Elster's time: they should enable us to appreciate that there are other ways of thinking about and using the texts that we call 'literature.'"[23] Certainly, contemporary notions of the transnational constitute a new way of thinking about literature. However, if the "progress of *Weltliteratur*" to which Clüver refers is to be a positive development in the *teaching* of world literature, then its progress from its Goethean beginning to the present day must be a matter of which both student and instructor are aware. For a historically informed insight into Weltliteratur as grounded in the subnational-transnational dialectic will facilitate the most comprehensive possible appreciation of world literature. Goethe's concept of Weltliteratur encompasses both the universal and the particular, and an acquaintance with Weltliteratur will help students develop the ability to identify and appreciate culturally specific, diverse elements of literary works while still recognizing the universally human aspects that first enable and inspire genuine hermeneutic engagement.

It is my hope that this book will help facilitate such an enabling process. The chapter immediately following this introduction focuses on Goethe's articulation of the paradigm. Although Wieland perhaps first coined the term (if it did not appear even earlier in the now lost or forgotten manuscript of a more obscure German writer[24]), Goethe's oeuvre constitutes the concept's true locus of origin; his scattered remarks were foundational for subsequent critical discussion and continue to be seminal for virtually all engagements with Weltliteratur (again as opposed simply to "world literature") up to the present day. The circumstance that Goethe's Weltliteratur adumbrations are scattered throughout his later oeuvre,[25] so that the concept is never the object of a sustained discussion on Goethe's part, has contributed to the difficulties and disagreements on what he intended precisely to signify with the term, and my own interpretation will not and should not end these debates. However, by placing these remarks in the broad historical context of Goethe's own time, an essential element in my project of writing a *history* of Weltliteratur but one that has received heretofore only tangential treatment, I hope to provide a productive framework for future theoretical discussions and for the engagement of the paradigm in the World Literature classroom.

Some of Goethe's views are self-evident; he defined Weltliteratur as a dawning epoch of useful interchange between authors and critics in foreign lands, an interchange facilitated by recent improvements in book and journal production, communication technologies, and transportation, in his day. However, this circumstance already raises a significant question; because the improvements Goethe witnessed were restricted to Europe, and because his descriptions of this expanding literary interchange among nations considered only this continent, is Goethean Weltliteratur "Eurocentric?" There is no unanimity of critical views on this point, but exploring the nuances of this issue is fundamental to how we can and should engage Weltliteratur in today's World Literature classroom, where the curriculum has expanded beyond the traditional European and American pantheons. Because Goethe viewed Weltliteratur as constellated through a national-international dialogue, what allows us to regard it as inscribed by a subnational-transnational dialectic? In articulating an answer to this question, an answer which will principally engage the voice of Bakhtin as a unique reader of Goethe, surprising parallels—parallels highly relevant to World Literature's pedagogical praxis—will emerge between the European geopolitics of the mature Goethe's age and the broader-scale "globalization" that characterizes our own.

This second chapter will conclude with a brief consideration of the role played by the German Romantics in the history of Weltliteratur. Conventional literary periodization makes even such a fleeting consideration implausible; most critics equate the end of Romanticism with Goethe's death in 1832, and because his principle adumbrations concerning Weltliteratur were not published until 1836 and after, the Romantics would not have responded to the concept as such. As Steinmetz has noted, the Romantics intensified the focus on *national* attributes in literary works, a focus which began in the second half of the eighteenth century, through a consistent critical recourse to the primal, mystified origins of diverse populaces, in spite of the international character of their general poetic theories.[26] If one were to pay attention solely to this fact, one would have to conclude that German Romanticism existed prior to (or at least in ignorance of) the commencement of Weltliteratur's age. But according to Ernst Behler, Friedrich Schlegel, early German Romanticism's principal literary theorist, was the first to recognize that in the modern age "a history of literature could not be carried out on the basis of a separate national literature. If the spirit of poetry is to be investigated in all its possible expressions, a national literature is too limited for this task." Though Behler goes on to note that "Schlegel's literary history is also not outright a world literature" because in spite of his forays into Sanskrit and other non-European literatures he is Eurocentric in his "range of vision,"[27] Schlegel's seminal comparatism helped *enable* a Weltliteratur dynamic in subsequent compositions of literary history.[28] Perhaps more importantly for our purposes, the Germanist Andreas Huyssen established in 1969 a unique linkage in early German Romanticism between a translation theory quite distinct from Goethe's and an idealistic and equally singular conception of Weltliteratur,[29] and chapter two will examine this liaison.

Given the circumstance that Goethe's Weltliteratur is connected to increased transnational communication and interchange, the question of agency is raised. A central postulate of chapter three is that Heinrich Heine was the *only* mediator of Weltliteratur *as Goethe understood it* to have received international recognition, even though Heine never directly discussed the concept. While chapter two will establish affiliations between the technological/cultural/political atmosphere of Goethe's age and our own, chapter three, in highlighting Heine's unique role as an agent of Goethean Weltliteratur, underscores the differences. Heine's contemporaries in the *Junges Deutschland* (Young Germany) movement were the first intellectuals to critically debate the paradigm, as Goethe's principal remarks on Weltliteratur were initially published after his death and during the fullest flowering of *Junges Deutschland*'s existence. "Young Germany" authors were united, indeed defined, as a cohesive literary movement by their commitment to a unified, liberal Germany, free from the repressions characteristic of the Restoration age from 1815 (the end of the Napoleonic Wars) to the 1830s (a decade when the fight for national unity and greater freedom became quite intense). While Heine's admirers attempted for political reasons to promote Weltliteratur as an ideal, his detractors, through scathing criticism of the concept, ensured its utopian dimension would be buried until after 1945, when Germany's desire to be reaccepted into the world community brought about the paradigm's reemergence. The virulent nationalism of Heine's opponents made literary cosmopolitanism anathema, and their views held sway until the end of World War II. In examining Weltliteratur's status among German-language writers from the end of *Junges Deutschland* through the twentieth century in chapter four, I will touch on relevant works by such well-known figures as Georg Brandes, Ernst Elster, Thomas Mann, Fritz Strich, Erich Auerbach, Hans-Georg Gadamer, and Hans Robert Jauß.

In the late phase of *Junges Deutschland,* Weltliteratur became associated with canonicity and commerce, a circumstance that affected its reception in America. Chapter five focuses on this American reception of Weltliteratur in the nineteenth century, and on the subsequent history of World Literature as a pedagogical domain in this country. The noted New England Transcendentalist Margaret Fuller published her translation of the *Gespräche mit Goethe* as *Conversations with Goethe in the Last Years of his Life* in 1839, and thereby introduced the concept of Weltliteratur into the United States, much as the publication of the German original in 1836 stimulated discussion of the paradigm in Germany at that time. It is possible to see the influence of Goethe as mediated by Fuller in what is perhaps the earliest attempt to articulate a pedagogical ideal of World Literature, Thomas Wentworth Higginson's 1890 essay "A World-Literature." Not coincidentally, Higginson was one of Fuller's earliest biographers. Among the influential early texts for the teaching of World Literature in the United States was Richard Moulton's *World Literature and Its Place in General Culture* (1911), notable for its prescient effort to develop a "cultural studies" approach to this topic in combination with an immanent methodology. Moulton was quite open about the Anglo-American bias informing his praxis. We will also examine the debates on canonicity and "great books" orientations in World Literature pedagogy. This debate was already evident late in the 1950s, when Haskell Block (citing Lionel Trilling's unhappiness with the organizational problems and over-ambitious dimensions of what Trilling termed "so-called World Literature courses") announced in his introduction to the proceedings of a 1959 conference on "The Teaching of World Literature" that "'World Literature' is not a happy term."[30] The culmination of these debates in the substantive inclusion of non-Western works in World Literature in English Translation curricula, a culmination propelled by the late twentieth-century desire that such curricula be informed by the twin ideals of multiculturalism and the recognition of alterity in diverse ethnic populations, constitutes a significant element in this chapter. The vexed issue of the relationship between Comparative Literature and World Literature at American universities and colleges will also be treated.

A key figure in the contemporary pedagogical practice of World Literature in English Translation is Sarah Lawall, and her ideas and influence will also be discussed in this fifth chapter. In her introduction to *Reading World Literature,* she summarized the unique dilemma of this pedagogical domain in America as follows: "Frozen by academic history into the image of a great book list that offers simultaneously the wisdom of the ages and the accumulated experience of societies around the globe, it has not been able to fill either role."[31] In my opinion, introductory World Literature courses *cannot* fill either of these enormously ambitious roles. A genuine immersion into such wisdom and experience can only be attained through a lifetime of committed study. I believe that one of the fundamental desiderata of a World Literature course should be the inculcation of an *appreciation* for the nuances of alterity, of a belief that life and literature outside the United States are inscribed by unique linguistic/cultural matrices perhaps no longer defined at the national level, but capable of being glimpsed through the filter of the subnational-transnational dialectic. At the same time, those universal themes and lessons evident in all great literature, and which first inspire cross-cultural readings, must be emphasized in the World Literature classroom so that students can relate to the texts they read. This dual goal supports the proposition that the Weltliteratur paradigm—which, in its Goethean formulations, underscores the dialectic between the universal and the particular—must be introduced into the curriculum of the World Literature classroom.

In *Writing Outside the Nation,* Seyhan demonstrates how Syrian-German writer Rafik Schami's *Erzähler der Nacht* draws on the Arab world's oral storytelling customs in order to evoke Damascus's now vanished cultural plurivocality. As with her other readings, Seyhan foregrounds the bilingual nature of Schami's novel, highlighting its interweaving of the German language and Arabic nuances, exilic and motherland frames of reference. These elements make *Erzähler der Nacht* a paradigmatic instance of contemporary transnationalism for Seyhan.[32] In the sixth and final chapter, while drawing on Seyhan's reading, I will slightly alter the prism through which she observes the novel. By resolutely articulating

Lokalität in *Erzähler der Nacht* and reinscribing it macrologically into the world, the comprehensively global, as Bakhtin did in the interpretation of Goethe delineated in chapter two, I will show how contemporary transnational works can be productively interpreted and taught through the dialectical filter of Weltliteratur, thus sustaining textual alterity in its discrete particulars and in its plenitude. In so doing, I will have recourse to the work of another Turkish-born American Germanist, Ülker Gökberk. Her examination of "*Ausländerliteratur* between Relativism and Universalism"[33] demonstrates a productive balance between the universal and the particular in highlighting textual diversity, especially in the minority discourse literature in Germany of which Schami's novel is an example. In conjunction with the Germanist and editor Uwe-Michael Gutzschhahn, Schami published a fictional treatment of Goethe entitled *Der geheime Bericht über den Dichter Goethe, der eine Prüfung auf einer arabischen Insel bestand* (The Secret Report on the Poet Goethe, Who Passed a Test on an Arabian Island, 1999). This book, which thematizes Goethe's Weltliteratur paradigm, establishes the basis for a kind of textual reciprocity: I will read Schami through the eyes of Goethe and Goethe through the eyes of Schami.

My experiences in teaching World Literature in a metatheoretical manner will be described in the afterword. In introducing this conclusion, some personal background is in order. I am a professor of German and Comparative Literature. Almost all of my teaching and scholarship has been in the field of Germanics, with occasional comparative undertakings. Teaching a beginning-level World Literature in English Translation course was a new foray for me. At our university, I had the choice of teaching this course through the Honors College or the English Department. I wanted to test my pedagogical theory on the typical population of beginning students because I believe that World Literature courses should provide an early *introduction* to the globe's literature in its broad temporal and cultural diversity. Therefore, I chose to teach World Literature as an English course, and the Department of English at my university was gracious enough to allow me to teach the class as a lower level "Studies in Literary Traditions and Themes" class in the Fall 2002 and 2003 semesters. Despite its large size, the Louisiana State University Department of English had not offered

World Literature classes in recent memory, so it was a calculated risk for this department as well as for myself. The afterword thus presents my class-room experience and practice as I made this unique attempt to introduce a metatheoretical dimension to teaching World Literature. In introducing this dimension, I still attempted to teach world literature *as* literature, paying close attention to artistic elements in the works, but also examining how these elements were informed by the distinct cultural/linguistic nuances grounding their production.[34] I hope my experience can serve as a guide to others who teach this subject.

Some thirty years ago, René Etiemble posed the question "Faut-il réviser la notion de 'Weltliteratur'?" (Do we need to revise the concept of Weltliteratur?). Surveying what he believed to be a universal imbalance in the world literary canons of diverse nations, he proposed a truly cosmo-politan approach to the paradigm. He advocated the training of a new breed of literary "workers" who would be versed in at least one language of the globe's language families instead of possessing a broader knowledge of, for example, German, Romantic, or Slavic languages. Such uniquely educated generalists might attempt a genuinely world literary historical synthesis. Citing Goethe's own admonition that the master reveals him-self in limitation ("Beschränkung"), Etiemble admits his scheme is utopian, perhaps impossible.[35] Perhaps it is also utopian to believe that a metatheoretical approach to teaching World Literature can attune Ameri-can students to the nuances of what is diverse, unique, "other" in both English and non-English language culture while concomitantly enhancing their ability to discern those universally human elements that first enable cross-cultural reading. However, if we observe Goethe's precept on limita-tion by combining a curriculum consisting of a small but culturally and temporally broad corpus of literary works, along with key texts that articulate the principles of Weltliteratur, then I believe our students may master this talent.

The Emergence of *Weltliteratur*
Goethe and the Romantic School

WHEN GOETHE BEGAN TO issue his pronouncements on Weltliteratur in the 1820s, the dreams of a united Germany which had helped stoke the fires of resistance to Napoleon earlier in the nineteenth century were but a distant memory. Germany was not one unified country at this time; unification did not occur until 1871. Instead, it was a loose confederation of largely independent entities, called "Kleinstaaten," or small states. The early German Romantics, referred to by Heine as "The Romantic School," had lost much of their idealism. The Congress of Vienna, convened in 1815 after Napoleon had been conclusively vanquished, resolved to maintain a divided, fragmented Central Europe. Only by preserving the extreme diffusion of political power in this region, it was believed, could European stability be restored. Naturally, German nationalists objected. The fiery Friedrich Ludwig Jahn, better known under his pseudonym "Turnvater Jahn," caused quite a stir in the Austrian capital when he showed up to press the cause of a united German state. However, astonishment at his antics turned into bemused contempt, and nationalist fervor was effectively held in check until the 1830s, when the Young Germany movement arose. The absence of political unity in Goethe's homeland occurred in concert with a renewed spirit of cosmopolitanism in Europe and advances in communicative media and transportation infrastructures, as well as increased translation activity.

During the Restoration age, there was a fascination among intellectuals and journalists that the written word could be transmitted to all corners of Western Europe with relative immediacy. Censorship became strict during this politically repressive period, but censors themselves were frequently incompetent. They often were unable to decipher thinly veiled dissent, and not infrequently lacked the capacity to contend with technological advances enabling the rapid spread of the printed word. Perhaps this is why Prince Clemens von Metternich himself, primary author of the restoration measures at the Congress of Vienna, was rather pessimistic about the long-term sustainability of the Restoration regimes. The improvements in publishing technologies and transportation conditions led to expanded international dialogue and literary reception on the continent. Such circumstances provided the perfect intellectual atmosphere for the emergence of Weltliteratur. As Goethe himself noted in 1830, the validity of speaking of a universal "Weltliteratur" was enabled by the fact that all (European) nations, shaken by war and then left to their own devices, realized that they had already adopted foreign influences. This led to a desire for greater contact with one's neighbors, for a free exchange of ideas (14:934).

Nationalist passions and ethnic enmities did not much concern the worthies who assembled at the Congress of Vienna. The term "Restoration" to describe this epoch from 1815 to the 1830s is apt. Those convened in Austria's capital essentially wanted to return to prerevolutionary political stability, to a monarchic system of checks and balances where popular sentiments held little significance. Hagen Schulze characterizes this epoch as "the last time in the history of Europe that statesmen were in a position to pursue a rational policy that balanced the interests of all the parties and kept the peace without taking account of the emotions of the masses and the hatred of one people for another."[1] Though nothing equivalent in scale to the Congress of Vienna took place when the Soviet Empire collapsed in the late 1980s and early 1990s and what was then termed a "new world order" emerged, European and American politicians also believed that they could make rational assumptions concerning post-Soviet behavior in Europe, assumptions which also failed to take ethnic sentiments into account. As we now know, these surmises that popular feelings would be governed by economic self-interest rather than ethnic pride were far more disastrous, and far more *immediately* disastrous, than the geopolitical calculations made in 1815. In the twenty-first century, globalized culture and globalized economics intersect with tribal solidarities to which the world's peoples seem to be clinging with ever greater tenacity, at least partly *in reaction* to globalization and a concomitant loss of distinct identity.[2] This is why the subnational-transnational dialectic adumbrated in the introduction, a dialectic which grounds Goethe's Weltliteratur paradigm, is relevant in considering the state of world literature today, as well as in dealing with how world literature and Weltliteratur should be addressed in the World Literature classroom.

Of course, there are dangers in exaggerating the parallels between the political/cultural milieu of the *Goethezeit* and that of our own age. In considering the potential of a universal idea of the social, which he makes the central element in his analysis of contemporary globalization, Martin Albrow has reflected on Goethe's Weltliteratur concept. He stresses Goethe's optimism that the tension between universalist and nationalist tendencies in his day could be productively and creatively harnessed. Albrow sees two central ideas at work in Weltliteratur as Goethe conceived it. One is that the diverse forms of human existence evident in national literatures could be made reciprocally beneficial through a world literary dialogue. This dialogue would bring to life the second central Weltliteratur ideal, a universal striving toward mutual goals. Albrow does not perceive such optimism in the current global age. While Goethe associated Weltliteratur with the unlimited potential of human interaction, the contemporary concept of globalization underscores the circumstance that globalism *limits* our actions. The other major difference between globalization today and how Goethe envisioned it in his Weltliteratur paradigm is one of dimensions. While Goethe stressed the interaction of social groups, whether nationally or internationally oriented, globalization in the current age constitutes the frame for *all* social relationships, in Albrow's view.[3] Naturally, this circumstance inevitably lessens our awareness of, and appreciation for, social and cultural alterity. The circumstance that Goethe and his age were unencumbered by this problem makes the adroit consideration of Weltliteratur all the more potentially efficacious today.

Goethe's Weltliteratur concept attained popularity in Europe in the early nineteenth century not simply because a cosmopolitan political climate and technological improvements at that time created a fertile ground. Goethe's own enormous political stature was equally important in establishing a receptive audience. Goethe first gained fame in Europe with the epistolary novel *Die Leiden des jungen Werther* (*The Sorrows of Young Werther,* 1774). Chafing under the perceived cold rationality equated by many with the dominant Enlightenment philosophy in the late eighteenth century, young people in Western Europe were enthralled by this tale of star-crossed passion leading to the title hero's suicide. Indeed, many young men followed Werther's fatal example, and Napoleon always kept a copy of the novel with him on his travels. Though none of his subsequent works matched this early popularity, Goethe enjoyed even greater prestige among Europe's artists, intellectuals, and nobility later in life, when he resided in Weimar. British travelers sought an audience with Goethe there in particularly large numbers, and this personal intercourse was quite beneficial for the furtherance of Weltliteratur as a mode of cosmopolitan interchange.[4] Though Goethe's remarks on Weltliteratur are scattered throughout his correspondence, essays, and in the published conversations with Eckermann, a core motivating factor links them all: the desire for a productive and peaceful coexistence among the nations of Europe after the divisive and destructive Napoleonic Wars. Such fraternal yearning reached beyond Europe, and helped spur the composition of the *West-östlicher Divan,* though Goethe's embrace of the foreign informed his entire poetic career. Todd Kontje has summarized the link between Weltliteratur and Goethe's own creative endeavors as follows: "Goethe's scattered comments about *Weltliteratur* in the late 1820s provide a theoretical justification for his lifelong poetic practice. From the beginning Goethe had demonstrated his ability to feel his way into foreign literary forms; his pseudo-Persian poetry of the *Divan* is only one phase of a career that included Shakespearean drama, Pindaric odes, and Roman elegies."[5] Goethe's receptivity to the foreign, in turn, enhanced his prestige among foreign journalists and intellectuals, further aiding the reception of Weltliteratur during his lifetime as a transnational ideal.

To be sure, Goethe's generous aesthetic outlook did not encompass all nations or cultures. Kontje calls Goethe "the outspoken enemy of everything Indian,"[6] and it is indeed the case that he loathed Indian statuary for its polytheistic representations, which Goethe associated with idolatry. He deplored Indian depictions of gods as variegated animals (1:615, 618), and even praised the zeal of a Muslim in the Middle Ages, Mahmud of Gasna, for destroying such religious art (3:438–39). As privy counselor to Duke Carl August in Weimar, Goethe strongly supported the suppression of democratic ideals linked to the French Revolution. He helped formulate policies designed to crush enthusiasm for such ideals among peasants, students, and professors in the Duchy of Saxony-Weimar-Eisenach. Thus, his cosmopolitanism was not all-encompassing, and his politics showed a strongly intolerant streak.[7] This is why National Socialist propagandists, embarrassed by Goethe's cosmopolitanism, focused on his loyal, un-questioning service to an absolutist German state. This circumstance also explains why the Young Germany author Ludwig Börne famously called him a "princes' lackey" three years after Goethe's death.[8] However, these realities do not diminish the contribution Goethe made to transcultural understanding through his Weltliteratur paradigm, a contribution that can be harnessed in the praxis of the World Literature classroom.

In a letter to Sulpiz Boisserée dated 12 October 1827, Goethe noted that Weltliteratur would come into existence when national particularities were balanced and resolved through international interchange.[9] While Goethe disapproved of the sort of global cultural uniformity he called "sansculottisme,"[10] scholars who have wrestled with Goethe's Weltliteratur concept have increasingly articulated its relevance within the globalized literary context implicit in the term "cultural transnationalism." Goethe introduced the term Weltliteratur in 1827, in the context of a response to discussions of his oeuvre in French newspapers, in the journal *Über Kunst und Altertum* (On Art and Antiquity). After translating a passage from a favorable review of a French adaptation of his drama *Torquato Tasso* (1790) in the Paris *Globe,* Goethe notes his extensive quotation is not merely intended to remind readers of his own work:

> ich bezwecke ein Höheres, worauf ich vorläufig hindeuten will. Überall hört und liest man von dem Vorschreiten des Menschengeschlechtes, von den weiteren Aussichten der Welt- und Menschenverhältnisse. Wie es auch im Ganzen hiemit beschaffen sein mag, welches zu untersuchen und näher

zu bestimmen nicht meines Amtes ist, will ich doch von meiner Seite meine Freunde aufmerksam machen, daß ich überzeugt sei, es bilde sich eine allgemeine Weltliteratur, worin uns Deutschen eine ehrenvolle Rolle vorbehalten ist. (14:908)

[I have something higher in mind, which I want to indicate provisionally. Everywhere one hears and reads about the progress of the human race, about the further prospects for world and human relationships. However that may be on the whole, which it is not my office to investigate and more closely determine, I nevertheless would personally like to make my friends aware that I am convinced a universal world literature is in the process of being constituted, in which an honorable role is reserved for us Germans.]

Goethe's vision of a new literary modality emerging from the progress generated by the increasingly international nature of discursive interchange reflects the holistic perspective that guided his forays into the natural sciences.[11] However, while Goethe's personal authoritativeness is strongly projected into much of his scientific writing, he deliberately masks the discrete, subjective component of his announcement concerning Weltliteratur through the use of the subjunctive case and through the impersonal pronouns "es" and "man." Goethe *as an individual* does not perceive what he describes. Rather, *one* sees and hears of progressive globalization, and one experiences this trend everywhere. Even when Goethe expresses in the first-person a conviction that a universal Weltliteratur is in the process of forming, he uses the indirect discourse subjunctive "sei" to note this belief. It is as though Goethe wishes to disappear into the background so that the impersonal, universal essence of a world literary scene can, conversely, be foregrounded. This is an initial, subtle hint at the death of the author as an independent literary "agent" in both senses of that term, Goethe's perhaps unintended way of announcing that world media (and, by extension, world markets) will weave a writer's products into a transindividual, indeed transnational grid, a grid Goethe terms Weltliteratur.

To be sure, Goethe's discovery of an emerging Weltliteratur is not intended to be read as announcing the demise of discrete national literatures. Indeed, he conveys in the same sentence which carries the newly enunciated discourse a belief in the positive role the Germans will play in its formation. However, he goes on to note that German literature is constituted from so many heterogeneous and contradictory elements that only a common language makes it a coherent field (14:909). This view of German literature as marked by disunity and a lack of cohesion is consistent with remarks Goethe set down in a much earlier essay, "Literarischer Sansculottismus" (1795), where he makes Germany's fragmentary political construction, its *Kleinstaaterei,* responsible for the nation's lack of "classical" authors. A truly classical author must be infused by a national spirit, and both internal factiousness and a concomitant overabundance of foreign influences makes such an infusion impossible in Germany. However, Goethe does not wish for the political upheavals which would make such classicism possible, and only bemoans the lack of a political-cultural center where German authors would be freed from subjection to the highly variegated whims and influences of their individual homelands (14:179–85). Given Germany's own lack of a strong, immanent, infrangible national identity in his time, it is not surprising that Goethe was particularly aware of and open to the possibility of a super- or transnational literary modality. Perhaps Goethe's insights into the contemporary impossibility of creating a "classical" (national) German literature made the formulation of a Weltliteratur desirable as the only possible alternative to cultural fragmentation.[12]

Another obvious political factor in Goethe's enunciation of a Weltliteratur concept was his experience of the Napoleonic Wars. As René Wellek has noted, Goethe believed the desire for greater literary traffic was rooted "in the weariness of strife" after these wars.[13] To be sure, in Goethe's age as in our own, strident nationalism resulted from globalist tendencies, and Goethe's battle against political and cultural xenophobia in Germany is evident in his engagement with Weltliteratur.[14] Nevertheless, in the wake of the Congress of Vienna and prior to new nationalistic outbursts in the 1830s, Europeans could reasonably sense a decline in the significance and autonomy of the individual nation-state, much as the "new world order" which emerged in the wake of Soviet Communism's collapse has led to a globalization of economics, politics, and culture. Thus, if Goethe's Weltliteratur concept anticipates current cultural transnationalism, a certain parallel between the geopolitics of the last phase of the Goethezeit and those of the contemporary age is, in some measure, responsible, though such trends in Goethe's age were restricted to Europe. Indeed, Goethe specifically equated Weltliteratur with "European litera-ture" (14:907). Nevertheless, he also commented that Weltliteratur was a domain being constituted by the ever increasing rapidity of (transnational) interchange and traffic ("Verkehr"). He further noted that what is popular among the masses would spread out into all zones and regions, a tendency serious-minded thinkers ("Die Ernsten") would strive in vain to resist. Such individuals must therefore form their own modest "church" (14:914–15), presumably in order to attain the sort of "aesthetic autonomy" Martha Woodmansee has shown was constructed precisely as a site of critical resis-tance to nascent literary mass marketing strategies in the age of Goethe.[15] Again, Goethe's remarks anticipate both the postmodern mass global mar-keting of culture and conservative reaction against this trend, though here too Goethe's thinking is primarily informed by European rather than truly universal tendencies.

When Goethe prefaces a schematic list of some European nations and their strengths and weaknesses in the emerging world-literary age with the cryptic subtitle "European, which is to say World-Literature" (14:907), our instinctive reaction would be to assume a Eurocentric perspective. Gail Finney has noted that "for Goethe, world literature meant only European literature, a fact that significantly differentiates his enterprise from the discipline of comparative literature today."[16] The relationship between Comparative Literature and Weltliteratur will be examined in chapter five, but Finney's remark might make us question the relevance of Goethean Weltliteratur for the contemporary World Literature classroom, where such narrow transnational cultural geography appears decidedly anachronistic. Two essays written in the 1980s by the Moroccan-born Germanist Fawzi Boubia establish the genuinely global dimensions of Goethe's Weltliteratur postulations and foreground their seminal and precocious embrace of alterity in the hermeneutic dialogue among the world's literatures. In Boubia's view, Goethe attempted in his formulations to arrive at a means by which one could highlight what is genuinely "other" in works of foreign literature and by which one could approach this alterity with genuine respect and open-mindedness. Because my primary theses in this book are that the goals of recognizing this alterity and encouraging this openness should be paramount in the introductory World Literature classroom, and that a metatheoretical approach to teaching World Literature in English Translation courses is the most efficacious means of achieving these desiderata, a somewhat extended meditation on Boubia's essays is in order here.

In "Goethes Theorie der Alterität und die Idee der Weltliteratur: Ein Beitrag zur neueren Kulturdebatte" (Goethe's Theory of Alterity and the Idea of World Literature: A Contribution to the Contemporary Cultural Debate, 1985), Boubia noted the concern already being expressed in the 1980s that intercultural exchange was in danger of giving way to hegemonic influence by one partner in the dialogue, a danger, we should add, far greater and more obvious in our current global age. Thus, one must be aware that the "other" is historically manifest in one's *own* literary heritage; only then can the framework for a recognition of true reciprocity be established. This insight could prove valuable when one reflects on how to teach Anglo-American literature in the context of a World Literature class. Unlike Hegel and Marx, who presupposed a leveling of discrete cultures to a sameness through dialectical evolution, Goethe never lost sight of the unique, specific aspects of divergent nations and peoples, according to Boubia. Indeed, Goethe spoke in his enunciations on Weltliteratur about deeply embedded national particularities ("Eigentümlichkeiten") that variously attract and repulse people in their intercourse with one another (14:913). Such psychobiology may appear outmoded today, but it helps explain Goethe's immunity to Hegelian assimilationist predilections. This is not to say that Goethe did not recognize the problem of an emerging homogenization among diverse cultures. As Boubia notes, precisely this recognition spurred Goethe to embrace the principle of alterity, the need to pursue insights into the legitimate particularity and identity of the Other.[17]

Boubia stresses in "Goethes Theorie der Alterität" that Goethe first developed his Weltliteratur paradigm in the context of reflecting on poetic production in Asia, and in considering that China in particular enjoyed a flourishing literary culture when Europeans were still wandering about in the forests. Indeed, like few others, Goethe regarded the "'continents oubliés' as an integral component of his own poetic creativity."[18] We can draw here on Boubia's somewhat unique recognition of this circumstance to note that

Goethe's equation of "European" with "World-Literature" was based on the profound *intra*-European intercourse he saw developing in his time; if the non-European world did not yet participate in a world literary dialogue, this was simply due to the fact that improved communication networks, transnational media exchange, and prolific translation activities were still restricted to his own continent. Goethe's insights into the conditions enabling Weltliteratur were based on contemporary circumstances. Only in the late twentieth century did the technological infrastructure first expand to a degree allowing for a genuinely global rather than merely European Weltliteratur as Goethe understood it. In this sense, Goethe's Weltliteratur paradigm is not Eurocentric, but rather merely reflects the realities and possibilities of international cultural mediation in his age.

Boubia concludes "Goethes Theorie der Alterität" with an examination of the intercultural and social dimensions of alterity in Weltliteratur, and how these dimensions are linked to tradition. Because Weltliteratur as a process of intercultural learning and recognition had existed for a long time already, Goethe believed that a critical relationship to the principle of tradition had to be established. This allowed Goethe to reveal the historically rooted nature of communicative and social interaction in the paradigm, thereby making them productive for the present. Unlike the Romantics, in Boubia's view, Goethe refused to separate what is innately one's own from what one has attained through acculturation of the foreign in the process of cultural history. Such a division would eliminate tradition's multivalence. For Goethe, identity and alterity are intertwined through history, making an autochthonous partitioning of culture into elements grounded in the polarities of national self and foreign Other inconceivable. In order to underscore this impossibility, Goethe had to establish Weltliteratur's culturally productive intermingling among nations and peoples as historically rooted, as already established by tradition.[19] In this sense, Weltliteratur is not a new byproduct of the 1820s, but only Goethe's recognition of its existence.

Boubia's essay "Universal Literature and Otherness" (1988) repeated and simply translated some of the salient points found in "Goethes Theorie der Alterität," but broke new ground in establishing the antichauvinist, dialogic purport of Weltliteratur as Goethe defined it. Citing Goethe's view, expressed in the journal *Über Kunst und Altertum*, that one must guard against any tendency toward leading nations to think in a uniform manner, Boubia emphasized that Goethean Weltliteratur is "a conception that is not confined within a blind Eurocentrism. On the contrary, it takes otherness into account and, consequently, the particularity and identity of peoples."[20] If students studying Goethe's paradigm in a World Literature classroom can be brought to understand and appreciate precisely this point—admittedly, no easy task—then their experience of the course will have lifetime value. Boubia's essay further grounds the dialogic element in Weltliteratur; the paradigm can be defined, in part, as a dialogue that will, ideally, lead to greater tolerance. Citing Goethe's tripartite translation scheme discussed in the introduction, and to which we will return at the conclusion of this chapter, Boubia noted that Weltliteratur is "other" directed. That is to say, Goethe's belief that translation in its highest, third, stage must approximate the rhythmic and grammatical nuances of the original language demonstrates that Goethe's paradigm sets as its highest ideal the movement of the self *toward* the Other, not a dominion over the Other or a leveling of the Other. This embrace of alterity, grounded in a unique principle of estrangement that forces the self to become foreign to itself, serves the twin causes of intercultural dialogue and respect for the foreign.[21] Boubia's insights in this regard demonstrate once again the importance of elucidating translation theory in the World Literature classroom if the appreciation of alterity is to be cultivated there.

Despite Goethe's somewhat antipathetic response to the mass aspect of Weltliteratur, his attitude toward what he articulated as an unavoidably emerging paradigm was generally positive. In 1828, after noting the friendly foreign reception of his Weltliteratur notion, a discursive formation he hoped would soon emerge through improved ease of communication in the turbulent present, Goethe elucidated the benefits to be gleaned through such inter-national literary interchange: "Eine jede Literatur ennuyiert sich zuletzt in sich selbst, wenn sie nicht durch fremde Teilnahme wieder aufgefrischt wird. Welcher Naturforscher erfreut sich nicht der Wunderdinge, die er durch Spiegelung hervorgebracht sieht?" (14:896) (Every literature dissipates within itself when it is not reinvigorated through foreign participation. What researcher into nature does not rejoice at the marvelous things which he sees brought forth through refraction?). In addition to confirming the tendency of Goethe's scientific perspective to permeate his Weltliteratur articulations, this passage adduces a dynamic quality inherent in the Weltliteratur paradigm, without the aid of which individual (national) literatures would simply dissipate. Referring to this commentary, Wellek defines Weltliteratur as "an ideal of the unification of all literatures into one literature where each nation would play its part in a universal concert."[22] This description captures the cosmopolitan spirit of the Weimar Classical milieu in which Goethe coined the term Weltliteratur while emphasizing its status as, in part, a teleological projection, a future goal. Certainly, Goethe was not in a position in the early nineteenth century to foresee the potential effects of the vigorous commingling taking place in the current age of multicultural exchange on a global scale. However, the "foreign participation" within and among the discrete nation-states he articulated must inevitably multiply on an infinite scale the "hybrid cultural space" Homi Bhabha sees inscribed in postcolonial literature.[23] This is one reason why, as we will see, Bhabha finds Goethe's Weltliteratur formulation a particularly valuable paradigm.

The geopolitical homogenization that emerged in the wake of the Congress of Vienna occurred in concert with a beginning internationalization of literary texts through a dawning mass market system, increased translation activity, and cross-national media coverage. While these circumstances allowed Goethe to sense the onset of Weltliteratur, he of course recognized that the constellation of a truly transnational literature, marked by thematic, stylistic, and even linguistic features drawn from the world and not anchored primarily in the traditions of individual nation-states, was at best, as Wellek puts it, "a distant ideal."[24] In spite of his conflation of "World-Literature" with "European literature," and in spite of a belief that early works of Egyptian, Indian, and Chinese literature could only be viewed as "curiosities," lacking the potential to enhance the modern European's ethical and aesthetic acculturation ("Bildung") (9:602),[25] Goethe's own poetic effort to approximate the ideal of hybridity in world literature is most evident in the *West-östlicher Divan*, inspired by his reading of the medieval Persian poet Hafiz. Drawing on both topical and structural features in the Persian's poetry and striving to appropriate even certain features in his language, the *Divan* represents Goethe's attempt at the "completion and confirmation" of the poetic self, a self enacted through a "return" to the Orient as a locus of both difference and origin, as Edward Said notes in *Orientalism*.[26] Thus, one can recognize another reason Weltliteratur as transnational interchange appealed to Goethe: it allows the development of the poetic self to the fullest possible degree, enabling it to approach the personal totality which finds its objective corollary in the ideal of a universalized poetic framework.

Aside from his antipathy toward the globalized mass marketing aspect of Weltliteratur, what accounts for Goethe's ambivalent attitude toward the world literary epoch? Why would he tell his secretary, Johann Peter Eckermann, in 1827 that Germans will slip into "pedantic darkness" if they do not attempt to look beyond their narrow geographic confines as he proclaims the need to move beyond "national literature" and to hasten the impending arrival of the epoch of Weltliteratur (24:229) and then, two years later, argue that Germans have the most to lose from this dawning age?[27] When he made his original pronouncement concerning Weltliteratur in 1827, Goethe assumed the Germans were assured of an "honorable role" in its formation due to current universal (that is, European) fascination with German literature (14:908–9). Gerhard Kaiser has cogently analyzed Goethe's ambiguous position; while the remarkable achievements of German writers in Goethe's age created the possibility that German arts and letters could play a substantive role in the nascent formation of a Weltliteratur, the particularisms that imbued German literature throughout its history, in contrast to the French, made it doubtful that German literature would be able to retain its unique, specific character as it became constellated within a world literary process.[28] When we consider the increasing globalization of commerce and culture at the present time, a trend that is beginning to render the notion of national literature obsolete and to create a transnational body of work on a truly universal scale, Goethe's concern about German national literature's ability to retain its specificity seems likely to become a worldwide issue in the coming years. Nevertheless, as I will argue, a heightened foregrounding of subnational cultural particularities in much current literature tends to obviate this danger.

Contemplating the problematic of subjective identity in the postcolonial age, Bhabha has posed, on a universal scale, the question of national
spiritual fragmentation in the face of all-encompassing cultural border
crossings, which Goethe had perceived as a purely domestic difficulty for
his people:

> How do we conceive of the "splitting" of the national subject? How do we
> articulate cultural differences within this vacillation of ideology in which
> the national discourse also participates, sliding ambivalently from one
> enunciatory position to another? What are the forms of life struggling to
> be represented in that unruly "time" of national culture, which Bakhtin
> surmounts in his reading of Goethe. . . . What might be the cultural and
> political effects of the liminality of the nation, the margins of modernity,
> which come to be signified in the narrative temporalities of splitting,
> ambivalence and vacillation?[29]

Such issues troubled Goethe as he wrestled with the concept of
Weltliteratur because of the "liminality" of Germany within Europe,
a liminality caused by Germany's political fragmentation, by the regionalism and particularism that made its national culture "unruly"
through creating a lack of intellectual cohesion. Goethe recognized the
concomitant impossibility of even *arriving* at a truly "national discourse"
through which a somewhat unified response to the trends generating a
Weltliteratur paradigm could be brought to bear. If Goethe was objectively
unable to overcome the "unruly time" of *his* national culture, and if
Bhabha has correctly ascertained that such fractionalism and instability
are general characteristics of our age, it becomes a matter of some interest
to investigate why Bhabha believes Bakhtin transcended this volatility
through his reading of Goethe.

According to Bhabha, Bakhtin was able to articulate an ambience of
stable, phenomenally manifest national temporality in Goethe's narratives
by demonstrating how Goethe invests the most regional, local spaces in his
work with a highly visible historical synchronicity.[30] Indeed, in the essay
to which Bhabha refers, "The *Bildungsroman* and Its Significance in the
History of Realism (Toward a Historical Typology of the Novel)," Bakhtin
demonstrates a dialectic interaction at work in Goethe's oeuvre between
temporal plenitude and concrete localized spatiality, which allows Goethe

to imbue world history with a rich, lived fullness, and, thereby, with an atmosphere of holistic teleologically anchored stability. Historical time in Goethe's prose becomes necessary time, according to this view. Bakhtin even suggests Goethe was the first author to evoke a sense of the "world" in its entirety through his spatiotemporal dialectics:

> The locality became an irreplaceable part of the geographically and historically determined world, of *that* completely real and essentially visible world of human history, and the event became an essential and nontransferable moment in the time of this particular human history that occurred in this, and only this, geographically determined human world. The world and history did not become poorer or smaller as a result of this process of mutual concretization and interpenetration. On the contrary, they were condensed, compacted, and filled with the creative possibilities of subsequent *real* emergence and development. Goethe's world is a *germinative seed,* utterly real, visibly available, and at the same time filled with an equally real future that is growing out of it.[31]

In *Writing Outside the Nation,* Azade Seyhan shows how contemporary bicultural authors who write in a diaspora sustain cultural memory at the transnational level. That is to say, she demonstrates that imposed or chosen exile prompts such "borderland" writers to articulate memory at the interstice between divergent cultural discourses. Such transnational writing is productively engaged by Seyhan to indicate how cultural memory can be creatively enacted outside national matrices. Precisely because globalization increasingly calls into question the viability of discrete, coherently definable national literatures, literatures of the nation-states previously regarded as the repositories of communal, collective history, the question of Weltliteratur is becoming once again relevant. Bhabha has drawn on this Goethean paradigm to suggest that "transnational histories" of colonized and minority groups "may be the [new] terrains of world literature."[32] Sarah Lawall finds "world literature" even more specific than "Comparative Literature" as a signifier for a pedagogical practice that leads to "the replacement of fixed [national] spaces and definitions with open or perspectivist space, where proportions are not established and must always be observed anew."[33] It is in this context that Bakhtin's reading of Goethe is particularly relevant. Indeed, Bakhtin's "chronotope" concept is ideal for suggesting such an "open space" in spite of its own practice of concrete fixation, for it signifies a wedding of temporal and spatial relationships so filled with discrete historical plenitude that the term inherently calls into question the artificial stasis of national literary terrains, terrains in this case too widely rather than too narrowly drawn.

Particularly in Goethe's "unrealized creative projects,"[34] Bakhtin saw a chronotopic totality so fully realized that he believed these fragments become microcosms of the world itself. Though Bhabha is not entirely incorrect when he sees in Bakhtin's reading of Goethe an emphasis on "the emergence of the nation,"[35] Bakhtin's interest in his *Bildungsroman* essay is in Goethe's ability to enact cultural memory in its spatiotemporal (chronotopic) fullness at the local, regional level. Thus, it is worthwhile to examine Bakhtin's chronotopic reading of Goethe's unrealized creative sketches, particularly the "Aufenthalt in Pyrmont" (Sojourn in Pyrmont, 1801), to suggest that in a future which promises the further erosion of discrete *national* cultures, cultural memory may be sustained and evoked in its rich lived totality at the subnational *as well as* transnational level. The Weltliteratur paradigm in Goethe's writing can be brought into play here, because, as we have seen, Weltliteratur emerges as a transnational phenomenon the articulation of which was largely inspired and informed by Germany's *subnational* status in the eighteenth and early nineteenth centuries. This will allow me to show why current theorists such as Lawall can still draw on the concept to call into question the viability of fixed national cultural spaces in the teaching of literature.

As we noted, when Goethe first coined the term Weltliteratur in 1827, he believed that the Germans would have an honorable role in this process. The world's nations appear to Goethe to cast their gaze at Germany, praising and criticizing, imitating and rejecting its output. Germany's national literature is derived from quite heterogeneous elements, unified only through its composition in a language which is gradually bringing to light the immanent quality of the German people. Goethe tacitly assumes Germany, in his age, lacks both military-physical and ethical-aesthetic cohesion (14:908–9). There was an external element to the political dimension of this initial Weltliteratur formulation. In suggesting Germany's lack of moral and physical unity, Goethe was reflecting on his country's psychological ambience in the wake of the Napoleonic Wars. During these wars, not only populists like Jahn but also German intellectuals such as the Romantic philosopher Johann Gottlieb Fichte were sustained by the hope that a liberated fatherland would emerge from French occupation not only spiritually but politically coadunated. However, Metternich's reactionary measures at the Congress of Vienna, which thwarted the ambitions of those seeking a unified Germany, dashed this optimism. While Goethe's prefatory Weltliteratur formulation evinces an implicit recognition of this circumstance, of a return by Germany to a prewar status quo which (before the 1830s) triggered widespread despair, it points to the positive side of non-nationhood, to an anti-nationalist cosmopolitanism culturally attractive to the world at large. Indeed, as Hartmut Steinecke has noted, the retardation of nationality in eighteenth-century Germany led to a relatively unimpeded view, in Goethe's estimation, of transnational, universally human contexts in his native land.[36]

This perspective is evident in the essay "Literarischer Sansculottismus," which therefore bears a brief reexamination. On the one hand, Goethe bemoans here Germany's lack of national cohesion, for political fragmentation renders impossible the development of "a classical national author." Such a fortunate being only emerges when he is able to find himself the son of a unified country that has enjoyed a history filled with events of great magnitude and a present populated by a resolute, purposeful citizenry (14:181). However, a worthy philosophy and an invisible school ("unsichtbare Schule") have evolved in Germany, helping the talented young poet to represent external objects with clarity and grace (14:184). Particularly compelling in Goethe's metaphoric language is the articulation of the invisible school, a school invisible, presumably, because Germany lacks a physically manifest sociocultural center ("Mittelpunkt gesellschaftlicher Lebensbildung") where young writers could undergo a cohesive, mutually supportive period of aesthetic maturation (14:182). Ironically, the invisible school allows Germany's contemporary writers to enter into a circle now more fully illuminated than in the past (14:184), as though a physical invisibility rendered necessary by Germany's fragmented political status has ultimately led to transcendent enlightenment in the literary domain. Bhabha has noted Bakhtin's foregrounding of optic, ocular tropes in Goethe's oeuvre when the Russian critic putatively attempts to underscore Goethe's rhetorical nation building: "The recurrent metaphor of landscape as the inscape of national identity emphasizes the quality of light, the question of social visibility, the power of the eye to naturalize the rhetoric of national affiliation and its forms of collective expression."[37] However, "Literarischer Sansculottismus" attempts to bring opacity at the geographic national level into a dialectic relationship with luminescence in the aesthetic-pedagogical sphere in order to underscore politically fragmented Germany's ability to sustain a vibrant literary culture. The continued impediments to Germany's political cohesion in 1830 constitute, perhaps, another reason Goethe envisioned the globe as but an expanded fatherland when he discussed the role of improved, accelerated, expanded traffic/communication infrastructures in the development of Weltliteratur (14:914).

This is not to say that Goethe regarded transnationalism and subnationalism as simply two sides of one dialectically productive coin. Goethe realized that the average German's lifetime confinement within the narrow boundaries of one of its multitude of petty states tended to result in pedantic narrow-mindedness among the citizenry. However, precisely this circumstance led him to issue his famous proclamation to Eckermann in 1827 that his fellow Germans should follow his lead in observing the culture of foreign lands, and that "national literature now does not signify a great deal, the epoch of world literature has arrived, and everyone must help to accelerate this epoch" (24:229). Only Germany's fractured political status permits Goethe to formulate a transnational cultural ideal through his Weltliteratur concept. As Bakhtin's reading of Goethe's creative fragments allows us to realize, sustaining cultural memory begins at the local level, and only in this subnational domain is it possible for literature to articulate the global, to become, in this sense, "world literature." Before examining this reading in greater detail, it is worth noting that Goethe himself used highly ocular language to mediate this relationship between the particular and the universal in his 1828 review of Thomas Carlyle's *German Romance* (1827). Though nationality is an element in the particular, Goethe does not qualify this term as corollary to membership in a politically unified nation. Otherwise, Germans would be excluded from participation in furthering the epoch of Weltliteratur, and we have already seen their politically fragmented status actually enhances the role which Goethe envisioned them playing in this regard: "In every particular, be it historically, mythologically, fabulously, more or less arbitrarily conceived, one will see that universal ever more radiate and shine through nationality and personality" (14:932). Hendrik Birus has shown that this comment and several others reveal a universal/particular dialectic at the heart of Goethe's Weltliteratur paradigm.[38]

Bakhtin most comprehensively elucidated his chronotope principle in the essay "Forms of Time and of the Chronotope in the Novel: Notes toward a Historical Poetics" (1937–1938). At the outset of this lengthy discourse, he defines the term as follows: "We will give the name *chronotope* (literally 'time space') to the intrinsic connectedness of temporal and spatial relationships that are artistically expressed in literature."[39] Though he adroitly and elaborately uses the chronotope as a heuristic device in the essay to almost literally map out such unique genres as the "Greek Romance" and the "Chivalric Romance," the concept most fully acquires its previously described concrete density and its concomitant ability to (paraphrasing Walter Benjamin's famous formula) explode the continuum of political nationality in "The *Bildungsroman* and Its Significance in the History of Realism (Toward a Historical Typology of the Novel)," a fragment from one of his missing books. Bakhtin demonstrates here that Goethe's ability to intensely focus on locality, to keep in mind its human historical dimension even when the local space was desolate or sparsely populated, led him to creatively infuse such domains with a synchronic resonance, to promote a "feeling of the past and the present merging into one."[40] This feeling is multilayered, inscribed by a struggle between historical-geographic realism and romantic ghostly uncanniness. Bakhtin believes the realist element in this struggle within creative consciousness emerges victorious,[41] and Bhabha equates this circumstance with the successful articulation of a discrete "national time," which "becomes concrete and visible in the chronotype [*sic*] of the local, particular, graphic, from beginning to end."[42] While Bakhtin does read Goethe's autobiographical musings on Alsace and Italy as a dynamic constellation of a "country's" geographic-social-historical topography,[43] he does not equate the country with a politically unified nation-state. In the case of Alsace and early nineteenth-century Italy, such an equation would have been inconceivable. Rather, Goethe's evocation of locality, in Bakhtin's reading, enacts cultural memory at a subnational level, even though such evocations may create tableaux suggestive of a broader ethnic and/or national populace. This is the case with Goethe's description of Wilhelm Tell during a trip through Switzerland in 1797. In this vision, according to Bakhtin, "Tell himself appeared to Goethe as an embodiment of the people (*eine Art von Demos*)."[44]

It is immediately after Bakhtin describes Goethe's creative engagement with the personage of Wilhelm Tell that he discusses the poet's inspired synchronic vision in and of Pyrmont. Goethe enjoyed a brief stay in the spa town (located in Lower Saxony) in the summer of 1801. He was particularly fascinated by its natural phenomena, especially its nitrogen gas–filled cave, but also by the human drama generated by the locale's gaming tables. In concert with his readings on Pyrmont history, these social and natural world experiences created in Goethe the impulse to concoct a tale set in the region in 1582, when a procession from all quarters of the world suddenly visits Pyrmont's spring. The unexpected arrival of a large body of international visitors instantiates a chaotic, but, for the reader, entertaining and instructive tableau, as the guests seek to accommodate themselves as best they can (11:684–88). In this brief description, one can already see a paradigmatic merging of the elements Bakhtin discerned in Goethe's artistic engagement with "Lokalität," namely, the fusion of contemporary social and natural domains with an episode of regional history, resulting in a project resonant with synchronic energy, with dynamic cultural memory. This is what Bakhtin means when he calls the Pyrmont sketch "profoundly chronotopic," evocative of a humanized, tightly drawn geographic site that suggests a history both predetermined and vital to the site's contemporary inhabitants, "like those creative forces a given locality needs in order to organize and continue the historical process embodied in it."[45]

The sketch itself, published under the title "Aufenthalt in Pyrmont," introduces a bold German knight who meets up with the mass of pilgrims streaming toward the spring and, with his page, helps organize and guide them. Much in the tableau is reminiscent of the region's earliest, indeed primal history. Despite disease and tumult, kindred spirits come together to erect a divine city with invisible walls in the midst of the world wave ("Weltwoge"). Inevitable discord within the cosmopolitan group is not destructive, for a virtuous group of knights ensures order and justice. All these events are duly recorded by the page, who makes short, apropos observations. The sketch ends with the arrival of three dignified males: a youth, a mature man, and an elderly man. In a secretive manner, they reveal the reason for their congregation and allow the crowd to perceive Pyrmont's future greatness (12:627–29).

Particularly striking in the sojourn is Goethe's ability to concisely merge past and future, the regional and the international, the spiritual and the geographic into one space, Pyrmont, thus filling the locality with a spatiotemporal (chronotopic) plenitude. The productive interaction between world (the international mass of pilgrims) and locale (Pyrmont) is reminiscent of Goethe's conjuration of Weltliteratur as a dialectic of the universal and the particular. In Bakhtin's view, as we have seen, the chronotopic definite space-time does not take away from the work's global sensibility, but enhances it. Bakhtin believed Goethe's creatively constelled chronotopic localities are so densely inscribed by synchronic detail, and the global so tightly interwoven with the site-specific, that the particular domain evokes the world at large, microcosm and macrocosm are productively, indeed necessarily, synthesized.

Bakhtin's monadic reading of Goethe's sketches is reminiscent of Goethe's own reflections on popular poetry. In his 1806 review of *Des Knaben Wunderhorn,* the famous collection by Achim von Arnim and Clemens Brentano of old German songs that also appeared in 1806, Goethe claims that "The lively poetic observation of a limited circumstance elevates a particular ('ein Einzelnzes') to an indeed limited but unconfined cosmos ('All'), so that we believe we are seeing the entire world in the small space" (14:458). This relationship, in turn, brings to mind the conclusion to Goethe's novel *Wilhelm Meisters Wanderjahre* (*Wilhelm Meister's Travels,* 1829), where "house piety" is seen to provide the foundation for "world piety"; the universal is thus grounded, and must be interpenetrated by, the local. Birus cites this passage in order to underscore Goethe's view that "advanced" (cosmopolitan) world literature is based on highly particularized "naive" or "nature poetry."[46] In the current age of globalization, with its emphasis on transnational literary history, when the enactment of cultural memory is negotiated in a broadly constructed, often homogeneous space, conjurations of Goethe's Weltliteratur paradigm such as those performed by Bhabha tend to lose sight of this paradigm's original, seminally subnational, indeed localized, dimension. However, recognizing this dimension is key to exploring cultural difference in the World Literature classroom.

At the conclusion to *Writing Outside the Nation,* Seyhan issues the following precaution with respect to how transnational literature should be taught: "We need to bear in mind, however, that if our reception of transnational, emergent, diasporic literatures is mediated only through English, not only linguistic but also cultural differences and specificities will be lost in translation. And our newly developed transnational, postcolonial literature courses will not be very different from the traditional World Literature in English Translation course."[47] Seyhan is, of course, correct, but the complex linguistic and cultural nuances of bi- and transnational literature can only be approached after the discrete, chronotopic elements in literary works are elucidated. To paraphrase Seyhan, we might call this a pedagogy focused on a writing *below* the nation. Ironically, perhaps, a metatheoretical introduction of Weltliteratur as Goethe understood it will be a prerequisite for such research and the teaching, *in particular,* of World Literature in English Translation courses. This Bakhtinian approach will not only complement the transnational method of postcolonial literary pedagogy, but will micrologically promote the questioning of fixed perspectives advocated by Lawall in elucidating world literature, a calling into question that transnational literary study accomplishes on the macrological level. Chronotopic concretization as critical praxis will also help sustain cultural memory, which is threatened by the antithesis of this praxis, a tacit acceptance of cultural globalization as a *fait accompli,* an acceptance that inevitably distorts our examination of past cultures.

If, as Bhabha correctly suggests in spite of somewhat misunderstanding the significance of the "nation" in the "*Bildungsroman*" essay, Bakhtin was able to overcome the flux and indeterminacy of national culture when viewed from a diachronic perspective through his analysis of Goethe, it seems equally plausible to suggest Goethe's *own* telos in striving toward the evocation of a comprehensive and stable geographic matrix rooted in the local was triggered by the desire to imaginatively compensate for the genuine instability, fragmentation, and lack of cohesiveness that characterized German politics and letters in his time. If Germans had the most to lose in the dawning age of Weltliteratur because of the country's geopolitical and cultural particularisms, then Goethe must configure the world and conjure stability and plenitude within the regional and the particular in his narratives. If we believe Bakhtin's elegant argument that Goethe succeeded in doing just that, then Goethe might be plausibly suggested as a role model not only for those who teach World Literature, but also for authors who seek to come to grips with the demise of their national identity in a transnational, multicultural age.

As we will see in chapter three, German national identity itself began to coalesce in the 1830s and 1840s, just as it had during the wars of liberation against Napoleon. The political quietude and war weariness marking the Restoration period in the 1820s when Goethe evolved his Weltliteratur concept created the intermediate lull between phases of intense nationalism in Germany and in Europe in general. This brief epoch was thus marked by an ambience of internationalism that formed the natural political environment in which the Weltliteratur paradigm could emerge. Nevertheless, a deep *undercurrent* of nationalism is evident in much of the critical and creative discourse of a literary movement contemporary to that age, German Romanticism. Indeed, scholars of Weltliteratur frequently contrast Goethe's cosmopolitanism and future-directed thinking with Romantic chauvinism, obscurantism, and an unhealthy obsession with the past. On occasion, the fulcrum used for juxtaposing their divergent views on the principle of Weltliteratur is constituted by their respective observations on translation and translation theory.

According to Hans Joachim Schrimpf, Goethe saw in the world's wide variety of languages and ethnic characteristics not a source for alienation and division among nations, but a medium that unites them. Weltliteratur does not signify suppression, but is a means to bring the (nationally) particular into the global domain and subject it to international scrutiny. Translation first makes this universal mediation possible. For this reason, in Schrimpf's view, Goethe rejected Romantic subjectivity, its nationalistic focus on the past in general and the German Middle Ages in particular.[48] Boubia also stresses Goethe's fear that the principle of Weltliteratur was undermined by the Romantic fixation with Germanic traditions in the Middle Ages. While Weltliteratur seeks to bring clarity to the Other, elucidating alterity by revealing the Other's discrete particularities, nostalgic Romantic obscurantism achieves the opposite result, blanketing alterity in a subjective, egoistic fog. Thus, in Boubia's view, Goethe rebuked the Romantics "for not using the other as an end but only as a means." As an example, Boubia cites Goethe's harsh evaluation of Friedrich Schlegel's putatively mystifying approach to Indian language and culture in *Über die Sprache und Weisheit der Indier* (*On the Language and Wisdom of the Indians*, 1808).[49] Extrapolating Boubia's perspective, the Romantic engagement with foreign tongues is antithetical to Goethe's. While, in Goethe's adumbration of ideal translation, one alienates and obscures personal identity in bringing the alterity of the translated language to the forefront, the Romantics further obscure, render strange and exotic, foreign idioms such as Hindi for subjective purposes.

A more differentiated view of the relationship between Goethean Weltliteratur and Romantic translation theory has been expounded by Andreas Huyssen and Antoine Berman. However, before analyzing their works, it will be worthwhile to briefly consider the single most celebrated critical text of German Romanticism, the 116th of Friedrich Schlegel's *Athenäumsfragmente,* which begins with the assertion that "Romantic poetry is a progressive universal poetry." It is progressive, according to Schlegel, because it continuously moves toward a global synthesis of all discursive and imaginative genres. This movement is never arrested by Hegelian sublation because the antitheses it subtends are never synthesized, but simply balanced through juxtaposition. The continuous self-cancellations this balancing sets into motion in Romantic works provide the foundation for the movement's most frequently discussed literary device, irony. Romantic irony in the movement's *imaginative* literature frequently counteracts the univocal, egoistic, nationalistic orientations of the sort decried by Schrimpf and Boubia in Romanticism's critical discourse, as even a superficial reading of works such as Ludwig Tieck's *Der gestiefelte Kater* (*Puss in Boots,* 1797) and Friedrich Schlegel's novel

Lucinde (1799) will attest. Schlegel also claims that only Romantic poetry can, like the epic, "become a mirror of the entire surrounding world, an image of the epoch."[50]

While such a goal certainly does not suggest the elucidation of the particular in its national, cultural alterity evident in Goethe's Weltliteratur paradigm, it does evince Schlegel's desire to reflect modernity in its global dimensions. For Schlegel, Romantic poetry is decidedly, self-consciously modern. The self-cancelling, unsublatable mechanisms, anchored in irony, that negotiate Romantic poetry's global mirroring are enabled by modernity's open, fragmented character, which Schlegel consistently contrasted with the totalized but self-enclosed nature of premodern, Classical culture. Thus, according to Schlegel, Greek poetry is paradigmatically objective and completely lacking in irony.[51] Moreover, Schlegel argued that the poet's endless striving to expand both his poetry and poetic theory, his attempt to reach sublimity by integrating his work with poetry as a whole, must be carried out in the most particular manner possible ("auf die bestimmteste Weise"), for poetic generalization has a deadening, contrary effect. Paul Gordon cites this passage from Schlegel's *Gespräch über die Poesie* (*Dialogue on Poetry*, 1800) in arguing that "romanticism has its roots in a concern with the symbolic relation between individual and universal."[52] Though Schlegel's failure to cogently address the national/international poles of this relation makes Gordon's treatment of Goethean Weltliteratur as a paradigm of early Romanticism untenable, he is correct to infer that the unsublatable balance between the universal and the particular in both domains informs the critical practice of Comparative Literature.[53]

The Romantics never directly engaged in a discussion of Goethe's Weltliteratur concept, and it would therefore be impossible to assert that they consciously proposed any alternative to it. Nevertheless, Schlegel's attempt to articulate a progressive universal poetry rooted in a comprehensive literary history is informed by a truly original, global approach. According to Huyssen, Schlegel's postulate that progressive universal poetry is capable of the highest and most comprehensive acculturation ("Bildung") not only from inside out but from outside in presupposes the appropriation of foreign poetry through translation, criticism, and historical thinking. Universality, in Huyssen's view, is Schlegel's highest ideal, and spurs his attempts at establishing a comparative world literary history ("Weltliteraturgeschichte"). The history of world literature ("Geschichte der Weltliteratur") would be the most appropriate vehicle, in Huyssen's reading of Schlegel, for establishing the historical-cultural foundation for binding the human race together.[54] Through translation, the Romantics hoped to establish a dynamic world literary canon in Germany.[55]

A general fixation on Germany is what causes the Romantic perspective on Weltliteratur articulated by Huyssen to be radically at odds with that of Goethe. Indeed, Birus suggests Goethe invented the term *in response* to Romantic critical predilections.[56] Like the Romantics, Goethe never lost sight of Germany's potentially seminal role in the commerce and dissemination of world literature in the age of Weltliteratur. Those who know German, in Goethe's view, find themselves in the midst of the world literary marketplace, and enrich themselves by playing the role of interpreter (14:932–33). However, German nationalism lay at the root of the Romantics' focus on the relationship between translation and Weltliteratur to a degree that would have been intolerable to Goethe. Citing a passage from Novalis's novel fragment *Heinrich von Ofterdingen* (1801) that establishes Heinrich's world travels as being squarely in devotion to the fatherland, Huyssen shows how translation in the Romantics' view is intertwined with—and stands in the service of—Germany. Translation for the Romantics is an act imbued with a kind of patriotic eschatology; Germans are master translators, and they translate not only world literature, but also the past into the future. German talent at translation and, thereby, at appropriation, preordains the German nation to lead Europe into a future Golden Age. Thus, Huyssen closes his book with a reference to a "literary spiritual utopia of a 'German *Weltliteratur*'" conjured by the Romantics.[57]

This vision obviously reverses the priorities and goals in Goethe's Weltliteratur formulations, which, while they presume an honorable role for the Germans and an even more intense degree of participation than is the case with other nations, presuppose a genuine dialogue of equals leading to the benefit, acculturation, and enlightenment of all involved. Equality among languages and nations is presupposed in Goethe's assertion that "these connections from the original to the translation are those which express the relationships of nation to nation most clearly and which one must especially know and judge for the promotion of the predominating and ruling universal *Weltliteratur*."[58] As George Steiner has remarked, the utilitarian, indeed commerce-oriented vocabulary Goethe employed in his Weltliteratur formulations was designed to counteract the chauvinist valorization of the German language that began with Johann Georg Hamann and Johann Gottfried Herder in the second half of the eighteenth century and reached alarming dimensions after 1813, which is to say, at the height of the Romantic age. Indeed, Steiner shows that Goethe's decidedly antinationalist concept of estranging the German language from itself was not just a theoretical postulate, but a principle he actually attempted to put into practice. In translating Alessandro Manzoni's *Il Cinque Maggio* (1821; Goethe's translation 1822), Goethe deliberately distorted his mother tongue, imbuing it with Italian rhythms, syllabification, and phrasing.[59]

A rather different view on the respective attitudes taken by Goethe and the Romantics with respect to translation, and how Goethe's attitude toward Romantic translation theory affected his Weltliteratur principle, has been adumbrated by Antoine Berman. Berman stresses the modernity of Goethean Weltliteratur, its grounding in a present where a world literary market is emerging and where national literatures therefore meet and act communally through translation. Because translation has traditionally played such a central role in German culture, Goethe believed that German would play a central role in Weltliteratur's universal exchanges, but Berman also notes Goethe never went so far as to allow these views to assume nationalistic overtones. However, contrary to other critics, Berman does not contrast Goethe and the Romantics along the lines of a cosmopolitan/nationalist dichotomy. With respect to estranging the German language in the process of translation, to the ideal attempt to translate the untranslatable which lies at the heart of the third mode of translation in the *Divan,* Berman sees a virtual congruence between Goethe's views and those of the Romantic thinkers August Wilhelm Schlegel and Friedrich Schleiermacher. Berman cogently argues that Goethe's objection to Romantic translation praxis in general and to A. W. Schlegel's in particular is based on a perception that the Romantics focused on form at the expense of content, engaged in a hazardous syncretism, and were too obsessed with the past. Goethe's own anchoring of Weltliteratur in the present, in Berman's view, is based on the conviction that his age was the first to stand in a radically open hermeneutic relationship to the foreign. In the dawning epoch of Weltliteratur, one does not seek merely to capture the foreign in one's work, but, sensing the incomplete character of one's own native culture, the individual in the contemporary age is open to being possessed by the foreign. In a Weltliteratur-informed dialogue, the self *participates* in—interacts with—the foreign, and is not simply, passively, *influenced* by it.[60]

Berman's reading is consistent with Novalis's definition of Romantic poetics as "the art of alienating in a pleasing manner, of making an object foreign ('fremd') and yet familiar and attractive."[61] Such a view is related to the dialectics of Goethean Weltliteratur in general, and to his third level of translation in particular, but is more specific with regard to the dynamics of highlighting alterity in the practice (and, we can extrapolate, teaching) of literature than one finds in Goethe. Thus, this aphorism is an effective expression of what I believe to be a major goal of the presentation of foreign literature in the World Literature classroom.

Nevertheless, Novalis's aphorism lacks a cosmopolitan, intercultural dimension; he uses the term "fremd" here in the broadest possible sense.[62] Whether one believes Goethe created his Weltliteratur paradigm at least partially in response to Romantic syncretism, Romantic nationalism, Romantic obsession with the past, Romantic formalism, or some combination of these, it is clear that Goethe's dialectical approach, in which Weltliteratur is constituted at the contemporary interstice between the universal and the particular on the one hand, and the subnational and the transnational on the other, strongly differentiates him from his Romantic contemporaries. Even if, as Huyssen maintains, early Romantic theory can be extrapolated to suggest a Weltliteratur utopia, this utopia lacks an impartially cosmopolitan dimension. Indeed, both Novalis and A. W. Schlegel proclaimed universality and cosmopolitanism to be distinctly *German* attributes.[63] Friedrich Schlegel's attempts at establishing a progressive universal poetry and a comprehensive literary history aside, a genuinely relevant engagement with Weltliteratur in the World Literature classroom must be rooted in a focus on Goethe's prophetically global, non-nationalistic understanding of the term, an understanding grounded in a principle of radical alterity based on a novel view of translation. Only thus will this engagement both make sense to American students reared in an age of globalization dominated by the United States and help them to appreciate and learn from the alterity they will encounter, in translation, in world literature. To be sure, an awareness of Weltliteratur's further adventures in Germany and the United States is paramount in a self-aware dialogue with world literature as well, and to these we now turn our attention.

The Mediation and Contestation of *Weltliteratur*

Heine and Young Germany

LET US RECALL AND briefly elaborate upon Goethe's comments concerning the role of the Germans and other German speakers in the age of Weltliteratur. In his review of Carlyle's *German Romance,* Goethe notes that a genuinely universal tolerance ("eine wahrhaft allgemeine Duldung") will be most efficaciously achieved if we accept at face value the unique particularity ("das Besondere") of diverse individuals and peoples while sustaining the conviction that what is truly worthy ("das wahrhaft Verdienstliche") comes to expression precisely by virtue of its belonging to all of humanity. Here, again, Goethe is attempting to define the proper parameters for articulating the correct relationship between the universal and the particular, an effort we have seen inform much of his commentary on Weltliteratur and which, for that reason, makes his paradigm particularly valuable in today's World Literature classroom. Nevertheless, a question emerges here. How do elements in culture inherently possessing universal merit but embedded in the practices and expressions of one, perhaps isolated, group, one civilization, come to the attention of the world at large, first making the global adoption of these values and ideas possible? It is here that Goethe sees the Germans as playing a particularly useful role. Germans have already contributed to such transnational communication, such mutual recognition, for a long time, in Goethe's estimation. Thus, it is those who speak and understand German who find themselves in the world literary marketplace, where all nations offer their goods. Therefore, those with a command of German play the role of interpreter on a universal scale (14:932–33).

Of whom is Goethe thinking when he extols the role of those who know German in the age of Weltliteratur? Certainly he has Carlyle in mind, who did so much in the way of translation and commentary to spread Goethe's fame, and that of Friedrich Schiller, in the English-speaking world. Among his own countrymen, he might have thought of his mentor Johann Gottfried Herder, who opened Goethe's eyes and those of educated Europe to the splendid riches of relatively "uncivilized," non-Classical cultures. He may have had Joseph von Hammer-Purgstall in mind, who helped popularize Near Eastern literature in Europe and whose translations of Persian works first enabled Goethe's dialogue with Hafiz in the *West-östlicher Divan*. He may even have had Romantics such as Tieck and the Brothers Schlegel under consideration, the quality and diversity of whose translations were undeniable even for Goethe despite Goethe's philosophical and aesthetic differences with the Romantic movement.

Whomever he had in mind among the Germans and other German speakers when he wrote his review of Carlyle's book, it certainly was not Heinrich Heine. Goethe and Heine only had one, awkward meeting,[1] and their relationship can be characterized by disinterest (Goethe's attitude toward Heine) and dislike (Heine's attitude toward Goethe). However, in considering Goethe's musings on Weltliteratur *in their historical specificity,* this chapter will attempt to substantiate the following two propositions: (1) Despite his personal and political antipathy toward Goethe, Heine was a mediator of Weltliteratur as Goethe understood the concept. (2) Though, as far as is evident, Heine himself never directly mentioned the concept, the *Junges Deutschland* (Young Germany) writers who did analyze it often made Heine a central figure in their discussions. Their writing, influenced as it was by rising nationalism, allows Heine to emerge as the *only* mediator of Weltliteratur in its specifically Goethean constellation to enjoy international, historically transcendent renown. If the previous chapter elaborated on the contemporary relevance of Goethe's Weltliteratur paradigm and its potential applicability in the World Literature classroom, this one will focus on its temporally limiting and fixed aspects in examining its subsequent mediation and reception in

Germany until 1848. Such knowledge is as important as the establishment of contemporary relevance for a hermeneutically valid engagement with any venerable concept. This will help us to better situate its reception and pedagogical manifestations in the United States. Thus, we will explore the early reception of Weltliteratur on its home soil in this chapter, and its vicissitudes in Germany from the end of the 1848 revolution through the present in chapter four.

We begin with the somewhat unusual proposition that Heine was Weltliteratur's only internationally renowned mediator. To be sure, the thesis that Heine played a significant role in the development of Weltliteratur as Goethe understood it is not entirely novel. As the title of Bodo Morawe's 1997 monograph *Heines "Französische Zustände": Über die Fortschritte des Republikanismus und die anmarschierende Weltliteratur* (Heine's "Conditions in France": On the Progress of Republicanism and the Advancing Weltliteratur) indicates, Morawe believes the articles written by Heine for the *Allgemeine Zeitung,* which contain his views on French politics and society in the early phase of Louis-Philippe's regime and which were published under the collective title *Französische Zustände* ("Conditions in France," 1833), constitute a paradigmatic example of what Goethe meant by the term Weltliteratur. Morawe's book borrows the term "advancing Weltliteratur" from Goethe's letter to Karl Zeller dated 4 March 1829,[2] though he ignores its negative connotation. The letter suggests that Parisian theatrical excesses are causing damage to German drama through the steadily advancing process the expression "advancing Weltliteratur" connotes.[3] Morawe underscores the technical progress, improved communication, enhanced intellectual exchanges, broader journalistic information, and increasing translation activity evident in Goethe's notion of Weltliteratur and sees Heine's work as an exemplary instance of these trends. In Morawe's view, Goethe's understanding of "advancing Weltliteratur" is immanent to the genre ("Werkform") of the *Französische Zustände*; Heine is engaging in journalistic reportage, providing the perspective of a German writing in France on French events and tacitly holding up that nation's Republicans as a political model to the citizens of his own native land. In his final brief analysis of the Goethean Weltliteratur dimension of the *Französische Zustände,* Morawe alludes to the work's consciously conceived reception aesthetics, which draw on new communicative and integrative processes. These create Heine's ability to provide immediate "feed back" (Morawe's term) to his audience on the conditions in France as they evolved, a dynamic practice which then retroactively impacts the ongoing development of the work and its author.[4]

Cursory though it is, Morawe's analysis of the *Französische Zustände* as an early exemplar of Goethe's Weltliteratur is valuable in underscoring Heine's highly developed awareness of the communicative and technical media, and of the stylistic and generic proclivities stemming from the development of these new mòdalities, inherent in Goethe's understanding of the term. To be sure, Goethe did not have political reporting in mind when he articulated his concept; in most instances, he employs it in connection with imaginative literature. However, Heine's political leanings can never be left out of account even when he is considered a mediator of *belles lettres,* and considerations of Heine's relationship to Weltliteratur since the appearance of Morawe's book continue to consist mainly of influence and comparative studies that do not take into account Goethe's understanding of the concept,[5] so Morawe should receive due credit for his original insights.

Another Heine scholar who has productively broached the subject of Heine's role as a mediator of Weltliteratur as Goethe defined it is Walter Hinck. In his monograph on Heine's poetry in the context of nationalism, Judaism, and anti-Semitism, *Die Wunde Deutschland* (Germany the Wound), Hinck stresses Heine's cosmopolitanism, his self-conscious role as a bridge between the German and the French peoples, rather than emphasizing his adroit manipulation of improved, more rapid communicative possibilities, the focus of Morawe's analysis of Heine's role in the "advancing Weltliteratur." Hinck cites Heine's well-known letter to a friend from April 1833 in which he describes his goal of making the French familiar with German intellectual life, of bringing the Germans and the French closer together. This is the letter in which Heine describes himself as "der inkarnirte Kosmopolitismus" (the incarnation of cosmopolitanism). In analyzing this letter in the context of Goethean Weltliteratur, Hinck emphasizes that neither Heine nor Goethe denied the existence or significance of national literatures.[6] For our purposes, this is already an important step in historically contextualizing Heine's relationship to the Weltliteratur concept, for today "world literature" as a discursive signifier *is* associated with the breakdown of national literatures, that is, literatures putatively informed by the discrete customs, values, and languages of individual countries. We recall, for example, that Homi Bhabha drew on Goethe's paradigm to propose that: "Where, once, the transmission of national traditions was the major theme of a world literature, perhaps we can now suggest that transnational histories of migrants, the colonized, or political refugees—these border and frontier conditions—may be the terrains of world literature."[7] Heine, of course, was a political refugee of sorts in Paris, and his experiences as they shaped his exile writing may help Bhabha and others when they draw on historical precedent to help establish such world literary terrains.[8] Nevertheless, Hinck is completely correct in suggesting that Heine is an agent of Weltliteratur in the politically and culturally more restricted sense envisioned by Goethe. Hinck quotes Goethe's remarks from 1828 in *Über Kunst und Altertum* which assert that Weltliteratur does not connote a complete correspondence of thought among the various nations, but only that these nations should become aware of each other, understand and tolerate one another. Hinck justifiably sees an identity between these remarks on Weltliteratur's function as a cosmopolitan ideal and the goal Heine expressed in the letter from April 1833 of bringing the people of Germany and France closer together.[9]

To be sure, as Hinck also indicates, this letter displays a politically more radical sensibility than is evident in Goethe's remarks on Weltliteratur in *Über Kunst und Altertum* by associating patriotic narrow-mindedness with the aristocracy, who profit from fostering nationalist prejudices.[10] Privy Counselor Goethe could only subtly attack aristocratic machinations through the cloak of fiction. No one could accuse the noblewoman Germaine de Staël of wanting to foment discord between the peoples of Germany and France; her goal in writing *De l'Allemagne* (1813) was the furtherance of the same enlightened mutual understanding between the nations promoted by Heine in his letter and by Goethe in his remarks on Weltliteratur in *Über Kunst und Altertum*. Nevertheless, Heine composed his two primary essays written to inform the French about German literature and philosophy, published in their final German form as *Die*

Romantische Schule (*The Romantic School*, 1833), and *Zur Geschichte der Religion und Philosophie in Deutschland* ("On the History of Religion and Philosophy in Germany," 1834) and in French under the same title as Madame de Staël's book, largely in reaction to what he believed was the misinformation spread by Madame de Staël. It is unnecessary to rehearse Heine's exhaustively treated personal, political, and literary antipathy toward the French noblewoman, but a brief consideration of the two *De l'Allemagne* will allow us to see why Heine's work corresponds to Goethean notions of Weltliteratur's form and function far more closely than does Madame de Staël's. In this regard, the divergence in their views on German culture in general and Romanticism in particular is not nearly as important as their respective target audiences, and, concomitantly, their choice of literary venues. With respect simply to content, Madame de Staël may be said to come closer to the ideal of Weltliteratur evident in Goethe's first employment of the term in 1827, when he claimed that a universal Weltliteratur was in the process of being constituted and that it reserved an honorable role for the Germans.[11] If we are to believe Madame de Staël, the role of the German Romantics in European literary culture was far more honorable and worthy of emulation than Heine would have it.

Madame de Staël's role in inspiring *Die Romantische Schule* is evident in Heine's opening remarks. He notes her *De l'Allemagne* is the only comprehensive work the French yet possess on Germany's intellectual life. Rather than immediately attacking her views, Heine simply notes that much has changed in Germany since her book appeared. The most important event in the intervening period is said to be Goethe's death, which brought "the demise of the Goethean period of art" in its train. Heine's first use of sarcastic invective occurs as an allusion to *De l'Allemagne*'s style and mode of presentation. After labeling it a "Koteriebuch" (coterie book), Heine continues: "Madame de Staël, of blessed memory has, as it were, opened a salon here in the form of a book, in which she received German writers and gave them the opportunity to make themselves known to the French civilized world" (III:360).[12] Heine, of course, was not a foe of the literary salon. Indeed, he proposed entitling a book encompassing some of his poetry and prose "Salon" in 1833 (III:710), and he learned much through his participation in salon society conversations. Nevertheless, in labeling

Madame de Staël's *De l'Allemagne* a "Koteriebuch," he underscored what he believed to be the elitism of its intended audience, and, thereby, of the book itself. Unlike Heine, Germaine de Staël spent her entire life within the rarified confines of Europe's aristocracy and the small circle of the continent's bourgeois intellectuals. These were the individuals who frequented her isolated salon at Coppet (along with the occasional well-heeled American), and these were the people to whom *De l'Allemagne* was addressed.

This does not signify haughtiness or close-mindedness on Madame de Staël's part; she was, for example, a great admirer of Rahel Varnhagen, a Jewish woman who maintained her own well-regarded salon in Berlin,[13] a salon Heine frequented as a young man. Indeed, Heine praises those portions of Madame de Staël's book where her own voice is clearly manifest. It is the influence of German Romantics themselves which Heine finds objectionable, particularly that of August Wilhelm Schlegel, one of the few relatively permanent guests at Coppet. Heine believes their putative obscurantism must work against both Enlightenment values and the untrammeled intellectual traffic in Europe he wishes to further and which Goethe articulated as the key element in Weltliteratur, even though Goethe ascribed such unhindered exchange to improvements in communication, book distribution, and an increase in the quantity of literary journals rather than to greater political freedom. Such a journal— *L'Europe littéraire*—was Heine's venue for publishing portions of *his De l'Allemagne,* and it is his choice of this medium for this work that allows Heine to express the belief in his previously cited letter of April 1833 that he is engaging in the peaceful mission of bringing Germany and France closer together, and that he is the very embodiment of cosmopolitanism (III:845). Of such organs, Goethe noted: "Diese Zeitschriften, wie sie sich nach und nach ein größeres Publikum gewinnen, werden zu einer gehofften allgemeinen Weltliteratur auf das wirksamste beitragen" (These journals, as they gradually attain a wider audience, will contribute to a hoped-for universal Weltliteratur in the most efficacious possible manner). He stressed as well the importance of developing a common public spirit ("Gemeinsinn") for this same purpose of developing a Weltliteratur.[14] This goal presupposes the establishment of points of convergence, harmonious accords among the national literatures. Here, too, Heine more closely approximates Goethe's Weltliteratur ideal than does Madame de Staël. For as Renate Stauf has noted with respect to Germany and France: "It can be said that Madame de Staël based her ethnic-psychological comparison on the principle of contrast and emphasized the mutual foreignness of the literary and philosophical systems of both countries. Heine, on the other hand, is equally concerned with showing aspects which will help to overcome this foreignness."[15] Though Goethe and Heine—contrary to postcolonial, postmodern critical praxis—underscored the necessity, inevitability, and value of national particularities, they *both* felt that the "foreignness" of which Stauf speaks must be at least partially overcome if a productive literary interaction among the cultivated individuals of different nations was to take place.

As we have noted, one factor that historically dates Goethe's Welt-literatur concept and, at first glance, makes it less applicable to present-day considerations of this topic is his equation of Weltliteratur with "European literature," even though this equation was based on the practical realities of communication networks and literary marketplaces in his day and not on any innate Eurocentrism. In spite of the interest Heine displayed in the world outside his own continent in such poetic works as "Vitzliputzli" and in wide-ranging readings of Asian, North American, and South American literature,[16] his critical focus was European literature as well, and his interest in transnational intellectual exchanges can be seen, like Goethe's, to revolve around Europe. Nevertheless, in comprehensively treating Goethe's concept of Weltliteratur, critics almost always make at least a brief reference to the poetic cycle *West-östlicher Divan*. This is justifiable, for these poems are not only the most celebrated example of Goethe's cosmopolitanism on an international scale, but contain a theoretical apparatus that helps supplement and clarify his scattered remarks on Weltliteratur. Thus, in his essay "Goethes Idee der Weltliteratur"(Goethe's Idea of Weltliteratur), Hendrik Birus draws on Goethe's comments on translation in the *Divan*'s theoretical apparatus to show that Weltliteratur does not presuppose the submersion of national particularities ("Besonderheiten") within the Weltliteratur matrix. One cannot become acquainted with national particularities by reading in translation; as Goethe's views in the *Divan* make clear, such translations are mainly valuable in attracting and introducing the reader to a foreign culture.[17] Heine's comments in *Die Romantische Schule* that contrast the *Divan* with writings on the Orient by the Romantic school are therefore of interest for our purposes. This contrast is fully in accord with Heine's positing of a political antithesis between the Romantic school's supposed conspiratorial, narrow-minded patriotism, its reactionary support of aristocratic restoration, and the cosmopolitanism he associates with G. E. Lessing, Herder, Jean Paul Richter, Schiller, and Goethe; naturally, Heine identifies with this latter faction of German writers in the eighteenth and early nineteenth centuries (III:379–80).

Heine notes at the outset of his remarks on the *West-östlicher Divan* the relative French ignorance of this work. Madame de Staël could not have been aware of it before *De l'Allemagne* was published, as Goethe's poetic cycle appeared six years later. His assumption that France's lack of familiarity with the work is to be equated with its absence from Madame de Staël's discussions shows the supreme influence he ascribed to her with respect to the French reception of contemporary German literature. Heine assumes the *Divan* accurately reflects "the manner of thinking and feeling in the Orient," and his own exotic, metaphoric descriptions of Goethe's imagery in the verse reflect the European view that Asia's manner of thinking and feeling is rooted in profound, intoxicating sensuality. Because such liberated sensuality was consistently a key element in Heine's utopian formulations, his approval of Goethe's sensualism is unsurprising. Indeed, Heine describes the *Divan* as a "Selam," as a greeting and gift of the Occident to the Orient, but also as a sign the West is weary of its ethereal spiritualism and wishes to recover by refreshing itself through an immersion into the Orient's "gesunden Körperwelt" (healthy physical world). Heine emphasizes this carefree but healthy voluptuousness in the *Divan* in order to contrast it with the Sanskrit studies of the Brothers Schlegel.

According to Heine, the Brothers Schlegel found Indian religion and customs attractive because of Hinduism's putative bizarreness, vagueness, and indulgence in mortification of the senses, as well as its character as a civilization rooted in a strict caste system. The Schlegels' penchant for India's culture is grounded in this culture's apparent parallels with

Catholicism. It must be emphasized that Heine does not claim these parallels exist. Rather, he believes the Schlegels discovered these attributes in Indian society and viewed the region as the originary locus of Catholic order and practices (III:402–4). While Goethe engages in a genuine interchange with Persian Islam, the Schlegels, in Heine's view, mold India into the shape most amenable to their Catholic perspective. As Azade Seyhan puts it: "In contrast to the Schlegels' ideological appropriation of the Indian identity that served to promote a false consciousness of the subject, Goethe's representation of the Islamic Orient resists identification with a textual construct." Thus, in Heine's interpretation of the *Divan,* "the subject institutes an exchange, a kind of dialogue with the object."[18] Engagement in such intersubjective dialogue is at the heart of Goethe's Weltliteratur ideal, and in embracing such congress while refuting its relational antithesis in the Schlegels' supposed confiscation of Indian ideology for the promotion of their religious agenda, Heine tacitly shows his own ideological affinity to the Weltliteratur concept as Goethe formulated it. Heine also clearly associated the Schlegels' Catholicism with conservative, nationalist politics and Goethe's pantheism with his cosmopolitanism and genuine openness to cultural and religious alterity. These latter perspectives are obvious preconditions for enacting the Weltliteratur paradigm in its broadest aspect.

As we noted, Goethe's enunciation of Weltliteratur does not signify a diminished interest in understanding discrete national attributes through the act of reading foreign literature. Such particularities can only be correctly appreciated through reading such literature in the original language, but translations can at least draw a reader to an initial interest in and acquaintance with a foreign culture. This may in turn inspire the reader to attain a reading knowledge of the original idiom and thereby a more genuine comprehension of its unique elements. Heine, too, was attracted to the "beautiful particularities" of different cultures. As Stauf maintains in citing this expression from *Über Polen* ("Essay on Poland," 1823), this tendency stands juxtaposed with Heine's desire to disempower national discourses in favor of a European discourse, a dichotomy which he shared with Goethe, Herder, and others.[19] Michel Espagne has cogently argued that, late in life, Heine passionately embraced translation, which is, broadly speaking and ideally in Heine's view, an act enabling a productive flight into the Orient both as a locus of oblivion and as a way to critically confront contemporary Europe's quotidian philistine realities.[20] This would certainly help to explain Heine's appreciation for the *Divan,* which he believed was capable of transporting the reader into a sensual space of genuine revivifying alterity rooted in exotic particularities. This allows the reader, in Heine's view, to forget frigid Europe, but also to critically reflect on the restrictions it sets to the life of the spirit and the senses.

Heine felt this liberating potential was lost in the Schlegel Brothers' treatment of India. Heine is capable of praising both the Romantics' critical investigations of world literature and the quality of their translations; he rates Friedrich Schlegel's lectures on literature as second only to Herder's writings in their comprehensive overview of the literature of all the world's peoples, and he extols A. W. Schlegel's translations of Shakespeare (III:410, 411). Nevertheless, his cosmopolitanism and his embrace of translation as a means for both imaginatively escaping and critically reflecting upon Europe in general and France and Germany in particular inevitably put him at odds with the linkage of German nationalism, translation, and Weltliteratur by the German Romantics.

To be sure, the cosmopolitanism of Goethe and that of Heine vary in many particulars,[21] and this circumstance has led Benno von Wiese to assert that Heine's left-wing politics manifest a clear break with Goethe's Weltliteratur concept. One can summarize Wiese's views as follows: while Europe, the locus of Weltliteratur as articulated in the early nineteenth century, constituted for Goethe an already existent universe in harmony with his spiritual, intellectual proclivities and was thus a region simply in need of broader cosmopolitan development, this continent was for Heine, after Goethe's death, a primarily political domain, the site of revolutions he optimistically hoped were portents of worldwide emancipation. Like Hinck, Wiese cites Heine's letter of April 1833 with its announcement of Heine's mission to bring the world's people together. However, while Hinck sees in this letter Heine's tacit embrace of Weltliteratur's ideal of productive transnational interchange, Wiese reaches the opposite conclusion. He does not interpret the letter's pronouncements as expressing a cultural goal inscribed with the spirit of peace. Rather, he believes the letter expresses the sentiment that what can and should unite the world's diverse peoples is not the idea of Weltliteratur but the idea of a world revolution to be realized sometime in the future.[22] Given Heine's bellicose pronouncements in the letter of April 1833 against an aristocracy served by Goethe and which actually took him into its ranks, Wiese's contrast is plausible. Nevertheless, this letter, as Hinck indicates, underscores what Heine's journalistic activities promoting transnational understanding of German and French culture firmly establish: Heine was an agent of Weltliteratur as defined by Goethe. The justification for Wiese's point of view is grounded in the diachronic perspective he establishes. However, I believe the truth about Heine's relationship to Goethe's Weltliteratur paradigm can only be expressed when we synthesize Hinck's and Wiese's antithetical perspectives. This leads to the following conclusion: while Heine mediated Weltliteratur in the manner elucidated by Goethe, Goethe's death during the early phase of Heine's life in Paris marked the *beginning of the end* of Weltliteratur as a distinctly Goethean paradigm. For in the period immediately before and after Goethe's death, the Young Germany movement, with Heine in its midst, literally wrote this paradigm off. Heine was not just its only mediator to achieve immortal distinction, he was also a key inspirer of its demise.

Before we take up why Heine and Young Germany can be said to bring Goethean Weltliteratur to an end, it is worth considering in somewhat more detail why Heine's activities not only mark its beginning, but the only genuine phase of its existence as a national-international dialogue. We have already cited Morawe's suggestion that Heine was perhaps the first pan-European writer to exploit the technological and communicative improvements at the core of Goethe's definitions of the term. The most significant organ to embody these improvements and inspire in Goethe the belief that the age of Weltliteratur was at hand was the Parisian journal *Le Globe*. As we noted, Goethe was first inspired to use the term after he read a *Globe* review of a French adaptation of *Torquato Tasso*; particularly the *Globe* essay and others he read in this magazine instilled in him the belief that a genuine transnational dialogue was taking place with respect to literature. In general, Goethe held the contemporary journalistic media of his time, especially the daily newspapers to which he had access in Weimar, in low esteem. But in *Le Globe,* he believed the spirit of the time was given clear and powerful expression. It became his press organ of choice for keeping up with current political and cultural events and opinions in Europe, and he made copious notes on its articles.[23] As Jeffrey Sammons has remarked, Heine became an avid reader of *Le Globe* as well around 1828. Sammons even suspects that the paean printed in this journal to mark Heine's arrival in the French capital was actually written by him.[24] Heine also expressed the belief that the cosmopolitan spirit of his century was given clear expression in the journal. Its scientifically democratic writers precisely dictate ("genau diktieren") what Heine termed "die Welthülfsliteratur" (II:903). This is a difficult neologism to translate, but it signifies a sort of literature Heine believed was in the process of emerging and which would promote the interests of humanity on a universal scale.

The tone and vocabulary of Heine's praise reflect his pleasure at France's intellectual upheavals, and point to a significant difference between his cosmopolitanism and that of Goethe. In this regard, it is significant to note that in October 1830 the socialistic Saint-Simonians took over the editorship of *Le Globe,* and while this shift only increased Heine's high regard for it, its new partisan spirit provoked Goethe's displeasure.[25] Both men were uniquely confluent in their prescient esteem for early nineteenth-century press organs like *Le Globe,* transnational with respect to content, ideals, and (because of new technology) transmission. However, Heine's nascent Saint-Simonian leanings led him to recoin, consciously or unconsciously, Goethe's already cosmopolitan term. "Welthülfsliteratur" reflects the movement's activist, utilitarian spirit, its belief that all social means—including literature—must serve and promote the interests of the world's masses, not just those of the aristocratic and intellectual elite. Heine's employment of the term in the context of praising the objective, research oriented, scientific young democrats who wrote for *Le Globe* helps to justify Wilhelm Gössmann's reference to "the coupling of Weltliteratur and science achieved by Heine in his work."[26]

The distinction in tone and purport between the terms "Weltliteratur" and "Welthülfsliteratur" should not be taken to signify that Goethe's paradigm lacked a societal dimension. This dimension is evident in the following remark from 1828:

> Wenn wir eine europäische, ja eine allgemeine Weltliteratur zu verkündigen gewagt haben, so heißt dieses nicht, daß die verschiedenen Nationen voneinander und ihren Erzeugnissen Kenntnis nehmen, denn in diesem

Sinne exisitiert sie schon lange, setzt sich fort und erneuert sich mehr oder weniger. Nein! hier ist vielmehr davon die Rede, daß die lebendigen und strebenden Literatoren einander kennenlernen und durch Neigung und Gemeinsinn sich veranlaßt finden, gesellschaftlich zu wirken.[27]

[If we have ventured to proclaim a European, indeed universal Welt-literatur, this does not simply mean that the different nations become acquainted with each other and with their products, for it has already existed in this sense for a long time, is continuing and is more or less renewing itself. Rather, what is meant is that the living, striving men of letters get to know each other and find themselves spurred to act socially through inclination and the sense of a common public spirit.]

However, as Victor Lange has noted, this passage cannot be understood outside its historical context, and does not equate Weltliteratur with a contribution to concrete political reality or to social criticism. Rather, it signifies that writing is only world-literary in scope if its author composes in a conscious spirit of communal understanding, possesses an awareness of the great tasks before the world as a whole, contributes to and is open to his epoch's knowledge.[28] Because he believed *De l'Allemagne* contributed to such transcultural understanding and promoted knowledge of Germany abroad, Goethe, unlike Heine, gave unqualified praise to Madame de Staël's book (11:736). Though Heine's own *De l'Allemagne* does veer into the social critical role highlighted as un-Goethean by Lange, it is nevertheless imbued with the same cosmopolitan spirit of understanding and contributing to intercultural knowledge Lange associated with the Weltliteratur paradigm in its historically restricted, early nineteenth-century ambience.

In summarizing and concluding my argument that Heine was the first writer of note who was a mediator of Weltliteratur in Goethe's sense of the term, I find several points bear repeating. As Morawe has indicated, Heine was one of the earliest writers to become aware of and exploit technological, communicative, and distributive advances highlighted by Goethe in his adumbrations of the paradigm. Heine's employment of these improved media allowed him to reach a larger, more diverse audience than was the case with predecessors such as Madame de Staël, whose own *De l'Allemagne* targeted and reached only a select group of aristocrats, intellectuals, and others who frequented literary salons. This more comprehensive and freer intellectual commerce is a key element in Goethe's understanding of Weltliteratur. Heine's unique two-way role in not only furthering the transmission of German literature and thought in France through his own *De l'Allemagne,* but reporting to the Germans his impressions of French events and culture in such works as *Französische Zustände, Französische Maler* ("French Painters," 1831), and *Über die französische Bühne* ("Concerning the French Stage," 1837) must also be mentioned in this regard. Given France's political, linguistic, and cultural status in the eighteenth century, one can find far more journalistic reporting on France in Germany than on Germany in France prior to Madame de Staël and Heine. However, the target audiences of such reporting on the French scene were generally the personages of European courts. I am thinking here particularly of the readers of Friedrich Melchior Grimm's famous eighteenth-century *Correspondance littéraire.* Other transmitters of French culture to Germany were primarily academics and intellectuals writing and toiling for other academics and intellectuals in relative obscurity.[29] Heine was the only writer working at the close of the *Goethezeit* committed to Weltliteratur's cosmopolitan, universalist ideals who personally enjoyed (and still enjoys) world literary status.

It remains to elucidate why Heine was not just the *first* but the *only* internationally renowned purveyor of Weltliteratur as a Goethean construct, and to this end we must examine the Young Germany engagement with this paradigm. Hartmut Steinecke, who has devoted an article to this topic, has pointed out that a response to Goethe's elucidation of the term only began to become widespread in 1836, four years after Goethe's death. In this year, the *Gespräche mit Goethe* were first published. It is here that Weltliteratur received its most famous articulation.[30] Steinecke notes that the Young Germany adherents, with their interest in combining literature and science, were initially predisposed in favor of Weltliteratur as an ideal, since such a comprehensive concept presupposes not only the transcending of national borders but of the traditional divisions between imaginative literature on the one hand, and scientific and political writing on the other.[31] Heine's coining of the term "Welthülfsliteratur" in praising the scientism of *Le Globe*'s writers (II:903) reflects the synthesizing inclination of which Steinecke speaks. In his essay "Goethe und die Welt-Literatur" (Goethe and World-Literature, 1835), Ludolf Wienbarg lauds Goethe's principle that art and life are inseparable.[32] Such approval reflects Young Germany's objectifying tendency and its embrace of Goethean Weltliteratur for this purpose, even though the movement is, with respect to literary criticism, most famous for its pillorying of the privy counselor. However, Wienbarg's praise also has a political dimension; the enunciation of the paradigm allows him to express certainty that a universal brotherhood binding the peoples of the world will continue to grow stronger, bringing about an ever more cordial interchange among the earth's literatures.[33] These are the same dreams that sustained Heine and allowed him to become Weltliteratur's premier mediator.

Despite Wienbarg's expression of a cosmopolitan spirit shared by Heine and others affiliated with Young Germany, it was primarily the movement's nationalist strain that put an end to Weltliteratur as Goethe understood it. This nationalism was partly sincere and partly a tactical response to the relentless jingoist diatribe directed against the group, particularly by Wolfgang Menzel, whose loathing for Goethe was partly based on the latter's universalist tendencies.[34] Heine tried to counteract such virulent "Teutomanie" through both ironic satire and positive prophetic visions that would channel nationalism in a positive direction.[35] A year after Wienbarg's essay was published, Karl Gutzkow's treatise *Ueber Göthe im Wendepunkte zweier Jahrhunderte* (On Goethe at the Turning-Point of Two Centuries) appeared. In this work, Gutzkow cautiously defended Weltliteratur by highlighting what he saw as its productive relationship with national literature. He argues in Weltliteratur's defense that it neither displaces nationality nor forces one to renounce homeland mountains and valleys in favor of cosmopolitan images. Indeed, Weltliteratur secures the viability of nationality. Given the absence of political preconditions for a national literature in Germany, the world literary condition ("weltliterarischen Zustand") justifies Germany's native literature, for the outside world acclaims this literature while it is condemned to death at home (i.e., through censorship). Gutzkow proceeds to rebut the calumny endured by Heine, who has achieved fame throughout Europe with his extraordinary talents.[36]

Gutzkow is clearly trying to sustain here the dialectic and dialogue of national and international literature that was so central to Goethe's Weltliteratur paradigm and to Heine's unique, albeit unconscious, practical realization of it. Gerhard Kaiser sees in Gutzkow's essay an early instance of the narrow-minded nationalism soon to be so prevalent in Germany,[37] but it seems more likely that Gutzkow is taking a defensive posture, reacting to the polemics of Menzel and his followers as well as to the repressive political atmosphere that culminated in the edict against five members of the Young Germany movement on 10 December 1835. A truly pronounced partisanship for national literature vis-à-vis Weltliteratur is more evident in Theodor Mundt's discussion of Goethe's paradigm in the former's *Geschichte der Literatur der Gegenwart* (History of the Literature of the Present, 2nd ed., 1853). Here Mundt claims Weltliteratur has primarily a commercial and political significance and asserts:

> Die schärfste Ausprägung der eigenthümlichen Nationalität ist vielmehr in jeder Literatur als der wahre Kern und der höchste Reiz zu betrachten, und ein überhand nehmender universalistischer Geist der Bildung, der eine Verallgemeinerung der Nationalität zuwegebringt, kann nur die Verderbniß und Verschlechterung der Literatur erwirken.[38]

> [The sharpest expression of characteristic nationalism is, rather, to be considered the true essence and greatest charm in every literature, and an ever more predominating universal spirit of acculturation, which is bringing about the leveling of nationality, can only bring about the ruin and deterioration of literature.]

This perspective reverses a trend found in earlier Young Germany engagements with the paradigm, namely, the tendency to label those works with the label Weltliteratur which are qualitatively superior to others. As Steinecke notes, the equation of value with world literary status was addressed only indirectly by Goethe (and, we might add, by Heine), but it has influenced discussions of world literature from the 1830s to the present day,[39] when works supposedly deserving of this appellation are still equated with the canon. More importantly, Mundt's comments mark a definitive break in German literary criticism with Goethe's paradigm as he defined it and as Heine put it into practice. Mundt's view that Weltliteratur is fundamentally a commercial rather than aesthetic signifier was an exaggeration of Goethe's views, but was also repeated in the twentieth century, as we will see in the next chapter.

A contemporary of Mundt's, Georg Gottfried Gervinus, was one of the first to reject the cosmopolitan element in Weltliteratur for political reasons. Gervinus was a pioneer in analyzing German literary history from a nationalistic perspective; indeed, he viewed the writing of a history of German literature as a patriotic responsibility. This makes his views toward Weltliteratur ambivalent; on the one hand, citing Goethe's comments on the centrality of German and Germany in the dawning age of Weltliteratur, he indicates that the paradigm's emergence reflects positively on the fatherland's increasing cultural stature and influence among its neighbors. However, he maintains that one must guard against the spirit of universalism signified by the term. He sees the damage brought about by its embrace in the imitation of foreign models by young German writers in the contemporary epoch. Thus, the gains in prestige achieved by German literature subsequent to the age of Goethe can only be sustained, in Gervinus's view, if Germans remain steadfastly committed to nationalism and to an advancement of German political goals.[40]

In the period between Goethe's death and the 1848 revolution, such nationalism became strongly established, and Heine's name became a fulcrum for both opponents and proponents of both Young Germany and the ideal of Weltliteratur. We have already noted Gutzkow's defense of Heine in the context of his argument for the efficacy of a universal literature-national literature dialogue. Those who held antipathetic views toward Goethe's concept and the Young Germany movement drew on Heine and his Francophile leanings to sustain their argument. Steinecke notes, citing Menzel, that for these conservative nationalists: "Weltliteratur means in practice—viz. Heine—the praise of what is French, and thus the delivering up of German culture to French culture and submission to the dangerous political ideals of the revolution."[41] Steinecke's inference that these opponents of Weltliteratur equated its practice with the name of Heine evinces 1830 Germany's correct grasp of the veracity of a central thesis of this chapter, which since the nineteenth century has been lost sight of: Heine was *the* foremost practitioner of Weltliteratur as Goethe defined it. At the turn into the twentieth, Germany's eager xenophobic embrace of imperialism made genuine critical support for Goethe's ideal almost inconceivable, and tirades against Heine continued to be a benchmark of this perspective. By this time, the difference between "national" and "nationalistic" literature was largely effaced.[42]

Of course, there continued to be writers in the late nineteenth and early twentieth centuries in the German-speaking world and elsewhere who promoted a cosmopolitan spirit in literature, a dialogue among the writers of the world that, ideally, would promote peace and the universal betterment of mankind; one can cite, for example, the ubiquitous international mediating engagements of Stefan Zweig and his good friend Romain Rolland. The mature Thomas Mann, who saw the need to promote international cosmopolitanism when its only alternative became a silent acceptance of Nazi and fascist principles, is another such figure. Such engagements, however, were reactive responses to an infrangible nationalism, not an attempt to promote a national-international dialogue at least partly in the service of *national* interests, as was the case in the ages of Goethe and Heine.[43] As Steinecke has noted, Goethe believed the articulation and development of Weltliteratur took place in Germany for a particular reason; Germany's retarded development of a discrete national identity in the eighteenth century sharpened its openness to and perception of international contexts and connections ("Zusammenhänge"). Adherents of Young Germany, such as Wienbarg, also saw Germany's lack of political unity as a positive force for cosmopolitanism.[44] Though Heine contrasted his own philosophical cosmopolitanism with the old German "philistine feelings" residing in his breast (III:614), his youth in the disunified political milieu described by Goethe undoubtedly contributed to his pan-European perspective.

Quite possibly the last positive expression of Weltliteratur as an ideal prior to its revival at the end of World War II is to be found in the 1848 *Manifest der Kommunistischen Partei* (*Communist Manifesto*) of Karl Marx and Friedrich Engels. This manifesto, the imagery of which was probably influenced by Heine,[45] maintains that in the age of international interdependence, intellectual productions of individual nations are shared by all, national narrow-mindedness and one-sidedness become impossible, and a "Weltliteratur" is taking shape out of the diverse national and local literatures.[46] Contrary to this utopian prophecy, nationalism became so virulent that Weltliteratur lost its idealistic resonance after 1848 and became, as we have seen, associated primarily with canonicity and commerce. Prior to this time, Heine was its most exemplary mediator. In the post–World War II age of mass communication, largely anonymous marketers and reviewers took over this role. As this trend has only been enhanced in the current era of the Internet, Heine will probably remain history's only agent of Weltliteratur in its Goethean sense to have achieved timeless international stature.

It is not difficult to summarize the fate of Weltliteratur from the end of the *Goethezeit* to the end of the nineteenth century. During the Young Germany period, leading cosmopolitan thinkers such as Gutzkow who supported the ideal of Weltliteratur had to argue that it was consistent with and even guaranteed nationality and the nationalist spirit. Literature written in Germany continued to be acclaimed *as* German literature in the world at large while being castigated at home, and this world-literary condition thus provided a primary impetus and justification for a German national-cultural identity, in Gutzkow's view. However, the more xenophobic and virulent form of nationalism that overtook Germany and most of Europe after the failed 1848 revolutions created a decisive break with the idealist, universal, cross-cultural aspect of Weltliteratur, which is to say that it ceased to function as a genuinely transnational paradigm. This circumstance, and the revival of Weltliteratur in the second half of the twentieth century, will be explored in the following chapter.

Nationalism and Revival

Weltliteratur from 1848 to the Present

CONTRARY TO THE PREDICTIONS of Marx and Engels, narrow-minded nationalism became more and more predominant in Europe after 1848, when the continent-wide revolution against the repressive, reactionary Restoration regimes was crushed. From the end of the 1848 revolution until the end of World War II, most German thinkers eschewed the cosmopolitan perspective as an impediment to the rise of Germany as a national state. Intellectually, this trend culminated in Friedrich Meinecke's highly influential study *Weltbürgertum und Nationalstaat* (*Cosmopolitanism and the National State*), first published in 1907. Though it may strike one as odd from the perspective of our contemporary age, given its tendency to valorize transnational alliances and global networks as clear manifestations of historical progress, Meinecke saw cosmopolitanism as a necessary but outdated principle that had to be transcended in order to bring about the emergence of German nationalism. Meinecke traces the conceptual rise of nationalistic thinking in Germany from the late eighteenth century to the present day. Each intellectual he examines is analyzed on the basis of how his thinking contributed to the theoretical foundation of the German nation-state. While he recognizes that cosmopolitanism and a nationalist perspective are not mutually exclusive, Meneicke clearly regards nationalism as the progressive end toward which historical thought has tended. For example, he regards the Romantic political thinking of Novalis and Friedrich Schlegel as a groping toward the foundation of the national state, but as a search enfeebled by its grounding in a Christian universalism still based on cosmopolitan Catholic dogma.[1] While somewhat unique in its concise yet elaborate teleology, Meinecke's book reflects generally held views in Germany between 1848 and 1945 concerning the relationship between nationalism and cosmopolitanism, and thus typifies this long age.

To be sure, Weltliteratur as a cosmopolitan concept had its defenders in the years following the failed 1848 revolution. In his encyclopedia article on Weltliteratur, Erwin Koppen cites the example of Johannes Scherr, who, in 1869, defended Goethe's concept in decrying the grandiose nationalism and xenophobia of his own age.[2] However, as Kaiser notes, Goethe's Weltliteratur concept was largely drained after 1848 of its historical-philosophical-humanistic substance and came to signify canonicity or comprehensiveness. This late nineteenth-century evisceration of the cosmopolitan character of Goethe's paradigm can be attributed not only to the age's nationalism, but to its positivism as well. The materialist strain resulting from this positivism led to the representation of Weltliteratur as purely additive, the compilation of works from diverse nations. Thus, anthologies of Weltliteratur first began to flourish at this time. The idea of Germany as the great mediator among world cultures, linked by Goethe to the nation's fragmented political status, was revived in the second half of the nineteenth century, but this was a phenomenon concomitant to Germany's sense of cultural superiority, an attitude that was especially widespread after the victory against France in the Franco-Prussian War in 1871, which led to German unification.[3] We have already noted the rejection of Weltliteratur as a cosmopolitan concept by former Young Germany adherents such as Mundt after the revolution. The nationalistic poet August Heinrich Hoffmann von Fallersleben even wrote a poem in the year of the founding of the Second Empire (1871) in which he denounced "the dream of Weltliteratur" as presupposing complete spiritual and cultural identity among all the peoples of the world.[4] To be sure, Comparative Literature as a cross-national discipline began to take shape in Germany late in the nineteenth century, and a lively debate began at that time on the relationship between Goethe's notion of Weltliteratur and the new discipline of Comparative Literature,[5] a debate carried on well into the twentieth century.

Nevertheless, the nuance of global transnationalism inherent in Goethe's articulation of his construct rarely if ever came to the fore in these fin de siècle discussions. Even the eminent, still-celebrated, and influential Danish critic Georg Brandes, who wrote a brief essay entitled "Weltlitteratur" for the periodical *Das litterarische Echo* at the behest of its editors in 1899, does not get beyond a "great works"–oriented definition. He admits at the outset that he has forgotten the context in which Goethe used the term. However, he goes on to argue that only a handful of authors "belong" to Weltliteratur; Shakespeare is a member of this exclusive club, for example, while Marlowe and Coleridge only possess the status of "English" authors.[6] Brandes assumes no automatic connection between world literary status and the merit of all in its pantheon. Fellow Dane Hans Christian Andersen attained this distinction, denied more deserving countrymen such as Johan Ludvig Heiberg, solely because of Andersen's worldwide popularity.[7] Clearly, Brandes's notion of Weltliteratur, not uncommon in his age, has only a tenuous connection to the paradigm as Goethe understood it.

Ernst Elster's influential 1901 essay "Weltlitteratur und Litteraturvergleichung" takes a rather one-sided view of the Weltliteratur paradigm, but the aspect he most clearly discerns in Goethe's formula parallels and anticipates the seminal immanent factor that is bringing about the increasing contemporary predominance of nonmonolithic cultures. These are cultures *not* primarily generated by, or focused on the concerns of, discrete nation-states. According to Elster, the term Weltliteratur signified for Goethe only the expansion of literary interests beyond the confines of national borders as driven by a broader sphere for literary commerce. Elster argues that Goethe did not intend his term to signify cross-national influences among the world's authors, nor (at least in the foreground) the issue of how literary wheat separates from chaff and exerts an influence beyond the time and space of its origin. According to this view, Goethe's term even excluded the impact on literary history made by past works; Weltliteratur signifies only the present, and Goethe "only wants to emphasize that the international market is open."[8] Comparative Literature, on the other hand, involves juxtaposing works (usually marked by temporal and spatial proximity to each other) and, through determining their differences and concordances, comprehending the "great current" of literary life.[9] Though Elster's conceptualization of how Goethe understood his own term is overly narrow in scope, his correct focus on the internationalization of the literary marketplace as central to Weltliteratur as a discursive formation suggests that even at its origin it has a closer structural affinity to contemporary transnational literary studies than does "Comparative Literature."

Another scholar who emphasized the international marketing element in elucidating Weltliteratur as a specifically Goethean construct, the individual who was its greatest twentieth-century adherent as well as its most prolific investigator, was Fritz Strich. At a relatively early stage in his career, Strich followed the lead of Elster and other turn-of-the-century analysts in examining the interrelationship between "Weltliteratur und vergleichende Literaturgeschichte" (World Literature and Comparative Literary History) in his thusly titled essay, published in 1930. At the outset of this piece, Strich rejects the assumption that "comparative literary history" is to be equated with the study of international relationships among the world's literatures, since literary studies confined to a single land also inevitably resort to comparisons between different authors and works in that one country.[10] He proposes the term "Weltliteratur" to signify what we continue to call "Comparative Literature." Strich's essay was progressive for its time in stressing that "world literature" was not to be equated with "European literature," and in promoting a belief that renewed attention to "world literary science" ("Weltliteratur-Wissenschaft")[11] could build bridges of understanding, tolerance, and productive exchange among diverse populations. However, the article is generally rooted in a *Geistesgeschichte* mentality common to the 1930s, obsessed with differentiating between discrete national spirits and insisting on how the unique mentality of a "Volk" is reflected in immanent literary production and in the dynamics of cultural interchange.

A strongly nationalist spirit between the two world wars is evident in the considerations of Weltliteratur which took place at that time. The writing of Thomas Mann provides a paradigmatic instance of such discussions. To be sure, Mann would come to draw frequently on Goethe's political cosmopolitanism in rallying his countrymen against the Nazis. However, he asserted in his pre–Third Reich essay "Nationale und internationale Kunst" (National and International Art, 1922), after underscoring what he believed were the uniquely German elements in Goethe's Weltliteratur concept, that there was no such thing as cosmopolitanism pure and simple, that only "national cosmopolitanisms" existed.[12] He spoke of the contemporary realization of the cosmopolitan element in Goethean Weltliteratur in highly derisive terms:

> Goethe's Verkündigung der Weltliteratur ist heute in hohem Grade verwirklicht. Der Austausch ist allgemein, der Ausgleich—man könnte gehässigerweise sagen: die demokratische Einebnung—beinahe erreicht. Es gibt Franzosen, die den breiten Humor Britanniens an den Tag legen, ins Pariserische entartete Russen und Skandinavier, die die Synthese von Dostojewski und Amerika vollziehen. Dergleichen darf man Internationalisierung der Kunst nennen.[13]

> [Goethe's proclamation of Weltliteratur has been realized today to a great degree. Exchange is universal, balance—one could, in a mean-spirited manner, say democratic leveling—has practically been achieved. There are French people who display the broad humor of Britain, Russians and Scandinavians who have degenerated into the Parisian, who have brought about the synthesis of Dostoevski and America. One may refer to such things as the internationalization of art.]

Much like contemporary analysts of Goethe's paradigm who fail to take into account that he could not possibly have foreseen the emergence of such globalizing instruments as the World Trade Organization or the Internet, Mann in his early conservative phase conveniently ignored the antinationalist context in which Goethe's formulations on Weltliteratur came about, and many intellectuals both prior to Strich and today altogether fail to reflect on the term's Goethean derivation. The comment on a degeneration "into the Parisian" points to a modernist association between Weltliteratur and a homogenizing urbanism also evident in the thought of Oswald Spengler.[14]

With the looming advent of Nazism, Mann's view of Weltliteratur drastically changed. In the essay "Goethe als Repräsentant des bürgerlichen Zeitalters" ("Goethe as Representative of the Bourgeois Age," 1932), written on the eve of Hitler's assumption of power in Germany, Mann drew on Goethe's cosmopolitanism in order to dampen the virulent xeno-phobia that had taken root in his homeland. In this essay, Mann argues that Goethe intended his term to signify the most illustrious literary works. Regardless of the home soil on which these creations came to bloom, they attained in Mann's opinion a universal value and became recognized as being the possession of all of humanity.[15] Mann praises the prophetic character of Goethe's views, his articulation of universal literary interchange spurred by an improved technological infrastructure, and clearly wishes the "humanistic-classical" expansiveness of the sage of Weimar could once again prove influential in Europe.[16] Uniquely, Mann engages in this essay the normative element one can plausibly find in Goethean Weltliteratur for liberal political purposes. In the context of the World Literature classroom, however, Mann's association of Weltliteratur with canonicity will strike most contemporary teachers as rather dated.

Of course, during the reign of the Third Reich, an embrace of Welt-literatur as a cosmopolitan ideal was inconceivable in Germany. Instead, Eurocentric and patriotic elements in Goethe's writing were distorted so that his thought could be made to conform to the regime's nationalist, racist ideology. Thus the National Socialist adherent Kurt Hildebrandt argued that Goethe's Weltliteratur principle was grounded in Aryan values rather than internationalist politics: "'Weltliteratur' is for him the literature of peoples with an Aryan destiny, who went through the Renaissance." In Hildebrandt's view, even the *Divan,* in reality Goethe's most profound poetic expression of Weltliteratur as a bridging of ethnic and cultural divisions, was "merely a reflection of the Aryan soul."[17]

The cosmopolitan ideal of the paradigm first reemerges in the work of Strich. Strich's magnum opus, *Goethe und die Weltliteratur,* appeared in 1946, not long after the end of World War II. Not surprisingly, given the renewed globalist hopes of that time, Strich's book reflects the same somewhat prophetic ambience of collapsed cultural borders, an emerging internationalization of the literary marketplace, and transnational aesthetic exchange on a universal scale characteristic in Goethe's own Weltliteratur paradigm and in contemporary articulations of postcolonial, post–Cold War hybridity. Nevertheless, Strich's global vision is Eurocentric with respect to center and origin: "A European literature, thus one between the literatures of Europe and which mediates and is exchanged between the European peoples, is the first stage of Weltliteratur, which, beginning from here, will continue to spread and will develop into a complex which finally encompasses the world."[18] Obviously Strich, like Goethe before him, is wedded to the notion of discrete national literary identities, but the comprehensive, world-embracing complex he envisions suggests a globalization of the forces driving literary production, marketing, and interchange.[19]

An even more powerful sense of actualized contemporary globalization than is evident in Strich's study is manifest in essays contributed to his festschrift, published in 1952 and titled simply *Weltliteratur.* In "Die Entfaltung der Weltliteratur als Prozess" (The Development of World Literature as a Process), Anni Carlsson argues that Goethe signified through his neologism those works which transcend national, temporal, and linguistic borders and address a universal audience. At the end of Goethe's age, the world becomes accessible and capable of being experienced as a totality. Carlsson draws a picture of an ever more comprehensive communication network mediating a world literary discursive formation.[20] Erich Auerbach bemoans such trends in his "Philologie der Weltliteratur," for he believes they are leading to a homogenization that will be destructive to all distinct cultural traditions. He even envisions a rapidly approaching age when only a handful of literary languages, perhaps just one, will be in evidence; such an event would constitute both Weltliteratur's ultimate realization and its destruction. Writing in the coldest phase of the Cold War, Auerbach indicates such standardization bears "European-American" and "Russian-Bolshevik" imprints.[21] Not surprisingly, in this dual context of uniformity and enmity, he believes that the utopian notion of reconciliation through Weltliteratur is out of date,[22] and he finds the connection of Goethe's paradigm in the 1950s with necessity and the imprimatur of mass movements to be highly un-Goethean.[23] In both Carlsson's rather positive and Auerbach's highly pessimistic vision of Weltliteratur at mid-century, we can glimpse the onset of cultural globalization as mediated by transnational marketing and rapid worldwide communication.

Hans-Georg Gadamer's magnum opus, *Wahrheit und Methode* (*Truth and Method,* 1960), played a seminal role in establishing the limits and possibilities of a dialogue with literary texts. The title of his book is ironic; because all understanding is historically conditioned, in Gadamer's view, there *cannot be* a method for determining the truth of a text. Instead, a profound metacritical awareness of comprehension's situated character, a knowledge that our being-in-the-world is circumscribed by the time and place in which we live as well as by our personal backgrounds, first enables a genuine openness to a hermeneutic engagement with a text. An awareness that our own historical horizons inevitably create interpretive prejudices first makes possible an understanding that the text itself is informed by the historical conditions under which it was composed, as well as by the author's own unique experiences. Because such metacritical reflection is as fundamental as a metatheoritical awareness of Weltliteratur's historical development for establishing the parameters of a successful World Literature course, it is of particular interest to explore Gadamer's view of Goethe's paradigm.

Gadamer begins his discussion by foregrounding the hidden historical nature of the literary text. Literature's being-in-the-world ("Dasein") cannot be considered a lifeless relic simply handed to the present for its consideration. Instead, "classical" works are living documents whose vitality is established through their historical reception and mediation as exemplary texts for the acculturation ("Bildung") of subsequent generations. This sustained engagement through the ages allows a text to be considered canonic. However, the development of historical consciousness calls this normative character of classical works into question. Such is the nature of literary history. If Weltliteratur can be characterized through its canonic status as a "living unity," historical consciousness counteracts this normative element by indefinitely postponing interpretive closure. Gadamer mistakenly assumes that Goethe himself underscored the normative dimension still evident in contemporary understandings of the paradigm, as though Goethe was responsible for still current equations of Weltliteratur with canonicity. Though Goethe did believe the global mediation of literature in the new age of Weltliteratur tended to separate the wheat from the chaff, the equation of Weltliteratur with canonicity first begins in the late phase of Young Germany.

Based on his assumption that Weltliteratur refers to works that have proven their current validity by standing the test of time and thus assuming a place in the classical pantheon, Gadamer must confront a fundamental dilemma; if a canonic work is marked by timeless relevance, how does one come to terms with both its historical horizon and that of its contemporary audience? According to Gadamer, works of Weltliteratur, by virtue of their normative status, remain capable of speaking ("sprechend bleiben") despite the divergent nature of the world to which they speak at any given time. A work that belongs to Weltliteratur possesses a dynamic historical mode of being. This imbues canonic works with a vitality that allows them to transcend the alienating elements of history and translation. On the one hand, while Gadamer's notion of what merits the status of Weltliteratur is so normative as to substantially constrict the purport of the term, on the other hand he implicitly broadens the contours of the concept to include non-poetic works. All texts mediated through tradition and enjoying canonic status, Gadamer suggests, belong to Weltliteratur.[24] Nevertheless, Gadamer's equation of canonicity with innate, historically proven merit seems somewhat naive to us today when we realize exclusion from the canon has been traditionally based on factors such as an author's race, gender, national affiliation, and language(s). There is, however, a hermeneutic value in Gadamer's adumbration of Weltliteratur that can be gleaned from the commentary of Joel C. Weinsheimer: "Literature that belongs to a world—world literature—discloses not merely what once was thought but what still is to be thought. It is not simply material to be learned or written about in literary histories but to be understood and learned from, even in worlds remote from that of the work's origin."[25] Better than *Wahrheit und Methode* itself, Weinsheimer's interpretation of the discussion of Weltliteratur in Gadamer's book establishes a key principle that must be brought to the attention of students in the World Literature classroom if they are to appreciate the present-day relevance of texts from the seemingly distant past.

Hans Robert Jauß built an international reputation in the 1960s and 1970s when he attempted to recuperate the somewhat discredited discipline of literary history by developing a historically grounded model of literary reception. Under Gadamer's influence, Jauß and his colleague at the University of Konstanz, Wolfgang Iser, sought to illustrate the historically conditioned nature of literary mediation, influence, and reading itself. Jauß's "aesthetics of reception" (*Rezeptionsästhetik*) has a strong sociopolitical dimension absent in Gadamer's hermeneutics; both author and audience must be critically situated within the broader context of their age if literary history is to reattain any contemporary relevance, in Jauß's view. Literary works must be examined in the light of everyday life experience, as a response to other artistic forms and to general societal concerns. A knowledge of this background allows the critic to comprehend the "horizon" (*Horizont*, a favorite term of both Gadamer and Jauß) within which literature was and is produced and read. This knowledge also enables the critic to judge the work's historical effect. Thus, toward the conclusion of one of his most influential essays, "Literaturgeschichte als Provokation der Literaturwissenschaft" ("Literary History as a Challenge to Literary Theory," 1970), Jauß traced the origin of the enormous scandal provoked by *Madame Bovary* in mid-nineteenth-century France to Gustave Flaubert's novel use of free indirect style, which shocked a reading public used to omniscient, objective, and thus morally grounded narration. Accustomed to such a narrative style, Flaubert's prosecutors in the famous trial provoked by the novel's publication and initial appearance assumed the author shared and promoted his heroine's putative moral turpitude.[26]

Such a radically contextualized approach to reading inevitably calls into question the sort of normative approach to Weltliteratur evident in Gadamer's *Wahrheit und Methode*. At the outset of an essay entitled "Goethes und Valérys *Faust*: Zur Hermeneutik von Frage und Antwort" ("Goethe's and Valéry's *Faust*: On the Hermeneutics of Question and Answer," 1976), Jauß strongly challenged the very principle of a non-historically grounded notion of Weltliteratur. He begins the essay by harshly criticizing contemporary comparatism, which, he believes, has adopted a naive principle of hermeneutic objectivism sustained by the hope that its disparate, methodologically suspect investigations will one day be synthesized into a totalized comparative compendium. Jauß believes this utopian goal is equivalent to what his contemporaries call Weltliteratur. Citing Goethe and Marx as godfathers of this movement, he claims that the adoption of Weltliteratur as an ideal means of getting beyond the simple comparison of discrete national literatures and establishing a universal context for critical analysis must first recognize the historical fluctuations to which literature and the formation of literary canons are subject. Thus,

Jauß foregrounds what Gadamer's hermeneutics overlook: Weltliteratur (understood as the transnational canon) is constituted by a fluctuation between preservation *and* forgetting, admission ("Anerkennung") and dispossession ("Aberkennung"). In the genuine world literary course of events, in Jauß's view, contemporary judgement is constantly engaged in a process of accepting or rejecting past experience. Before beginning his historically contextualized comparison of Goethe's and Valéry's *Faust,* Jauß notes that contemporary literature departments, still organized on the basis of national linguistic affiliations, continue to ignore this methodologically necessary recognition of how Weltliteratur develops. The historical problem of Weltliteratur remains to be worked through before the paradigm can be established as a "Relevanzachse" (fulcrum of relevance).[27]

Though Jauß somewhat exaggerates the 1970s embrace of Weltliteratur as a means for establishing the foundations of a postnational comparatism, he contributes a valuable historical dimension to the problem of canonicity suggested by Goethe's paradigm. While, for Gadamer, the ability to transcend epochal fluctuations in taste is at the very core of Weltliteratur, Jauß calls the principle of timeless "great works" into question by radicalizing the historical dimension of the hermeneutic dialogue with literature. Jauß's aesthetics of reception help make us realize that the decision on what we wish to include in the World Literature curriculum, indeed the very criteria we use to make such curricular decisions, is subject to constant revision, and that we should be aware of the sociohistorical contexts that, sometimes unconsciously, underlie these decisions.

One of the three papers cited by Jauß as evidence that Comparative Literature in the 1970s was in the process of embracing Weltliteratur as the synthetic, totalized domain of comparatist praxis was authored by one of the premier literary scholars in the former German Democratic Republic, Claus Träger.[28] As the title of his essay—"Weltgeschichte—Nationalliteratur, Nationalgeschichte—Weltliteratur" (World History—National Literature, National History—World Literature, 1974), indicates, Träger attempts to mediate between national and international modalities in order to show their dialectical connections. He argues that this task should constitute the proper domain of Comparative Literature. Träger tries to show how German literature's trend toward inwardness

("Innnerlichkeit"), usually the object of derision in Marxist critical circles, actually reflects and interacts with world historical and world literary tendencies. Thus, the inward poetic universe of a Rainer Maria Rilke or Friedrich Hölderlin is, in Träger's view, deeply linked to the literary as well as concretely real experiences of the international working class. Criticism must pay attention to the moments when literature emerges from itself   · and becomes integrated into the world literary and historical domain, for this attention will imbue literature with an international historical effectiveness. Träger argues that the sort of communal, socially effective engagement of those concerned with *belles lettres* idealized by Goethe in one of his Weltliteratur formulations was impossible in the post-Goethe and post-Marx but pre-socialist epochs, when the bourgeois ideologies of nationalism and chauvinism took the form of a cosmopolitan focus on maximum profits on the world market. However, Träger believes that the putative dawning of a new age of worldwide peaceful coexistence makes it possible for scholars of literature to revive the concept of Weltliteratur (without, of course, giving up the ideological class struggle). In one of the two "world systems," that of socialism, Träger believes this process is already under way.[29]

Träger's perspective was obviously undercut by subsequent, post-Soviet developments. Not only has the world market, greedy for maximum profits, pilloried by this Marxist critic as a disguised, outmoded capitalist venue for nationalist depredations, subsumed national economies, but globalism in literary and other marketplaces has brought about a new age of not always peaceful but somewhat denationalized, intermingled coexistence among cultures. Thus deterritorialized, "world literature" is increasingly coming to signify works with an *immanently* global character rather than indicating the canonic "great works" supposedly representative of the best creations, over time, that this planet's men and women of letters have produced. Thus, we will conclude this chapter with a brief look at how today's German scholars and critics view Weltliteratur under the sign of contemporary globalization.

In a book published in 1988 concerning the relationship between national literature and Weltliteratur from a Goethean perspective, the philosopher, rhetorician, and Germanist Walter Jens took note of Goethe's prophetic belief that the internationalization of technology and communication was leading to the epoch of Weltliteratur. While the advent of this epoch was a desideratum for Goethe, a concrete possibility for Marx, and an evolving state of affairs for Thomas Mann, its actualization toward the close of the twentieth century is regarded by Jens as self-understood. Jens equates the dominance of Weltliteratur with the extinction of discrete national literatures. He sees an emerging dialectic between global and regional literature, though he does not ground this dialectic in Goethe's own Weltliteratur paradigm, a grounding made possible in the second chapter through a Bakhtinian reading of Goethe. Instead, complaining of the American-induced worldwide cultural leveling in taste brought about through the global distribution of television shows such as *Dallas,* Jens simply offers thanks for the opposing trends being established in the world's provinces. Particularly in Latin America, Jens sees evidence of a regional literature that will counteract the universal cultural homogenization created by the United States. He expresses the hope that the interplay between "Third World"–led regional literature and Weltliteratur will lead to a humanistic renaissance. In order to realize the ideal of Weltliteratur in the age of *Glasnost* cosmopolitanism, Jens recommends André Gide, who attempted to attain a world literary dialogue with Goethe by learning the German language, as a model.[30]

With the collapse of the "Second World" (the Soviet Empire), *Glasnost* and (albeit to a lesser extent) the notion of a "Third World" became as much forgotten relics as *Dallas,* and it will be difficult in the current age of even more dominant American language and culture to persuade many of our World Literature students to adopt Gide as a model. Indeed, only two years after Jens's book appeared but after the fall of the Berlin Wall, which both symbolized and inaugurated the age of globalization dominated by the United States, Peter Coulmas followed *his* pronouncement that Goethe's proclamation of the epoch of Weltliteratur was prophetic by noting that literatures can now understand each other globally because of the worldwide spread of English. Not only do scientists of all nations and disciplines publish in English, but creative writers ("Schriftsteller") who compose in, or are translated into, English receive greater acclaim than those who do not, in Coulmas's view.[31] Thus, if the dialectic proclaimed by

Jens is to be truly efficacious and promote the informed cosmopolitanism he desires, those elements in the Weltliteratur paradigm which highlight alterity rather than homogenization and an undifferentiated universalism must be drawn upon.

In a 1993 article on how Weltliteratur should be regarded today, Hendrik Birus attempted to confront the problem of globalism, particularly as an issue to be considered in comparative studies. Birus argues that Goethe's notion can aid the discipline of Comparative Literature in recognizing both the limits and possibilities of its field of inquiry. Extensively drawing upon twentieth-century interpretations of Weltliteratur, he shows that this concept helps us to realize how individual comparatists can constitute their own discrete domains of inquiry, recognizing both the world's unity and the irreducible variety that forces us to make choices with respect to which texts we teach and research. He is certainly correct in noting that "a systematic situating of comparatism and, thereby, of Weltliteratur as its object of inquiry cannot, in spite of a necessary cognizance of universalization, do without a counter principle of restriction."[32] Birus's essay draws on the Weltliteratur paradigm to reexamine issues such as canonicity and cross-cultural literary interchange and shows that comparatists must regard the entire world as their homeland in coming to grips with the "necessary but endless task of treating the globe's imaginative texts in a comprehensive context."[33]

Birus's essay treats only tangentially the fact that literature is becoming *immanently* global; individual works are increasingly informed and constituted by social, political, and even linguistic trends that are not limited to a single nation or region. A greater recognition of literary transnationalism is evident in slightly more recent treatments of Weltliteratur, such as Manfred Schmeling's 1995 essay "Ist Weltliteratur wünschenswert? Fortschritt und Stillstand im modernen Kulturbewußtsein" (Is Weltliteratur Desirable? Progress and Standstill in Modern Cultural Consciousness). Schmeling maintains that contemporary discourse on Weltliteratur merges into the general discourse on literature in the age of (globalized) mass media. Information overload and deterritorialized cultural transference have led to a manner of writing so intertextual, according to Schmeling, that creative works have become world literature in the most literal sense, as "a kind of melting pot of international cultural experience."[34] Schmeling's essay is also valuable in underscoring the centrality of Goethe's notion of Weltliteratur, of "the birth of the Weltliteratur idea from the spirit of German humanism," even in contemporary non-German discussions of the concept,[35] and for demonstrating that dissatisfaction with Weltliteratur as a reflection of increasing cultural homogenization, particularly in Europe, has a long history, which Schmeling traces back to Nietzsche.[36] Nevertheless, Schmeling does not answer the question posed in his title: "Is Weltliteratur Desirable?" I believe this question can be answered affirmatively when the paradigm in its Goethean form is used to *counteract,* at least in the classroom, the cultural leveling of which intellectuals have complained since Nietzsche's time. However, the history of Weltliteratur in Germany has exposed its fundamentally dialectical character, the fact that the term subsumes and presupposes *both* alterity and homogenization. This circumstance must be appreciated before Weltliteratur can be introduced into the classroom with pedagogically fruitful results.

In an essay on globalization and literary history published at the beginning of the new millennium, Horst Steinmetz argues that Welt-literatur has come to an end. He associates Weltliteratur in this article with literary modernism. Culture for the modernists, in Steinmetz's view, was universalized and leveled, not bound to specific regions. Thus, Weltliteratur was addressed to everyman, no matter the national or ethnic background of the modernist writer. Steinmetz cites Kafka, Eliot, Joyce, Beckett, and Ionesco as representatives of such culturally homogeneous fiction, though, as we have seen, Thomas Mann most famously diagnosed modernity's infection by an amorphous Weltliteratur. What makes Stein-metz's latest engagement with this topic unique is his argument that the "literature of globalization" which is putatively replacing Weltliteratur is rooted in regional particularism. Such literature, associated by Steinmetz with postmodernism, is characterized by a dialectical tension between the universal and the particular. Steinmetz believes that the literature of glo-balization, unlike modernist Weltliteratur, confronts readers with the possibility that they are being exposed to experiences quite foreign to their own lives and destinies. Such exotic acts of reading are brought about through the circumstance that the culture articulated in contemporary fiction is not universal, but regionally bound.[37]

Steinmetz makes a cogent if perhaps somewhat sanguine case for the transmission of alterity in current literature. Ironically, his definition of the literature of globalization as marked by a dialectic of the universal and particular through which discrete subnational elements are foregrounded while a sense of the world in its overarching totality (and, sometimes in the current age, obtrusiveness) is concomitantly manifest brings to mind Goethean Weltliteratur as it was defined through Bakhtin's reading of works such as *Aufenthalt in Pyrmont*. Steinmetz's belief that the literature of globalization creates "the possibility that the reader once again can become a witness to destinies which are not also fundamentally his own or must be his own according to the intention of the authors"[38] articulates what I believe should be a key desideratum of the World Literature classroom, namely, the imbuing of our students with the recognition of why and how the "Other" *is* "other." There is no greater wisdom than knowing we are *all* caught up in the tension between the universal and particular, than truly recognizing how we are all bound together in one increasingly smaller world yet still experience that world differently from distinct cultural contexts. This lesson in the globe's culturally complex ambiguities can be derived in the World Literature classroom from more than just the contemporary literature of globalization. If Weltliteratur as a modernist phenomenon has come to an end, it may yet experience a renaissance as a pedagogical, hermeneutic principle.

Canonicity/Great Works/Multiculturalism
World Literature in America

IN A LETTER TO Carl Zelter dated 21 May 1828, Goethe wrote that the *Weltliteratur* he has called into existence is "streaming" toward him. Like the sorcerer's apprentice guilty of unleashing a torrent, he feels as though he is "drowning" from *Weltliteratur* discussions. He cites Scotland, France, and the Milan daily *L'Eco* as immersed in purveying the ideal he has promulgated. Ten days later, he wrote to the editors of *L'Eco* to congratulate them on their "friendly" contribution to *Weltliteratur*.[1] These letters demonstrate that, from the earliest days of its articulation, *Weltliteratur* was the object of discussion in Europe, even if public knowledge of the paradigm was not widespread until after Eckermann published the *Gespräche*.

Thus, Germany did not and does not have a monopoly on valuable contributions to this discussion. For example, the British scholar Hutcheson Macaulay Posnett, whose *Comparative Literature* (1886) contributed greatly to spreading the concept which gave the book its title throughout the English-speaking world, defined "world-literature" as "the severance of literature from defined social groups—the universalising of literature." Posnett's sociological view, which sees "world-literature" as marking an advanced stage in a distinct culture's evolution, a stage characterized by "the reflective and critical spirit,"[2] is certainly unique, and allowed him the prescient insight that Asian literature must be considered within the world literary pantheon. More recently, the Belgian professor José

Lambert drew on Goethe's paradigm to argue that the monolingual ordering of literatures was politically comfortable but inaccurate. He calls into question Weltliteratur's putative presumption of discrete alterities beyond national borders, and, anticipating current discussions of literary globalization, refers to national literatures as a "chimera."[3] In *What Is World Literature?* (2003), David Damrosch defines this domain as consisting of both individual texts and bodies of works that have enjoyed transmission beyond their original cultures and are often enriched by translation and an elliptical configuration. In this view, world literature is positioned both in an originary source and in the reception of subsequent generations. This elliptic hermeneutics is unique to world literature. Damrosch finds Goethe's engagement with Chinese texts to be exemplary for world literary reading. He believes this ideal reading, practiced by Goethe but productive for all those who partake in a dialogue with world literature, is driven by a pleasure in the difference of foreign works from one's contemporary cultural framework, a gratification in their similarity, and an exploration of "what is *like-but-unlike*—the sort of relation most likely to make a productive change in our own perceptions and practices." For Damrosch, this tripartite reading constitutes the fullest possible engagement with world literature,[4] and its inculcation in the World Literature classroom is one we should all strive to approximate. In showing how archival and archaeological research as well as divergent translations and critical discussions create modes of circulation allowing texts to become works of world literature, Damrosch engages in a remarkable chronological and geographic range of readings, beginning with *Gilgamesh* and concluding with the 1984 Yugoslavian (Serbian) novel *Dictionary of the Khazars.* Indeed, in his introductory essay, he shows how the *Gespräche mit Goethe,* a text central to the formulation and subsequent discussion of the Weltliteratur paradigm, became an actual *work* of world literature through the varied and contested modes of editing, circulation, and translation, as well as the controversies on authorial authenticity and intention, which mark the passage into world literature of the more properly poetic works he treats in subsequent chapters.

Such ruminations on what Weltliteratur signifies would have to be considered by any future scholars who might pursue the laudable goal of writing a comprehensive treatise that would analyze how the paradigm has been defined throughout the globe over the course of time. I have confined myself to adumbrating its development in Germany because only in that country did this development truly take place; its articulation by other writers when considered within a national context tends to have a scattered, incohesive character. As a distinct, coherent *concept,* Weltliteratur, despite its obviously cosmopolitan essence, was most fully and consistently articulated in Germany; it is, essentially, a German paradigm. But if Weltliteratur as a discursive paradigm is most closely and profitably associated with Germany, "World Literature" *as a pedagogical practice* is almost exclusively to be found in the United States. As Lawall has noted: "Courses in world literature are a uniquely American institution. World literature exists elsewhere as a scholarly topic or as the subject of ambitious global histories, but it is not an academic institution. Only in the United States do we find a systematic attempt to encompass the 'world' (however defined) in literature courses."[5]

It is a primary thesis of this book that our American World Literature courses would be greatly enriched by a metatheoretical approach. I hope teachers of these courses will benefit from the insights gleaned from the overview of Weltliteratur's development in Germany, for I believe their students can profit from an awareness of the paradigm's ideological contestations. However, I believe it is equally essential to have a grasp of the development of "World Literature" as a pedagogical domain in the United States if we wish to steer this "uniquely American institution" in the right direction and to enhance our students' appreciation for the significance and purport of what they are studying in the World Literature classroom. Thus, this chapter will explore World Literature's institutional history in America's universities and colleges.

To be sure, the initial offering of "World Literature" as an academic course in the late 1920s did not occur in an intellectual vacuum. World Literature's institutional origins were preceded by the introduction of Goethe's Weltliteratur paradigm in the United States. As we noted, the first widespread discussions of Weltliteratur in Germany took place in the wake of the publication in 1836 of the *Gespräche mit Goethe,* in spite of Goethe's protestations in 1828 that he was "drowning" in the sea of Weltliteratur discussions in Europe to which his ruminations had already given rise. The *Gespräche* were first translated into English in 1839 by Margaret Fuller and published under the title *Conversations with Goethe in the Last Years of his Life*. Fuller, a member of the New England Transcendentalist group, which also included Ralph Waldo Emerson and Henry David Thoreau, was Goethe's earliest and one of his most ardent adherents in this country. She strove enthusiastically to counteract the charges of immorality leveled against Goethe by his earliest American readers, and was in large measure responsible not only for popularizing his work among the Transcendentalist group, but within the United States as a whole.[6] Fuller's translation of the most influential passages on Weltliteratur was not entirely felicitous. She mistranslated Goethe's remark on his pleasure at consulting the works of foreign countries in order to escape pedantic narrow-mindedness. Fuller's translation of this comment, made just before Goethe proclaimed the arrival of Weltliteratur's epoch, makes it appear as though he enjoyed making actual "excursions" to these countries. Indeed, "pedantic narrow-mindedness" ("pedantischen Dünkel") is translated as "pedantic mistake." Despite these minor errors, the *Conversations with Goethe,* Fuller's first book publication, enjoyed a positive reception.[7]

Though Fuller does not appear to have actually engaged in a discussion of Goethe's Weltliteratur paradigm, scholars are in agreement that it profoundly influenced her own literary criticism, imbuing it with a cosmopolitan outlook almost unique in America at that time.[8] As Margaret Vanderhaar Allen puts it, "Goethe educated Margaret Fuller to be a citizen of the world," not least through his proclamation of the Weltliteratur epoch,[9] a circumstance which, given Fuller's great influence, helped to broaden the perspective of early nineteenth-century American letters in general. However, her introduction of the Weltliteratur concept to a wide circle of Americans did not have an impact on higher education in this country, though German (particularly Prussian) influence on American pedagogy from the 1830s up to World War I was, in general, quite profound.[10]

One of the Americans on whom Fuller's *Conversations with Goethe* made a positive impact was Thomas Wentworth Higginson. In his critical biography of Fuller, published in 1890, Higginson says that Fuller "made a delightful book" of the *Conversations,* and notes its great influence in making Goethe familiar to the English-speaking world. Higginson claims that the *Conversations* "brought him [Goethe] nearer to me than any other book, before or since, has ever done."[11] Thus, it undoubtedly influenced Higginson's article "A World-Literature," also published in 1890. This essay makes it quite evident that the Weltliteratur principle had not yet taken root in American universities at that time. Higginson begins his essay by citing Goethe's 1827 pronouncement that "the epoch of World-Literature is at hand (*die Epoche der Welt-Literatur ist an der Zeit*)." Higginson's citing of the original German assumes many readers at the turn of the nineteenth century would appreciate its nuances. Indeed, in a gesture unthinkable in any contemporary popular American media venue ("A World-Literature" was published in *The Century,* which was widely read), he later cites a passage from the *West-östlicher Divan* and a quote from Napoleon Bonaparte *without* providing translations from the German or French. It is probably not a coincidence that Higginson's translation of the passage on the arrival of the age of Weltliteratur is identical to Fuller's.[12] Higginson expresses a tacit agreement with the prophetic character of the original Weltliteratur paradigm by noting the free give-and-take of "the national models" in his own day, finding that English literature was taking on a French character while French critics were discovering in Jane Austen a model for the contemporary Realist school of Emile Zola. However, Higginson finds the promise of Weltliteratur's arrival in the guise of a new cosmopolitan era belied by its absence in the curriculum of American higher education. What is needed, Higginson believes, are courses that stress what is universal in literatures. His proposal for establishing World Literature courses is worth quoting in full, for his desideratum was ultimately reflected in the principle of canonicity generally accepted as binding for these courses until late into the twentieth century:

> Yet in looking over the schedules of our universities, one finds as little reference to a coming world-literature as if no one had hinted at the dream. There is an immense increase of interest in the study of language no doubt; and all this prepares for an interchange of national literatures, not for merging them in one. The interchange is a good preliminary stage, no doubt, but the preparation for a world-literature must surely lie in the

study of those methods of thought, those canons of literary art, which lie at the foundation of all literatures. The thought and its expression—these are the two factors which must solve the problem; and it matters not how much we translate or overset—as the Germans felicitously say—so long as we go no deeper and do not grasp at what all literatures have in common.[13]

Higginson's desire that World Literature courses impart to students those general values, ideas, and structures he finds at the root of all *belles lettres* became inflected some years later into the search for our "common Western heritage," particularly in the "Great Books" courses that began to develop between the world wars. What Higginson could not anticipate was the reversal of what he termed the "preliminary stage" and what he regarded as an ultimate end. World Literature in English Translation courses became early on a first step, for those interested in more advanced literary studies, toward the scrutinizing of national interchanges, a branch of learning requiring the knowledge of foreign languages presupposed by Higginson for World Literature courses. The "preliminary stage" developed into twentieth-century Comparative Literature, while World Literature was the subject devised for novices usually lacking a background both in foreign languages and in humanistic discourse. Of course, Higginson's assumption that his readers had enough knowledge of German and French to understand a smattering of Goethe and Napoleon, and to realize that his awkward term "overset" is a literal translation of *Übersetzen,* "to translate," underscores the circumstance that he was writing in an age when one could not be considered cultivated without some acquaintance with foreign tongues. Most significant, though, is Higginson's early advocacy of a synthetic approach that was to become standard in World Literature in English Translation courses in years to come.

In the second half of his article, Higginson blames the absence of World Literature classes at American universities on overspecialization. Though finding the earlier Classical curriculum somewhat limited in its purview, he believes it imparted the universal, fundamental elements of literary discourse. While he would like to see contemporary World Literature courses take over this task, Higginson agrees with Goethe that Greek thought, traditionally viewed as the bedrock of Western civilization, must (re)attain a certain pride of place in the general discipline of literary studies. Though he embraces the study of "the collective literature of the world" as a pedagogical ideal, he argues that the emphasis must be on "the nations which have brought their product to the highest external perfection."[14] Thus, while seeming to uphold the principle of diversity in the selection of texts, Higginson still inclines toward a principle of selective canonicity soon to dominate the World Literature curriculum.

As Ralph P. Rosenberg noted in an essay on the Great Books tradition composed when this approach enjoyed its greatest popularity (the 1950s), Great Books courses were instituted in response to the same perceived overspecialization resulting from the free elective system[15] which prompted Higginson to argue for the introduction of World Literature courses in American higher education. While the first classes offered under the title "World Literature" were not introduced until the late 1920s, the same focus on specialization and on a philological approach that motivated Higginson to advocate a pedagogical World Literature[16] inspired the eminent scholar Richard G. Moulton, born and educated in England but based at the University of Chicago, to compose his book *World Literature and Its Place in General Culture,* which was published in 1911.

Moulton was a versatile and prolific writer, an author of books on (among other things) the Bible as literature, Shakespeare, and Classical drama. Nevertheless, Moulton was deeply committed to the principle of mass education, particularly through extension courses, and his concept of World Literature is rooted in the broad-based pedagogical ideals, general rather than specialized in scope, which were soon to define American attitudes toward the World Literature classroom. Moulton makes it clear from the outset of *World Literature and Its Place in General Culture* that his perspective is governed by his target audience, the English-speaking world. World Literature for Moulton is literature perceived as a unity, and to this end, he believes, reading in translation is an entirely acceptable practice. Like Higginson, Moulton sees a radical disjuncture between philological studies and literary studies. Philology is concerned with the small picture, with information and facts. Literature, on the other hand, should make a great impact, developing the student's taste, spirit, and ability to think, indeed know, imaginatively. Like Higginson, Moulton believes a comparative approach to literature constitutes only a first step toward attaining a feel for literature's unity, toward developing a holistic approach to the study of *belles lettres*. Moulton also distinguishes between "Universal Literature," which is simply literature in its totality, and "World Literature," which presupposes a specific national perspective. Thus, World Literature conjures inevitably different visions, and will inspire quite disparate canons, in China, France, England, and Japan. Moulton's consistently underscored "English point of view" inspires him to see "the Hellenic and Hebraic" civilizations as most significant for the historical development of his and his audience's culture. Thus Classical and biblical works have pride of place in his world literary canon. Most other literatures are either "entirely extraneous" to the English-speaking world or stand "in the relation of collateral propinquity" to it.[17]

By consciously rooting his principle of Weltliteratur in a decidedly nationalist context, Moulton may appear to be an antediluvian chauvinist to students and teachers of World Literature in the contemporary age of globalization. Writing a treatise on Weltliteratur based on a specific national outlook was not unique in the years preceding the Great War, when perspectives were colored, indeed clouded, by nationalism; only two years after Moulton's book appeared, Richard M. Meyer published his book on Weltliteratur in the twentieth century "from a German perspective" (*Die Weltliteratur im zwanzigsten Jahrhundert: Vom deutschen Standpunkt aus betrachtet*). In neither the case of Moulton nor Meyer, however, can one speak of an attempt at making one's own national point of view appear superior to those of other lands. Indeed, as Lawall has noted, Moulton's perspective on Weltliteratur is "openly positioned" by considering the reality of different canonic schemes in the globe's various lands. Moreover, as Lawall points out, Moulton's position reflects Goethe's progressive views. While both Goethe and Moulton saw nationality as an inherent cornerstone of Weltliteratur, they were cosmopolitan in their optimistic view that familiarity with the literary works of the globe brings the world's people closer together through mutual acquaintance and interchange.[18] Indeed, when Moulton defends his relative lack of attention to contemporary literature by arguing that temporal proximity makes it difficult to adjudicate among the various assertions diverse literatures may make about their own merits, their qualitative nearness to the "great masters," he, like Goethe before him, notes that the "leading peoples of the world" are coming closer together in their choice of readings, are in the process of selecting "the best products of each people" on a transnational scale.[19]

Nevertheless, a distinction between Goethe and Moulton must be made with respect to the purport of their observations. Goethe believed that the very essence of Weltliteratur lay in the increasingly inevitable character of the national-international dialogue, enabled both by an improved communication infrastructure and by the relative political tranquility and war-weariness he observed in the 1820s in Europe. For Moulton, this cosmopolitan phenomenon was an ancillary feature to be observed in the present day and then set aside. Indeed, at the outset of his chapter on "World Literature as the Autobiography of Civilization," he returns his attention to "national literature." In this chapter, "autobiography" is primarily equated with the historical and cultural roots of England.[20] In the metatheoretically informed World Literature in English Translation classroom, Goethe rather than Moulton will have to have pride of place if we want to impart to our students a sense for the *history* of literary globalization, or, at the least, make them realize that literary cosmopolitanism does not begin in the *age* of globalization, or even in the twentieth century. However, as I have stressed earlier, this lesson is not as important in the current era of superficially homogeneous culture, worldwide linguistic Anglicization (or Americanization), and economic transnationalism as teaching our students to recognize and respect cultural diversity from a historical perspective.

In focusing on "World Literature and its place in general culture" from a specifically Anglophone point of view, Moulton wishes to reveal the literary foundations of Anglo-American civilization. This goal seems as important to him as that of developing taste, discernment, and the ability to think imaginatively in his students. To this end, the bulk of his book is devoted to analyzing the "Five Literary Bibles" fundamental to the cultural development of the English-speaking world. To each bible is devoted a separate chapter, beginning (after the book's introduction) with the "Holy Bible," and continuing with "Classical Epic and Tragedy," "Shakespeare," "Dante and Milton," and "Versions of the Story of Faust." A sixth chapter analyzes those works Moulton had described as collateral to, but not entirely divorced from, the universe of English civilization; these include, among others, James Macpherson's *Ossian* and the Finnish epic *Kalevala*. To each bible, Moulton devotes a detailed, immanent, but somewhat historically informed reading. Indeed, so much attention is focused on textual detail, and, to a lesser extent, historical setting, that each bible's specific significance for the English-speaking world tends to disappear. However, this is not always the case; in justifying the juxtaposition of Dante and Milton, Moulton puts forth the following argument: "What makes the combination of the *Divine Comedy* and the *Paradise Lost* into a literary bible is that they give us complete revelation in creative poetry of supplementary stages through which our own literary evolution has passed."[21] Because he has so thoroughly justified translation as a means of understanding and appreciating literary, if not always linguistic, merit in foreign masterpieces, Moulton is unselfconscious about expounding upon such elements as rhythm, meter, and even alliteration in works such as the *Kalevala*,[22] though he occasionally alludes to difficulties in rendering certain terms into English, as with "Ewigweibliche" (the "eternal feminine") in *Faust*.[23] As I argued in the introduction, it is necessary to distance ourselves from such cavalier attitudes toward translation and from an overly national perspective if we are to inculcate an appreciation for linguistic and cultural distinctions among our students.

I believe the greatest pedagogical merit of *World Literature and Its Place in General Culture* resides in the contribution of its final chapter, "The Place of World Literature in Education." Lawall has nicely summarized most of the strengths and weaknesses in Moulton's educational program. On the one hand, his all-too rigidly Anglophone perspective is tinged by a class-consciousness. His belief that language easily and clearly functions as a transmitter of ideas blinds him to problems inherent in the study of translated texts. One might add this problem may still arise today if World Literature instructors do not at least make their students aware that unique poetic nuances resist translation. Nevertheless, as Lawall also notes, Moulton both recognized diversity as an inevitable element in questions of the canon among the globe's different peoples, and perceived and attempted to adjust to the changing character of his own student body. Moulton causes us to reflect on how metamorphoses in student demographics, technological innovations, and educational policy must inevitably impact pedagogical praxis in the World Literature classroom. Indeed, Moulton demonstrates that "the idea of world literature is a catalytic concept that opens up literary, cultural, and personal horizons."[24]

While original in many respects, Moulton's view of World Literature as a leisure time activity designed to promote an awareness of diverse ideas and to help students think imaginatively and creatively reflects nineteenth-century German notions of *Bildung,* though his program of acculturation is more democratically pitched to a broad population segment (mainly the working class) and lacks the element of language instruction and educational travel. Moulton regards language learning and even the study of English literature as specialized branches of pedagogy, while he views World Literature as a general program to be taught on a universal basis. Though Moulton has no objection to specialization within literary studies, he argues that students in such narrowly focused programs can only succeed when possessed of the broader knowledge his ideal World Literature courses would afford. However, Moulton did not want to restrict World Literature instruction to students with a special interest in the humanities. Rather, he believed World Literature must ameliorate the neglect of generalized, universal educational programs, a neglect decried earlier by Higginson and, later, by university faculty and administrators who sought to remedy overspecialized post-secondary education by introducing Great Books curricula. Though World Literature did not ever become, at most universities, the mandatory course of study Moulton at least tacitly envisioned, it did become widespread in this country's universities and colleges as a discipline specifically directed toward a diverse body of primarily entry-level students (freshmen and sophomores), even if World Literature classes are not so frequently offered in the university extension programs for the working classes which he advocated.

Moulton's defense of World Literature is as valid today as it was early in the twentieth century:

> The perspective of the whole literary field, which is the essential point of World Literature, is that which gives to each particular literature when it is studied fresh interest and fresh significance. It is the common bond which

draws together the humanity studies into a single discipline. And for those whose main interest is widely removed from literature, who follow the physical or mathematical sciences or art, if their education touches literature at all, it is this World Literature that most concerns them, and not any single literature, even though that be the literature of their native land.[25]

Though we in the twenty-first century will not agree with Moulton's World Literature program in all its particulars, we must recognize that he was the first to develop such a program. His ideal of World Literature as a seminal element in a course of humanistic studies geared toward the beginning, nonspecialist student reflects the fundamental approach to World Literature in English Translation courses still evident in American universities and colleges today, an approach there seems no good reason to overturn.

As we will see, scholars of Comparative Literature came to denigrate World Literature because of what they perceived as its lack of attention to linguistic nuances. This is certainly a flaw inherent in Moulton's own praxis. Nevertheless, Moulton is accurate in arguing that World Literature courses lead to the development of "the comparative habit of mind, which acts as a lens to bring together resemblances and contrasts from all parts of the complex civilization."[26] Contemporary World Literature courses should primarily strive to educate beginning students in the complex diversities of the globe's cultures while concomitantly highlighting their universal elements. However, inculcating the comparative habit of mind at this early stage may inspire such students to pursue more advanced comparative studies and give them a notion of how such studies may be most profitably carried out. Though Moulton's proposal that World Literature be part of a core university extension program for self-directed, non-full-time learners enmeshed in their careers may be an unrealizable ideal in the current age, when few individuals in today's workforce have the leisure time Moulton saw as integral to the lives of nonslaves,[27] the basic thrust of his ideal may be applicable for the many nontraditional, retired, older students who enjoy learning for its own sake.

While Moulton was the first scholar to develop a pedagogical foundation for the teaching of World Literature, a foundation reflected even today in World Literature curricula, the first courses given under that title were taught by Philo M. Buck Jr. at the University of Wisconsin in the late 1920s.[28] According to Ralph Rosenberg, Buck was originally brought to Wisconsin in 1926 in order to assume a professorship in Comparative Literature, a great rarity in those days. Not long after arriving, Buck added elective courses specifically designed for undergraduates above the rank of freshman. Among these early offerings one could find titles such as "Masterpieces of Western Literature" and "World Literature in Translation."[29] Buck also edited one of the earliest World Literature anthologies, which first appeared in 1934. In the preface to the first edition, Buck expresses his regret at finding it necessary to exclude Chinese and Japanese literature, so that Asian literature included in the anthology is limited to a few works from India, Persia, the Arabian Peninsula, and Palestine. The reason for this restriction is explained as follows: "All national literatures have been excluded whose vital influence upon the European tradition has been negligible or very recent."[30] In the preface to the third edition, published in 1951, Buck notes he has enhanced the selections from the Far East with Chinese.[31] Nevertheless, selections from "The Orient" constitute less than 10 percent of the third edition; all the other works are of European provenance. Of course, the establishment of such a Eurocentric focus as a benchmark for text selection in World Literature anthologies became less acceptable later in the twentieth century.[32]

Even at this earliest stage of World Literature praxis in America, Buck feels compelled in his introduction to answer a question certainly familiar to contemporary World Literature teachers: what is the relevance of past texts for today? Presumably, he had experienced it in his own classroom. In answering, Buck cites "the great primal motives that make human nature" as well as "the question of questions, man's place in nature" in relation to mysterious, uncontrollable forces evident at all times. These inspire literature, making it of interest to the present.[33] Contrary to Moulton's perspective, Buck's anthology is entirely devoid of texts originally composed in English; not even Shakespeare is to be found there. Clearly, the first teacher of World Literature in America did not wish his subject to overlap with those of English departments.[34] By restricting his World Literature courses to undergraduates, he also established the still evident disconnect between World Literature as an undergraduate program and Comparative Literature as a domain for primarily graduate studies. However, despite opening a gap between World Literature and Comparative Literature that would lead to controversy in the coming years, Buck's background as a comparatist ideally suited him for his pioneering role as America's first World Literature teacher. When we consider this role, a further examination of his critical thinking is in order, for his writing provides clues as to how he approached the task of establishing World Literature as a new pedagogical domain.

In the introduction to his anthology, Buck established the bond between the present and bygone eras as part of his effort at demonstrating the validity of his new world literary enterprise: "We are bound by a thread to the past, a golden thread we can never hope to sever. Like the memories of past experience, individual or race, it enters potently into every act of the present. It is the richest heritage, this tradition of man's imagination."[35] Several elements in this passage are striking. One is a focus on the past; while Weltliteratur may have been rooted for Goethe in a present-day, national-international dialogue, Buck regarded World Literature as a classroom dialogue with yesteryear, though he wished to establish this dialogue, at least in part, in order to help understand contemporary trends. Indeed, only in the third edition did Buck include works of relatively recent vintage. His emphasis on the imaginative tradition underscores the onset of another important trend. While the Great Books class included (and still includes) works from a broad range of discursive domains in its curriculum, World Literature was to concentrate on what we have come to term "imaginative literature." Though Buck's anthology does contain passages from "Greek and Roman Philosophy," as well as essay excerpts from the post-Classical age, the vast majority of texts consist of excerpts from lyric poetry and prose fiction. Finally, the allusion to racial memory points to a phylogenetic view of history characteristic of Buck's age.

This racial element in Buck's thinking is also reflective of the attitudes of his time in its distinction between Occident and Orient (as is the complete neglect of Latin American and African imaginative literature). The "golden thread" metaphor he employs in the anthology's introduction to show the phylogenetic link between the past and the present is derived from the title of a book he published three years prior to the appearance of the first edition of his *Anthology of World Literature*. *The Golden Thread* exhibits Buck's profound knowledge of the writings he taught in abridged form in his pioneering World Literature courses. As in the anthology's introduction, he attempts in the introduction to *The Golden Thread* to establish the vital, dynamic link between the literary tradition and the thoughts and deeds of his own day. In so doing, he indicates that the golden thread is really woven of two distinct strands, those of "the contemplative Orient and the scientific and changing West."[36] In the introduction to the anthology, the East's inhabitants and their thought are mystified through a distancing trope, a reference to "the imagination of these peoples behind the barriers of desert and mountain."[37] One might assert that Europe is separated from America by a barrier, the Atlantic Ocean, more imposing than those between Asia and Europe, but Buck claims America "is only a transplanted Europe slowly adapting this [European] tradition to its own varied needs."[38]

Buck would certainly argue that the relative dominance of European texts in his World Literature classes and anthology would make this process of adaption more self-aware. This concomitant intertwining of Europe and the United States and obscurantist marginalization of the rest of the world links World Literature and Comparative Literature in their earliest manifestations as academic disciplines in America. As Edward Said has noted, Comparative Literature took Goethe's Weltliteratur paradigm and created from it a hierarchy that placed European/Latin Christian oeuvres front and center. From the time Comparative Literature gained departmental status in the United States at Columbia University in 1891, this hierarchy was tacitly adopted: "Academic work in comparative literature carried with it the notion that Europe and the United States together were the center of the world, not simply by virtue of their political positions, but also because their literatures were the ones most worth studying."[39] The eminent comparatist Philo Buck adopted this position when he realized the ideals of Higginson and Moulton by creating World Literature as an undergraduate offshoot of graduate Comparative Literature at the University of Wisconsin, though, at least in his anthology, he left literature originally composed in English entirely out of the picture.

While Buck's attitudes toward literature in general and World Literature in particular reflect the predilections of his age, there is no real sense, in his introduction to *An Anthology of World Literature* or in his other criticism, of institutional pressures behind his pioneering effort. Despite the social traditions Buck saw as a "golden thread" linking the European literary past with the contemporary American ethos, he still treated the rewards of reading in personal terms. In *Literary Criticism: A Study of Values in Literature* (1930), Buck asserts: "It is the value of literature, as of all art, that it helps to supply precisely the experiences that enable a mind thus completely to organize itself." While he sees this organization of the mind through literature as grounded in supraindividual experience, and thus views reading as an exercise in the transcendence of personal routine with its confined social liaisons, Buck still foregrounds the individual discoveries beneficial to the individual reader though the act of reading.[40] However, just as the end of World War I brought in its train the institutional flourishing of both General Education and the Great Books courses that had been developed by John Erskine for American soldiers in France,[41] so the end of World War II facilitated the proliferation of World Literature at American universities.[42] The reason for this has been summarized by Lawall: "World Literature courses grew apace in the period after World War II. More students were entering college, many of them veterans who had been abroad, and there was a general feeling that the United States should be better acquainted with the global society in which it had begun to play a major role."[43]

The sudden expansion of World Literature in English Translation courses in the United States meant that such courses could no longer be confined to the guidance of eminent comparatists such as Buck. At least at universities with fewer resources than the University of Wisconsin, World Literature became the province of English departments and World Literature courses were staffed by instructors who often enjoyed little training outside the Anglo-American domain. Just as the rise of General Education and the Great Books programs after World War I provoked a backlash by specialists (research scholars opposed to the supposedly ahistorical, nonscientific critical approaches these twin curricular models helped to proliferate between the wars),[44] so the proliferation of World

Literature gradually led to expressions of contempt from abroad[45] and objections at home. The latter trend is exemplified by Calvin S. Brown's 1953 essay on "Debased Standards in World-Literature Courses." Brown opens this brief treatise with the remark that Goethe's 1827 Weltliteratur "prophecy" has been fulfilled, though he claims that it is not worthwhile to precisely define Goethe's term. Brown notes the increasing tendency in twentieth-century America to provide or even require World Literature courses. He traces this trend to the falling off in popularity of Latin, Greek, and reading in general, and the concomitant lapse of the presupposition that the nation's students would familiarize themselves with certain canonic works. Because, despite this lapse, universities assume students should know those works most central to impacting American thought and tradition, World Literature courses are flourishing, in Brown's view. Brown believes that the anchoring of such courses in English departments is accidental; as they replaced more traditional English literature survey classes, the instructors who staffed those classes were retained to teach the new World Literature courses. There were few comparatists [such as Buck] to be called upon for such staffing, and departments of foreign languages tended to be recalcitrant when asked to perform this duty. Brown does not see this arrangement as a bad thing; in some cases, specialists in national literatures were brought in for guest lectures (though Brown feels that this can lead to a loss of continuity in the classroom), and the English teachers were often as competent as anyone else to teach World Literature courses.[46]

Brown's overview at the outset of his article on World Literature's proliferation is highly informative. Though, as he notes, there was a universal mandate to introduce World Literature into university curricula, little thought or resources were invested in accomplishing this task. English and American literature specialists simply had to become generalists who were to provide students with the introduction to the global cultures among which their country was coming to play a dominant role. It was believed, after World War II, that increasing interaction with these cultures made familiarity with them advisable, and the many veterans entering upon their university studies in the late 1940s and early 1950s undoubtedly had developed some interest in the cultures of the regions in which they had fought during the war. Considering the dominant role played by the

New Criticism at this time, with its focus on intrinsic reading and its general decoupling of criticism from broader social, historical, and cultural matrices,[47] the teaching of World Literature by individuals who lacked broad comparative and historical training could be justified. On the other hand, the intrinsic approach guaranteed that students failed to attain the sort of cosmopolitan cultural knowledge it was felt these courses should provide.

At any rate, Brown does not complain that World Literature was housed in English departments; as he points out, not many comparatists were on hand, and English teachers were as well-prepared to teach World Literature as German, French, or Spanish literature specialists. What alarmed him in the 1950s were the results of a questionnaire focusing on sophomore classes in literature which indicated that World Literature syllabi were coming to be dominated by contemporary works of American and British literature. Only 16 percent of the questionnaires, distributed in four states to English teachers, were returned, but this sample made it clear to Brown that educational democracy was getting out of hand. Brown felt that the dominance of literature made popular at the time through Broadway plays and Hollywood hits, such as Edmond Rostand's *Cyrano de Bergerac* and Arthur Miller's *Death of a Salesman,* in World Literature classes reflected a belief that students were not interested in difficult texts, and that teachers were pandering to their tastes. It seems equally plausible that the instructors were creating syllabi attuned to what we would term today their own "comfort level." Brown argues that comparatists, more readily available than in earlier years, should intervene, should demand the inclusion of more traditional, canonic works and, if possible, plan and teach the World Literature courses.[48] His comment regarding the trendy syllabi, that "the educational effects are disastrous from any point of view. The student necessarily finishes the course without that familiarity with the shaping forces of our civilization which he is supposed to get,"[49] is of interest in revealing a key desideratum of World Literature courses: a knowledge of America's cultural provenance. These goals were also clearly uppermost in the minds of Moulton and Buck, and remain influential today.

A few years after the appearance of Brown's essay, Lionel Trilling wrote an article that called World Literature courses into question from a quite different angle. In "English Literature and American Education" (1958),

Trilling's chief lament is the decline of the traditional, historically wide-ranging programs at American universities in English literature in favor of American Studies. He complains that few current literature majors are still able to engage in informed discussions of the Elizabethan and Restoration periods in England. He sees World Literature as another "rival" of the traditional English literature curriculum, tracing its influence to the "Humanities A" class developed at Columbia College. Trilling himself was a professor of English at Columbia University and had been Erskine's student there in the mid-1920s. Trilling praises the reasoning behind the humanities program introduced by Erskine, whom Gerald Graff credits with formalizing the Great Books approach to humanities education.[50] Nevertheless, Trilling expresses regret that the introduction of writers such as Homer and Goethe in the "Humanities A" course inevitably displaced certain canonic English authors, such as Chaucer and Fielding. Trilling also asserts that this course was highly influential in inspiring the introduction of World Literature, "now part of the argot of our collegiate education," at other American colleges, even though the Columbia College course was not created as a World Literature class.[51]

Trilling is no doubt correct that Erskine's Great Books approach was influential in paving the way for World Literature as a widespread pedagogical domain at American institutions of higher learning. Both movements were established in reaction to perceived scholarly and curricular overspecialization, though Great Books considerably precedes World Literature; Graff notes that Great Books was the name of a course taught at Berkeley beginning in 1901.[52] Trilling is also correct to note a major methodological distinction. The Great Books approach presumes the student will engage in readings from a wide range of humanities disciplines, while World Literature's range is usually limited to imaginative writing. As the name implies, Great Books courses require an intensive concentration on a relatively small number of frequently unabridged works, while World Literature, from the outset, has relied on a survey approach utilizing many abbreviated, anthologized texts or short works such as lyric poetry.[53] What Trilling leaves out of account is the circumstance that Great Books became popularized in the wake of World War I, while World Literature first became widespread after the Second World War.

Also, as the seminal example of Buck indicates, the departmental origins of World Literature are linked to Comparative Literature. While, to quote Gail Finney, Goethe "in essence invented comparative literature" through his Weltliteratur paradigm,[54] the flourishing of Comparative Literature in America is itself intertwined with the birth of World Literature as an institutional curricular offering.

If, as Lawall noted, America's increasingly significant role in the world at large after World War II led universities to introduce World Literature in order to help Americans understand that external world,[55] teachers of World Literature may have conceived of their role very differently. At least this is Trilling's assertion. Trilling believed that while Erskine's course was exclusively oriented toward the Western "Judaic-Hellenic-Christian" tradition, World Literature teachers felt this was too narrow a perspective. Trilling's World Literature teachers are attuned to global multiculturalism, sensitive to Western cultural imperialism and Eurocentrism, a sensitivity we might regard as *avant la lettre* of contemporary trends. What follows is the thought process Trilling ascribes to "a good many" World Literature teachers:

> For a time, we of the West have dominated the world. But we know that we can no longer dominate it, ought no longer dominate it, should never have dominated it. We thought we could teach and lead others: we have sinned the sin of pride. Now we must listen to new voices too long unheard. There is the voice of China, there is the voice of India, and very likely a good many others when we come to look for them. If we listen to these voices, then the voice of the Judaic-Hellenic-Christian tradition becomes but one in a great chorus. And of course any one national temporal part of that voice comes to seem small and thin indeed, let alone any personal part of it. Can we spend our students' time on Keats when all the Upanishads wait?[56]

Trilling's satiric intent in this precocious attack against what he perceived to be pious political correctness is obvious. It is impossible to ascertain how many of the 1950s World Literature teachers really held the views Trilling attributes to them, but his invective in defense of the centrality of English literature certainly foreshadows much rhetoric heard from conservatives during the culture wars which began in the late 1960s and continue to this day, an ironic circumstance given Trilling's fame as a leading liberal in his age. These debates deserve our attention, for World Literature as a pedagogical domain continues, unfortunately, to be implicated within them, but first it is worthwhile to consider the issues raised at the "Teaching of World Literature" conference held at the University of Wisconsin in April 1959. As I noted in the introduction, Haskell Block had Trilling's critique in mind when he referred to "World Literature" as "not a happy term" in outlining the conference's objectives. Block seems to agree with Trilling's accusation that World Literature courses are informed by cultural relativism which, by stressing "the equal value of *all* cultures," negates the value "of *any* culture," and emphatically agrees with Trilling that World Literature cannot be studied in a systematic fashion.[57]

Perhaps both Trilling and Block expected too much from a World Literature classroom. By their very nature, World Literature classes provide an introductory survey. World Literature courses should not and usually do not assert that all cultures are of equal merit. The merit of individual national literatures does not have to be an issue; students can learn to appreciate literary diversity without worrying if Chinese, German, and Italian works possess as much worth as English and American classics. Systematic study is perhaps impossible when one considers the literature of the globe at large, but this need not be a major concern. If a student develops a taste for the literature of a particular nation based on the brief sample to which she is exposed in a World Literature classroom, she can pursue a more systematic study of that literature. Employing a metatheoretical approach to World Literature will obviate its unsystematic nature at any rate; a focus on the meaning and significance of Weltliteratur will invest the World Literature classroom with an organizational center around which the study of the disparate individual works will revolve.

Certainly, issues such as translation, pedagogical training, and the choice of texts—issues raised by both Block and the others who made presentations at the Wisconsin conference—will always be controversial. Nevertheless, the other essays included in *The Teaching of World Literature* tend to be more upbeat in tone than Block's introductory remarks. Weldon M. Williams, for example, uses an extended tourism analogy in stressing the value of the World Literature course: "It may be that its quick forays into cathedrals and castles and mosques are too often like the achievement of the American tourist who boasted that he made it through the Louvre in ten minutes flat. Yet a summer's tour may have its own values. It may even infect some of the tourists with the desire (on some future and more independent trip) to linger in the cathedral and explore it."[58] Liselotte Dieckmann and Leon A. Gottfried underscore the value of interdepartmental World Literature offerings,[59] and this is certainly a desideratum when feasible, for aside from introducing greater expertise, students can be expected to develop a greater appreciation for diverse cultures if the pedagogical voices to which they are exposed are also diverse.

A more negative tone is struck by Werner P. Friederich in his essay "On the Integrity of Our Planning." Friederich addresses what had already developed into a dispute between World Literature and Comparative Literature adherents by noting that such squabbling would end if the disputants would recognize once and for all that World Literature in English Translation courses are designed for undergraduate students, while Comparative Literature is essentially a graduate program. Sometimes, but not always, the World Literature classes will allow the graduate comparative courses to develop. However, Friederich goes on to dismiss "World Literature" as an absurd term. He expresses opposition to "sweeping" World Literature survey courses because they infer low academic standards, incur the wrath of language departments, cannot truly represent the entire globe, and are shallow and presumptuous. Friederich proposes that if large-scale transnational literary surveys are mandated, Great Books courses should be substituted for World Literature. He cites the inexpensiveness of the paperback classics in defense of this perspective,[60] thereby invoking an argument that even the most ardent Great Books proponents could not make today! Despite his misgivings with respect to World Literature as a pedagogical approach, Friederich underscores the importance "of making American youth become aware of this throbbing and fascinating interplay with the rest of the world."[61] In the current global age, this task is even more important, and the World Literature classroom can help to accomplish it.

At the outset of his essay, Friederich notes that he became founding editor of the *Yearbook of Comparative and General Literature* in order "to build a bridge between Comparative Literature and World Literature."[62] The persistence of the animosity between these two disciplines is attested to by "The Levin Report" (1965), the first report submitted to the American Comparative Literature Association on professional standards in the field. Its authors articulated a fundamental opposition "between Humanities or World Literature or Great Books at the undergraduate level and Comparative Literature as a graduate discipline." Comparative Literature courses, the report argues, should include a "substantial" number of works in their original language, though readings in translation are found acceptable in such advanced courses in the case of "more remote languages."[63] Reading in translation versus reading in the original language is one polarity allowing the authors of the Levin Report to make a clear disciplinary distinction between World Literature and Comparative Literature, but the distinction has somewhat broken down in pedagogical practice today, when many graduate Comparative Literature teachers do not enforce the original language mandate.

The conflation of "Humanities," "Great Books," and "World Literature" in the report is, to some extent, justified by early proponents of World Literature as an academic subject. For example, in his 1940 *Preface to World Literature,* Albert Guérard had credited Goethe with coining the term "World Literature" and praised his cosmopolitanism, while simultaneously expressing a concern that Goethe's authority in this domain might cause World Literature to be regarded as an all-too "formidable subject, fit only for such a titan of culture as he, or, at second-hand, for his learned disciples." On the contrary, Guérard reassures his readers, World Literature arises in the nursery and not in graduate school,[64] for there is a clear distinction to be made between Comparative Literature as the study of cross-national relations, a study which clearly presupposes specialized knowledge, and World Literature as "the body of those works enjoyed in common, ideally by all mankind, practically by our own Western group of civilization."[65] This body of common works are those which traditionally constitute the Great Books curriculum. Both the Great Books approach and the definition of World Literature by Guérard create what François Jost has referred to as the conflation of Weltliteratur with *Wertliteratur,* which can be translated as "literature of merit." In Jost's view, Comparative

Literature frequently suffers from the opposite malady, the inability or unwillingness to conceptualize any standards of aesthetic value.[66]

The linkage between World Literature and the Great Books tradition has subsequently been challenged by several critics during the past thirty years. Robert J. Clements, for example, asserts in *Comparative Literature as Academic Discipline* (1978) that World Literature is "a much abused term in America"[67] and calls the definition of World Literature contained in the first ACLA report a "sanction to a misnomer invented largely by textbook publishers." He believes this "sanction" was finally corrected in a second ACLA report issued ten years after the first.[68] Indeed, "The Greene Report," noting an increasing interest in non-Western cultures, advises that we must never again conflate "'world literature' with the literature of our inherited culture."[69] Clements himself defines World Literature as "the maximum geographical dimension of comparative literature"[70] and argues that its realization as a discipline cognizant of a still developing age of cultural globalization should be the goal toward which contemporary comparatists strive.[71]

There continue to be practical reasons for maintaining World Literature courses as broad surveys of the globe's imaginative corpus while retaining Comparative Literature as the domain of a more specialized, narrow focus. If students are to direct their attention to one national literature or a set of national literatures, or even to contemporary transnationalism, they must be exposed to a wide range of cultures in order then to make informed choices at a more advanced level, and World Literature courses are ideally suited to providing this wide exposure. For that majority of students who are not interested in becoming literature majors, World Literature can at least provide an appreciation for the world's cultural diversity. However, Clements's comments raise an issue specific to World Literature in the contemporary age. Today, a postmodern literature marked by a blend of national identities, cultures, and even languages suggests that an artistic transnationalism propelled by globalized marketing, worldwide communication networks, and literary interchanges unimpeded by political and linguistic borders is no longer merely "at hand," as Clements, following the lead of Goethe, suggested in 1978.[72] Though the term "multiculturalism" signifies for many an ideal still to be crystallized (or, for conservatives, avoided) through critical studies and classroom praxis, it is in fact a reality.[73] Furthermore, the role of Weltliteratur as a paradigm within the multicultural matrix continues to be debated by leading scholars. Drawing on the communicative and travel advances which helped inspire Goethe's minting of the term, A. Owen Aldridge has noted that more recent technological advances, as well as political changes, have brought Asia and Africa into the world literary pantheon: "In other words, contemporary world literature has taken on a truly global dimension, no longer merely reflecting traditional cultural patterns of the West."[74]

Though Aldridge's study of East-West literary relations still associates world literature with "the great works or classics of all times" drawn from the globe's various nations,[75] his argument that the term must be taken to signify literature from the world in its entirety brings up the culture wars fought in the last decades of the twentieth century and that continue in this one. Goethe's paradigm is still brought up in these battles. At the outset of his 1987 essay "World Literature in an Age of Multinational Capitalism," a slightly revised version of an article first published in 1986 under the title "Third World Literature in the Era of Multinational Capitalism," Fredric Jameson notes: "In these last years of the twentieth century, the old question of a properly world literature reasserts itself." Distancing himself from conservative social critics such as William Bennett, who, Jameson believes, continue to associate this domain with a Western canon composed of a "Graeco-Judaic 'great books list,'" Jameson asserts that "the reinvention of cultural studies in the United States demands the reinvention, in a new situation, of what Goethe long ago theorized as 'world literature.'"[76] This reinvention entails coming to grips with what Jameson calls Third World literature, about which he makes a series of broad generalizations, arguing, for example, that Third World writers consistently strive to produce national allegories grounded in a materialist perspective. Although Aijaz Ahmad has rightly criticized Jameson's reliance on a "Three Worlds" model[77] that, because of the collapse of the "Second World" on a global scale, now seems completely anachronistic, Jameson nevertheless demonstrates, as did Clements and Aldridge before him, that, correctly understood, Goethe's paradigm can be employed to promote critical and pedagogical engagement with previously ignored bodies of work.

Indeed, Jameson's wish to link cultural studies to a new vision of world literature was realized at the University of California, Santa Cruz, where a combined "World Literature and Cultural Studies" curriculum was designed to allow the classroom presentation of unclosed, non-hierarchical, allegorically constellated relationships between diverse cultures, to overcome the putatively excessive reverence for narrowly focused disciplinary expertise found in most traditionally run departments devoted to specific national literatures, and to expose the fallacy of binary oppositions between "Third World" experience within and outside of the United States. Perhaps inevitably, the individual courses taught in this program seem to have a somewhat narrow thematic focus, even though the "World" in the title of the program was intended to signify the foreclosure of any disciplinary delimitation.[78] Whatever the merits of such World Literature *programs,* they cannot substitute for introductory World Literature courses where our beginning students will gain a sense of the *breadth* of the world's cultural diversity. This is particularly the case on those campuses, certainly in the majority, where in all likelihood the traditional model of national literature departments will continue to prevail. At present, such academic divisions are predominant even in the case of colleges and universities containing literature departments that have adopted cultural studies as a theoretical and pedagogical framework.

Conservatives are not quite so closed to non-Western texts in university humanities classes as Jameson suggests, though they clearly wish to see works representative of Western civilization predominate. Bennett has noted that "the college curriculum must take the non-Western world into account, not out of political expediency or to appease interest groups, but out of respect for its importance in human history."[79] Lynne V. Cheney has also argued for the study of "Other Civilizations" (separate from "Western Civilization" and "American Civilization" but inclusive of Latin America) as part of her fifty-hour core curriculum.[80] Nevertheless, conservatives such as Bennett and Cheney were in high dudgeon when Stanford University altered its "Western Culture" program in favor of a "Cultures, Ideas, and Values" approach to the core curriculum in the 1980s. Mary Louise Pratt gave an eloquent defense of Stanford's new program, which she helped institute, citing the radically pluralistic nature of the globe in general and American society in particular. In discussing Stanford's earlier Western

Culture approach, Pratt points to the seminal influence of the Columbia University Western Civilization course instituted just after World War I,[81] a course that, as we have noted, led to the widespread adoption of Great Books curricula. In seeking to mitigate the impression that Stanford's new approach has led to radical changes, Pratt asserts: "The actual consequences of the reform remain uncertain, however. With only minor alterations, the standard Great Books course *can* continue to exist at Stanford, and nobody is being required to reeducate him or herself."[82]

As Lawall has indicated, World Literature has become entangled in these debates on core curricula, Western Civilization, and "Great Books."[83] I would like to propose that, whatever one's stance on these curricular approaches, World Literature should become *disentangled* from them. Contrary to the Levin Report, one should not conflate Great Books and World Literature. Though the former paradigm influenced the latter as a pedagogical practice, World Literature can never lead to a profound insight into Western *or* Eastern civilizations. While Great Books courses presuppose educational depth, World Literature must focus on breadth. An anthology-based course cannot do otherwise. World Literature courses should emphasize an engagement with the imaginative works of the globe in its broad cultural diversity, the universalities and particularities of human experience that can be gleaned and critically pondered from all worthwhile texts. Unlike most Western Civilization and Great Books courses, World Literature has paid at least some attention to non-European, non–United States culture throughout its history in this country. It can only provide a nodding, indeed superficial acquaintance with the world's diverse literatures, but it can lead to an appreciation for this diversity at a time when Americans might find such diversity virtually imperceptible. At the same time, it must familiarize students with the increasing global trend toward cultural transnationalism. A metatheoretical acquaintance with Weltliteratur as a concept and World Literature as a pedagogical practice will invest students with a consciousness of why these are matters they should learn, and how directed reading, discussion, and their own writing can facilitate such learning.

We are already in the process of distinguishing World Literature from Great Books as institutional domains with their own discrete goals and practices. In the summer of 1987, an NEH-sponsored workshop was held at the University of Massachusetts in Amherst on the "Theory and Teaching of World Literature." The report generated by this workshop argued that a World Literature curriculum should ideally revolve around textual clusters marked by diversity with respect to nationality, culture, and genre. It also stressed the need to avoid conflating world literature with a purely Western canon.[84] Lawall, the workshop's director, elaborates these points in her introduction to *Reading World Literature* (1994), which she edited. There she stresses that the Weltliteratur paradigm was not initially marked by a canonic approach that valorized the study of a narrowly defined list of "Great Books." Instead, it needs to be understood within the context of Goethe's efforts to bring to the fore the humanity of Germany's neighbors after the Napoleonic Wars, and to enhance European intercourse of all kinds. Goethe's notion of Weltliteratur, Lawall continues, is thus imbued by a strong openness to, and provides a basis for interchange with, the cultural and linguistic Other. It is temporally dynamic and oriented toward the future rather than the past.[85] All of these elements in Goethe's Weltliteratur paradigm argue for its central inclusion in the World Literature classroom; at the very least, understanding Weltliteratur will lead students to a greater appreciation for World Literature as an open-ended dialogue given added vibrancy and currency through their participation in it.

What will be the nature of this dialogue in the twenty-first century? In an essay published at the beginning of the new millennium in *World Literature Today*[86] entitled "'World Literature' in the Age of Telecommunications," J. Hillis Miller argues that World Literature courses are proliferating, partly as a result of advances in telecommunications and the march of globalization. One might add that precisely such technological advances helped inspire Goethe to first coin the term Weltliteratur. Miller rehearses the obvious problems with World Literature courses: no one is truly (globally) competent to teach them, such courses tend to be Eurocentric (indeed, referring to all but post-Renaissance Western works as "literature" reflects a Eurocentric view, according to Miller), and the issue of translation in an age when English is becoming the universal language becomes especially acute. Miller focuses most of his attention on what the conditions leading to current practices in undergraduate World Literature mean for graduate studies in Comparative Literature, for he feels the "trends" in undergraduate courses will inevitably, and soon, impact graduate preparation in Comparative Literature. Though the tone of Miller's essay is pessimistic, he believes the return to World Literature "as a paradigm . . . is inevitable and in itself all to the good."[87] Miller does not explain why this flourishing of World Literature in the age of telecommunications is to the good; on the whole, advances in telecommunications are "shrinking" the globe, making it appear more homogeneous than it really is.

One might argue that what Miller regards as a return to the World Literature paradigm in the telecommunications age is a positive development because it will cause students to, borrowing the contemporary cliché, "think globally." Despite the dangers of homogeneous conceptualizations posed by such thinking, such an approach is essential at a time when the world's nations are becoming more interdependent and less independent both culturally and economically. If, at least ideally, Weltliteratur encompasses the dialectic of the universal and the particular, a Weltliteratur-informed engagement with the literature of the world in its temporal and geographic breadth will truly promote cosmopolitan thinking. Indeed, the telecommunications technology Miller regards as somewhat responsible for inspiring a new wave of World Literature courses can facilitate a knowledge of cultures *in their particularity*; today's students are visually oriented, and using the Internet to show images, say, of sixteenth-century China while a work of sixteenth-century Chinese literature is under discussion will certainly enhance a classroom's ability to perceptualize that particular culture. The afterword will provide examples of harnessing computer technology in the World Literature classroom.

The sudden trajectory of Miller's article away from the implications of World Literature for undergraduate education and toward an exclusive focus on how World Literature's supposed reemergence will impact graduate Comparative Literature programs illustrates a key thesis advanced by Damrosch's book *We Scholars: Changing the Culture of the University* (1995). Damrosch argues that most humanities professors who labor in departments with graduate programs are not interested in teaching introductory core courses traditionally grouped under the General Education rubric. It would be unjust, based on a short article, to assume that Miller shares this disinclination, but Damrosch is certainly correct to note that scholars gravitate toward specialized graduate courses because they tie in far more easily to one's research agenda, and to one's disciplinary comfort level, than do broad-based introductory classes. Damrosch's argument that this problem can be ameliorated through genuinely collaborative teaching is absolutely valid, and a World Literature classroom will certainly benefit when a group of faculty familiar with particular traditions creates a team-taught World Literature course.[88] This is not always feasible, and frequently the World Literature teacher will have to labor alone, or, at best, engage an occasional guest lecturer. To be sure, most World Literature classes are taught in departments without high-powered graduate programs, but what would motivate scholars in research-oriented foreign language departments to teach introductory World Literature? The answer is simple: the ensuing likelihood of future enhanced enrollments in more advanced foreign literature classes, which currently tend to be thinly populated. Introductory language courses attended mainly by students who are there because of degree requirements rather than by choice will not necessarily inspire a student to want to study Russian, German, French, Chinese, or other literatures in the original when they become juniors and seniors. A successful World Literature course, however, may very well provide the inspiration mandatory language courses may lack for many students. Such students will then study languages and foreign literatures in the original because they want to do so, not because they are forced to do so.

Perhaps the most well-known contemporary opponent of World Literature courses and anthologies is Damrosch's colleague at Columbia University, Gayatri Spivak. In her monograph *Death of a Discipline* (2003), Spivak argues that Comparative Literature is indeed dead in its traditional Western European orientation, and that comparatism can only be revitalized through a link to a depoliticized area studies discipline. Spivak argues that area studies can teach Comparative Literature scholars to be attentive to the languages and cultural practices of the southern hemisphere. She believes the comparatist of the future will have to learn some of this area's numerous languages, and that Comparative Literature linked to area studies will truly be open to, learn from, and move toward the Other of the subaltern world in its discrete particularity (though she rejects the traditional universalism-particularism model). She adopts Jacques Derrida's notion of teleopoiesis in articulating a model of Comparative Literature yet to come, which cannot be fully articulated and objectively constituted. She also finds telepoesis valuable as a model of reading indecisively, which is to say with genuine openness to the text's own open quality. There is much to admire in Spivak's ideas, marked as they are by nonclosure and a nonhegemonic, nonobjectifying approach to cultures other than our own. However, to reach such a goal, even an open-ended goal necessarily denied full articulation, one has to take a first step, and Spivak's attitude toward World Literature makes this first tentative step a near impossibility in this country. Even in the acknowledgments of her book, she makes dark prophecies concerning a future about to be marked by World Literature anthologies spreading onto the international market, so that even Taiwanese students will study *The Dream of the Red Chamber* as a few pages printed in a World Literature textbook published in America.[89] She argues that the possibility of a Comparative Literature open to the many languages traditionally ignored by this discipline "is undermined by U.S.-style world literature becoming the staple of Comparative Literature in the global South."[90] She objects to "the arrogance of the cartographic reading of world lit. in translation as the task of Comparative Literature"[91] and to the putative authoritarianism of the "world literaturists."[92]

Spivak is fundamentally incorrect in her remarks on World Literature. For one thing, there is no evidence that World Literature anthologies are widely marketed outside the United States. As we have repeatedly stressed, World Literature is a uniquely American pedagogic domain. Second, there is no basis for Spivak's assumption that editors of World Literature anthologies are authoritarians or cultural imperialists acting in bad faith. Like Spivak, they tend to be Comparative Literature scholars whose goal is, like hers, imbuing students with an openness to the alterity of the world's cultures.[93] Spivak's flawed view is based on a conflation of World Literature, which, as I have argued, must be oriented toward beginning college students, with Comparative Literature. Comparative Literature has traditionally been, and should remain, the preserve of those already proficient in different languages, already attuned to movement toward the Other of discrete cultures. If these languages are to include the numerous tongues of the southern hemisphere, as Spivak argues, then a first step must be taken toward creating an interest in them among American students early in their college careers. Otherwise, these students will never develop the inclinations and language skills Spivak cherishes. There is simply no better place for inculcating these interests in monolingual American students than the World Literature classroom.

In *We Scholars,* Damrosch notes that "the challenge now facing core courses and introductory surveys of many sorts is to do a better job of particularizing their material without sacrificing all unity to the multiplicity of events and cultural contexts."[94] A metatheoretically informed World Literature course can meet this challenge: if students become genuinely aware of how Goethe's Weltliteratur paradigm is *grounded* in the dialectical relationship between cultural unity and multiplicity, universality and particularity, then they can be motivated to learn how the world literature they are reading dynamically reflects *both* dimensions. Indeed, if they learn how to read in this manner, they may even become better world citizens. For learning to read under the sign of the Weltliteratur dialectic allows us to recognize the universal human ties that bind us all, while enabling us to discern and respect those diverse cultural elements which make the globe an interesting place.[95]

The Dialectical Filter of *Weltliteratur*

Reading Rafik Schami through Goethe and Goethe through Rafik Schami

IN DESCRIBING THE DEVELOPMENT of Weltliteratur as a discursive concept in Germany and of World Literature as a pedagogical domain in the United States, I have attempted consistently to keep in the foreground the practical consequences to be derived from these histories when considering approaches to teaching World Literature in the present day. What has not yet been addressed is the issue of applying Weltliteratur to the critical reading and teaching of imaginative texts. Simply reviewing the chronological progress of the concept's evolution in the classroom largely presupposes a process of distillation: one selects key texts suitable for the Introductory World Literature classroom and engages students in a discussion of Weltliteratur and World Literature by summarizing their developments. This process will be adumbrated in the afterword. However, another question remains: How does one apply the theory of Weltliteratur to an engagement with the literature of the world?

This chapter will offer an example of such an engagement by examining two novels by the internationally renowned author Rafik Schami through the dialectical filter of Weltliteratur. In other words, I will focus on the oscillation between the universal and the particular, and how they are synthesized, in these two texts. Schami is a contemporary writer whose work constitutes a paradigmatic example of literary multiculturalism and transnationalism. Additionally, Schami can be said to function as what the eminent literary scholar Harald Weinrich has termed a "Chamisso" author.

Adelbert von Chamisso was born in France and originally composed his works in French, but became one of Germany's great Romantic writers. Thus, Chamisso authors such as Schami originally wrote in a language other than German. Consciously echoing the position of Auerbach discussed in chapter four, Weinrich argues that the dominant position attained by English has tarnished Goethe's concept of Weltliteratur because only English now seems to be the world literary language. Thus, Chamisso authors have perhaps made a poor choice for their second literary language, for German, like all languages other than English, is subglobal. However, Weinrich expresses the hope that such subglobal writers will inspire intellectuals of all sorts to discern both similar and discrete elements among the world's literatures. Such literatures, produced outside the English mainstream of the global marketplace, may create "if not better world literature on this globe, then at least a better literature world, even if this world does not fit without remainder into economic calculations."[1] We will see that Schami is the sort of Chamisso author who contributes to such a better literature world.

The question naturally arises as to how effectively Weltliteratur can be applied to the broad spectrum of texts presented in current literature anthologies. Given the diversity of these texts with respect to genre, language, and historical-cultural background, can one employ one paradigm-driven approach to all of them? This question can only be answered affirmatively if the approach is oriented toward recognizing, highlighting, and articulating this diversity while still remaining cognizant of the universal themes and elements in great literature that continue to make historically and culturally distant works interesting and relevant to the nonspecialist student. In its Goethean character as a dialogue of the subnational, national, and international, Weltliteratur does just that. Wilhelm Dilthey noted the German attraction to methodologies alternating between the poles of "particularism" and "universality,"[2] and Weltliteratur provides a seminal instance of this inclination. Indeed, a consistent oscillation between these poles is what makes Weltliteratur a fundamentally German concept in spite of the theoretical interest it has attracted in other countries. By helping students to recognize both the universal elements rooted in the human condition and the particular elements rooted in language, culture, and history in the texts we teach, we will go a long way toward achieving the twin goals I believe should be paramount in the World Literature classroom: the creation of an interest in/respect for diversity and a recognition of the self in the Other.

I have chosen relatively recent works written by a contemporary author because, at first glance, recognizing and articulating diversity in today's globalized culture seems a particularly daunting task. In 2001, a telling political cartoon drawn by Jim Bergman was published in my local newspaper. It shows a car traveling around a globe. From one end of the globe to the other, the travel route taken is lined by a sequence of three signs painted with the respective corporate logos of the "Gap," "McDonald's," and "Starbucks." The caption contains the message the father gives to his children in the automobile, which is driving over the signs and has just reached the North Pole: "That's the value of travel, kids . . . you get to see how people in other cultures live."[3] Unfortunately, the cartoon's real message is correct: Americanization has produced such worldwide cultural conformity that travel itself may not allow one to penetrate beyond this superficial homogeneity and experience genuine diversity.

Nevertheless, this experience of self*sameness* in the Other does not have to be replicated in the act of reading contemporary literature if that reading is critically informed by the dialectics of Weltliteratur. Horst Steinmetz has noted that there is no longer an absolute antithesis between globality ("Globalität") and locality ("Lokalität"). The regional and the local are informed by their relationship to worldwide trends, and cultural articulations grounded in regionalism and localism are therefore caught up in the process of globalization: "Such articulations are therefore always two-dimensional, they contain elements of globalization next to those of the regional and the local." Steinmetz is not the first to note this contemporary intersection of the global and the local; he cites the social theorist Roland Robertson, who coined the term "glocalisation" to describe it.[4] The comparatist Robert Eric Livingston borrowed this term for the title of his recent essay "Glocal Knowledges: Agency and Place in Literary Studies." Livingston argues for a skeptical attitude toward the belief that locality is being displaced by the phenomenon of globalization. While he finds that transformations in the way place is perceived are indeed under way, he does not believe the human sensibility of and for the local is in the process of disappearing. Rather, globalization enacts copresences, the linking of discrete sites through communication networks and thus the multiplication of event horizons. As we noted, the dawning of such truly comprehensive network linkages can be traced to the age of Goethe, and helped inspire Goethe to coin the term Weltliteratur. Livingston, indeed, uses this term to describe the cultivation, annexation, appropriation, reworking, and translation of texts, a process he associates with Orientalism but which still reserves a place for regionalism. The state, in Livingston's view, can no longer define and secure a sense of place; narration is no longer driven by nation.[5] Social rationalization and engineering do not simply overturn, without resistance, literary-cultural affiliations with the local:

> What matters, however, in the comparative and competitive environment of *Weltliteratur* is the existence of a standard, a model for grasping and administering the relation among a global high culture (the classics), modern literary practices (the national canon), and popular, folkloric, or oral traditions (the vestiges of cultural heritage and local particularity).[6]

Combining the insights of Steinmetz and Livingston, we might say that a Weltliteratur-driven reading of contemporary "glocalized" literature must mediate among national, local, and universal contexts of place. Such a reading must show how discrete localities are imaginatively but realistically linked and transformed through discursive networks enabled by contemporary telecommunication technologies. This "two-dimensional" reading will indicate where the global and the local are enmeshed, but will also demonstrate where processes of globalization and uniformity are resisted and contested. In one instance, however, the true nature of glocalization suggests the reversal of Livingston's formulation of the current Weltliteratur environment, as the basic thrust of his own article makes evident; the "national canon" paradigm is itself on the way to becoming a "vestige," while "local particularity" is a reasonably vital, albeit somewhat threatened, element in "modern literary practices."[7] Recoining Rodney Livingstone's English translation of Theodor Adorno's famous term for what Adorno regarded as Georg Lukács's antimodernist critical praxis, "erpreßte Versöhnung," a phrase Livingstone translates as "reconciliation under duress,"[8] we might employ the term "particularity under duress" to describe the articulation of the local in the age of globalization. Particularity under duress is a seminal theme in Rafik Schami's *Erzähler der Nacht.*

Even if cultural studies reveal that the threat of globalization to the distinctive character of local/regional culture is somewhat exaggerated, the threat is perceived by many writers as very real. Of course, the notion of isolated, pristine regional cultures is itself somewhat of a chimera. Worldwide migratory patterns dating back to the beginnings of human life have guaranteed that few civilizations existed in complete isolation. Prior to the current age of globalization, political imperialism tended to eviscerate the unique character of many areas. In *Culture and Imperialism,* Said attributes worldwide cultural hybridity in some measure to imperialist colonizing:

> Partly because of empire, all cultures are involved in one another; none is single and pure, all are hybrid, heterogeneous, extraordinarily differentiated, and unmonolithic. This, I believe, is as true of the contemporary United States as it is of the modern Arab world, where in each instance respectively so much has been made of the dangers of "un-Americanism" and the threats to "Arabism." Defensive, reactive, and even paranoid nationalism is, alas, woven into the very fabric of education.[9]

As we have noted, Homi Bhabha drew on Goethe's Weltliteratur paradigm to undercut the principle of "national cultures" and to argue that the "transnational histories" of those groups previously marginalized, oppressed, and displaced by colonialism can be seen to constitute the proper "terrains of world literature."[10] However, in the work of Rafik Schami, the geographic particular is not so much the locus of hybridity as of multiculturalism, where divergent ethnic and religious groups blend socially but still maintain their distinct identities. The local site of such tolerant exchange and respect among these distinct cultures in Schami's texts is usually Damascus, Schami's native city.[11] To be sure, Schami's primary target audience is composed of German readers, and his works not only seek to dispel stereotypes about Arabs by showing the multifaceted character of the Syrian capital and its inhabitants, but to help sustain multiculturalism as a political and social ideal in Germany and elsewhere.[12]

In so doing, he must blend discrete, local cultural elements with the evocation of universal, timeless themes. He can thereby instantiate the process of self-Other identification among his readers, a process necessary for making multiculturalism a palatable, indeed appealing, desideratum. Schami's adroit linkage of the universal and the particular in the service of this goal thus makes his work particularly amenable to a reading informed by the dialectics of Weltliteratur.

In arguing for the inevitable character of cultural hybridity in the postcolonial universe in general and in the Arab world and the United States in particular, Said finds nationalism to be a reactionary, destructive mechanism which would undo social heterogeneity and differentiation. The "Arabism" Said sees as corrosive to tolerance of minority groups in much of the Middle East is in the process of becoming the dominant governmental ideology during the primary time frame of *Erzähler der Nacht,* August 1959. Thus, the novel mainly takes place during the brief period of Syria's union with Egypt under the leadership of Gamal Abdal Nasser. The merger of the two countries, which lasted from 1958 to 1961, led to the temporary formation of a new state at this time, the United Arab Republic. The xenophobia fueled by the alliance resulted in that weaving of nationalism into education articulated by Said; *Erzähler der Nacht* alludes to the circumstance that children were encouraged to report putative utterances of disloyalty toward the regime by family members to the authorities. Nasser's strident voice becomes omnipresent through the widespread introduction of transistor radios in areas where the public traditionally gathers, such as coffee shops. This new communication network acts as a blight on the Arab oral storytelling tradition, of which Damascus was a particularly vibrant center. The central figure in Schami's novel, the retired coachman Salim, is portrayed as one of the greatest of these storytellers. His sudden muteness puts the plot of *Erzähler der Nacht* into play. As Azade Seyhan indicates, Salim's inability to speak must be seen in the context of the governmentally instigated and controlled nationalist discourse which sought to drown out the capital's ethnically, religiously, and politically disparate voices: "The premise of the novel itself, Salim's sudden speechlessness, allegorizes the silencing of crucial truths under unstable and oppressive regimes, universal censorship, and senseless victimization of citizens to cover up state lies."[13] Such cover-ups include governmental silence on the outbreak of cholera in the northern part of Syria, when governmental media are confined to reporting the disease's spread in Iraq, a former ally which is now a declared enemy.

Schami's narrative is "glocal" in the sense that it firmly establishes Damascus as the locus of "agency and place," to again cite Livingston, while concomitantly highlighting the universally human elements of its inhabitants. *Erzähler der Nacht* creates a voice for, or at least establishes the presence of, those Damascus residents whose distinct identities are threatened in an age of nascent nationalism, such as Armenians, Jews, and Arab Christians like Schami. Schami consciously deexoticizes the Damascenes both by foregrounding their basic humanity (evident, for example, in Salim's deep affection for his deceased wife) and by showing that exoticism is in the eye of the beholder. Salim and his friends are astounded to learn from Tuma, a former resident of the United States who has repatriated to Syria, that Americans do not haggle over prices in stores and actually enjoy visiting cemeteries. The valorization of the universal and the particular in the novel imbues it with the dialectics of Weltliteratur. Though Goethe grounded his paradigm within the context of a national-international dialogue, the nation-state per se was almost irrelevant to the process, reflecting the circumstance that Germany in the age of Goethe itself did not enjoy (or suffer) this political status. As Hans Joachim Schrimpf has noted in a comment on the dynamics of Goethe's Weltliteratur concept at an early phase of its development: "National content utterly withdraws behind the cosmopolitan, is completely integrated into the overarching world-historical horizon."[14] As we have noted, Bakhtin's reading of Goethe's "Aufenthalt in Pyrmont," a reading suggestive for Bhabha of the overcoming of temporal instability in national culture, is enabled by this brief tale's fusion of the universal and local. In order to put the universal-local dialectic into play in the current age, the nation-state as destroyer of *both* global values and the discrete particularities of the local must be made the evil, negating agent, and Schami is very effective in demonizing the regimes of Nasser and his predecessors in *Erzähler der Nacht*. He thus contributes to undermining the principle of the "'sovereignty' of national cultures," a key desideratum in Bhabha's vision of a contemporary Weltliteratur.[15]

The "narrators of the night" named in the German title of *Damascus Nights* are the circle of Salim's friends, who weave their tales in an attempt to allow the master storyteller to regain his voice. According to the framework story provided by the novel's first-person narrator, who heard these tales while still a young boy growing up in Damascus's old quarter, Salim discovered and developed his storytelling talents as a coachman while driving the route between Damascus and Beirut. He found that his stories entertained the passengers during the two-day journey, and this helped him to gain an advantage over his competitors. Salim continues to regale his friends and neighbors with his tall tales long after his retirement, but one evening in August 1959 he is visited by his muse, the fairy who had made a "fairy-tale like tree" from his "dusty, wooden words" during more than sixty years of service.[16] She, too, has become old, and announces her retirement; after he utters twenty-one more words, Salim will become mute. However, because she is fond of him, the muse has persuaded the fairy king to be merciful. He will restore Salim's voice and his narrative talents, a young fairy muse will assist his tongue until he dies, if Salim can fulfill one condition. He must receive seven unique gifts in the space of three months. Otherwise, he will lose his speech forever. Using the remnants of his precious remaining words, Salim communicates his plight to his friends. They attempt to aid him by bestowing him with a series of material gifts: seven wines, seven pairs of pants and shirts, the scent of seven perfumes. This is all to no avail. Finally, one of the friends, a former finance minister named Faris who possesses the greatest experience in the group with respect to the vagaries of politics and nationalism, hits upon the solution with only eight days left before the deadline; Salim must hear seven tales before he can regain his voice. The bulk of the narrative consists of the tales related by the six friends: onetime Foreign Minister Faris, the coffeehouse owner Junis, the repatriated former America resident Tuma, an ex-prisoner named Isam who had been falsely convicted of murder and now sells songbirds, the barber Musa, and the geography teacher Mehdi.

The seventh in the circle, the giant locksmith Ali, is Salim's favorite because he talks little but loves to listen. However, this taciturn quality causes him alone among the elderly circle of men to relinquish his duty to narrate. Last in the order of storytellers through the luck of a card draw, he abdicates his role to his wife, Fatmeh, whose fairy tale metanarrative on the liberating potency of storytelling constitutes the seventh tale-as-gift and thus plays the ultimate role in freeing Salim from his muteness. Through her gender and as the teller of a tale of telling, Fatmeh is the novel's Scheherazade. This famous name, whose bearer tells the stories constituting *A Thousand and One Nights* to the calif, Sultan Schahriah (to whom she is consort), an hour before daybreak in order to avoid strangulation at his hands at dawn, is mentioned several times in the novel. Schami's intention to foreground the novel's proximity to her tales is evident in his constant invocation of the number 1001—the novel not only refers to 1001 stories, but to 1001 lies, 1001 flowers, 1001 professions, a 1001st year in which a god of demons finally grants a subject he had cursed an audience, and to Baghdad as the city of the 1001 nights, where Fatmeh's mother, Leila, a master storyteller who is the central, albeit mythologized, figure in Fatmeh's tale, met and fell in love with Fatmeh's father. Like the concept of Weltliteratur itself, *A Thousand and One Nights* suggests an ongoing discourse which cannot—must not—be broken off; complete narrative closure would have brought about Scheherazade's death. Indeed, *Erzähler der Nacht* concludes with the promise of another tale to be told another time (*EN*, 274). Schami's framework of a nocturnal narrative cycle is clearly invested in the structure of *A Thousand and One Nights,* though, as Seyhan indicates, the male narrators also bring to mind the Middle Eastern nighttime storytellers, the *confabulatores nocturni* discussed by Jorge Luis Borges in his essay "The Thousand and One Nights."[17] Goethe, too, was deeply influenced by *A Thousand and One Nights* and by the figure of Scheherazade. His lifelong preoccupation with the narrative cycle was seminal not only in influencing the narrative structure and symbolism of many of his works, but also in stimulating his interest in the art of the world at large, with expanding his perspective beyond European literary confines.[18] Such a global outlook was essential to the formulation of his Weltliteratur paradigm, despite its occasionally Eurocentric predilections.

Leila's gifts as both narrator and inspirer of narration free both a prince from a spell that made him a hideous giant (Fatmeh's tale is a therapeutic response to her stifling relationship with the taciturn giant Ali) and the many children who had turned to stone when they ventured into the giant's cave from a nearby village. However, confounding the villagers, the handsome prince, and, undoubtedly, many of *Erzähler der Nacht*'s readers, Leila spurns marriage to the prince, preferring to "move into the world" (*EN*, 266), as she does once again when Fatmeh is grown. Leila is a narrator in and of the world; as with her creator, Schami, and as with Goethe, her tales (and travels) are rooted in a strong sense of agency and place but seek to approximate the universal. Schami is very much "at home" with the cosmopolitan dimension of Weltliteratur. In an imaginative dialogue that was designed to illuminate certain of *Erzähler der Nacht*'s literary and extraliterary contexts, Schami is asked by a "wondrous" woman during a train ride why he does not simply categorize his works as "German literature." While he does allow that his tales ("Märchen") belong to the genre "Gastarbeiterliteratur" (guest worker literature), he responds by saying that "the world would be far more impoverished if it only consisted of Germans and non-Germans."[19] Clearly, Schami's transnationalism, as is the case with many other contemporary postcolonial writers, makes it impossible to simply add his work to the corpus of one discrete national canon, in this case that of German literature. As we are beginning to see, the parameters of this transnationalism are clarified through a recourse to the Weltliteratur paradigm.

What is the significance of the "Gastarbeiterliteratur" label in the context of this transnationalism? In her essay "Understanding Alterity: *Ausländerliteratur* between Relativism and Universalism," Ülker Gökberk uses the genre named in her title as a starting point for rearticulating the parameters defining the relationship between "minority" literatures and majority discourse. Gökberk claims that the term *Ausländerliteratur* (literature of foreigners) supplanted *Gastarbeiterliteratur* as Germany's preferred generic rubric for literature composed by foreigners and most non-ethnic Germans in that country in the 1980s, though Schami (whom Gökberk cites as a significant representative of the *Ausländerliteratur* genre) was clearly comfortable with the earlier term at the close of that decade. Gökberk uses the work of Tzvetan Todorov and of Gilles Deleuze and Félix Guattari as models for defining self-Other relationships in the context of minority-majority cultural exchange and interpretation, in coming to terms with the element of alterity in literature. Gökberk draws upon these three thinkers to show how critical engagement with *Ausländerliteratur* can steer a middle ground between the one extreme of elite condescension which focuses on cultural exoticism, and the other extreme of wallowing in a neurotic solipsism which assumes cultural marginalism is inevitably superior to art of the mainstream center. Gökberk emphasizes that, for Todorov, "'Otherness is never radical,'" and that experiencing the whole world as a foreign country, which is the experience of the exile, creates the most "'perfect'"—which is to say cosmopolitan—outlook.[20] Reading works by contemporary writers such as Schami, one of many bicultural authors who write in a genre signified by different monikers— postcolonial, transnational, *Ausländerliteratur, Gastarbeiterliteratur*—the reader experiences not only the whole world as a foreign country, but, as with Goethe's "Aufenthalt in Pyrmont" in Bakhtin's interpretation, the circumscribed locale as the whole world. Perhaps in order to compensate for the deracination exilic experience brings, writers such as Schami create works informed by a strong sense of agency and place, or, perhaps better, agency *as* place. Gökberk agrees with Todorov that "universality can be regained without giving up diversity,"[21] and in reading transnational literature such as that of Schami through the dialectical filter of Weltliteratur, both elements can be seen to come together in a productive synthesis that allows one the sense of having transcended both globalist cultural homogeneity and the exoticism one experiences when regarding the Other as inscribed by *radical* alterity. Such synthetic cosmopolitanism is the most positive element of Weltliteratur in the global age.

Schami is particularly capable of producing this experience in his readers, for his work is thoroughly grounded in Weltliteratur's universalparticular dialectic. As Iman O. Khalil has noted, *Erzähler der Nacht* "stresses the individual character of the Syrian capital and its inhabitants," but Schami "advocates a cosmopolitan outlook and a multicultural identity suitable for the 'global village.'"[22] This means eschewing an embrace of the nation-state. Probably reflecting Schami's own feeling toward his native space, Tuma indicates how he experienced his feelings of homesickness for his coastal hometown from American exile as follows: "I never had any yearning for homeland, fatherland, and shit like that, but

I absolutely wanted to get back to Latakia" (*EN*, 149). Tuma's vocabulary is consistently sprinkled with English words, and "shit" is the term actually used in *Erzähler der Nacht* to convey his (and Schami's) powerful feeling of antipathy toward the very principle of the nation-state as homeland. This is also underscored by the nomadic lineage of the novel's central character, Salim. Though he was not a world traveler, Salim's stories encompass the entire globe (see esp. *EN*, 9).

It is the tale told by Mehdi, the first narrated in the attempt to heal Salim of his muteness, which most powerfully enacts the dialectical fusion of the local and the global while debunking the nation-state as the appropriate site of a social cathexis. This circumstance is not surprising, for Mehdi spent thirty-five years as a geography teacher, acquainting countless students with the entire globe's countries and terrains (*EN*, 53). Schami's antipathy toward the domain of national and nationalist politics is evident early in the chapter devoted to Mehdi and his tale. As the former geography teacher leaves his house, dark clouds are gathering over Damascus. Mehdi greets an Armenian cobbler who uses a hand gesture to inform him that his new shoes will be ready in two days time. As he departs, Mehdi tries to remember the last time he saw the cobbler smile, and immediately thereafter sees a military convoy rumbling through the streets, exciting children who jubilantly shout "off to war!" (*EN*, 54). The juxtaposition here leads to an obvious conclusion; the Armenian has become melancholic because rising bellicose nationalism threatens those who, like himself, are marked by ethnic and linguistic alterity. The national threatens to suppress or eliminate the particular. Mehdi feels bitterness at the hypocrisy of his government and its voice, Radio Damascus; they had celebrated neighboring Iraqi president Abd al-Karim Kassem as a hero and now transform him, without explanation, into a pariah. Radio Damascus reports on war and cholera in Iraq while remaining silent on the evidence of such pestilence within Syria (*EN*, 54–55). The nation-state is clearly the domain of evil in *Erzähler der Nacht*, evoked as the agency that threatens both the local, particularized Other and the universal sentiments of solidarity between peoples who reside within different borders.

Perhaps because he is plagued by uneasiness at Syria's current circumstances, Mehdi is overcome by a desire to visit his childhood home.

He is shocked at its diminutiveness, particularly at the tininess of what is now a storeroom but where his father's apprentice had lived when Mehdi was a boy. The feelings generated by the brief visit to his boyhood home inspire Mehdi to base the tale he narrates to the circle of friends at Salim's house on that of Schafak, the shy, pockmarked former apprentice. Mehdi's tale is a retelling of Schafak's story concerning two amorous stars. They follow each other, and when they collide, 1001 pearls fall from the sky (*EN*, 61–62). The 1001 pearls metonymically evoke *A Thousand and One Nights,* with its cyclical framed structure, mix of the fantastic and quotidian domains, frequent use of interruptions within the narration, and multilayered narrative embedding. This style characterizes both the chapter devoted to Mehdi's tale and the structure of *Erzähler der Nacht* as a whole. Cyclicality and continuous breaks in the narrative flow allow for the arrest and highlighting of discrete, particular moments while investing the novel as a totality with an aura of holistic endlessness. There is thus a structural dimension to the universal-particular Weltliteratur dialectic that thematically informs Schami's novel. The same thematic ambience and unclosed, open-ended constitution is evident in Goethe's story cycle *Unterhaltungen deutscher Ausgewanderten* (*Conversations of German Refugees,* 1794–1795), the edifice of which was also strongly influenced by *A Thousand and One Nights.*[23] Goethe's lifelong affinity for this work is, then, perhaps related to the mindset that led him to compose his Weltliteratur formulations.

According to Schafak's story, the two amorous stars were once a human couple, an unnamed impoverished farmer and the beautiful village girl Sahar, who loves and marries him because of his mellifluous voice. The farmer is hopelessly inept at earning a living, and the poverty in which the young couple lives becomes truly dire. This circumstance prompts the farmer to sell his voice to a demon master in exchange for the ability to infinitely reproduce the gold liras the demon bestows upon him. The couple soon lives in great luxury, but the husband becomes despondent at his absolute inability to communicate. Not just his voice, but his hands and eyes no longer obey his will to signify. He thus begins a search, lasting many years, for the demon, in order to annul the bargain. After the farmer cleverly breaks the spell imprisoning a good demon, the latter turns him into an eagle so that he can fly to the evil demon's palace in order to liberate his voice and those of other victims, among whom is Sahar after she sells her speech to the devilish being in order to regain her vanished husband. The good demon instructs the farmer to find the evil demon's palace and to crash through its blue sky window, upon which time he will be transformed again into a man. He must keep a glass splinter from the window under his tongue. The farmer and the others cursed to voicelessness will lose their muteness by embracing their voice-Doubles, who are imprisoned in the palace. The farmer's key weapon is the splinter, for, as the good demon tells him: "The master will put his broken windowpane back together in order to hide his castle in the fog of eternity, but as long as the tiniest splinter is missing, he can no longer protect the castle against the power of time" (*EN,* 74).

The farmer succeeds in liberating his voice and that of Sahar by following the good demon's instructions, but is killed during a struggle over the splinter by the evil demon, who has metamorphosed into a scorpion. Dying, the farmer uses a kiss to convey the carefully wrapped splinter into Sahar's mouth. She succeeds in killing the demon, but the demon only expires after first fatally biting Sahar in the guise of a venomous spider. The two lovers die in each other's arms as 1001 voices escape the ruins of the castle. From this day on, the "fire-red star follows the brilliant Saharstar" ("Sahar" is Arabic for "dawn"), and 1001 pearls "fall into the open mouths of mussels" when they collide (*EN,* 81). After completing his well-received story, Mehdi is asked what became of the apprentice who first told it to him. Mehdi claims to have seen the apprentice dancing in the family's courtyard after being awakened one night by a cry of joy. He saw Schafak holding a glowing pearl in the palm of his hand. The apprentice had told Mehdi that if one catches one of the pearls produced when the stars collide, one should dance in a circle three times and then fling the pearl into heaven. This will bring the pearl thrower lifelong happiness. Mehdi witnessed Schafak perform this deed. Afterward, the apprentice disappeared forever.

Schafak's parable in Mehdi's retelling may plausibly be interpreted in a variety of ways. One meaning can be elucidated by articulating a metonymic relationship between the tale's two metaphors for microcosmic agency, the chamber which serves as Schafak's dwelling (the diminutiveness of which is underscored as a key factor in inspiring Mehdi's narrative) and the splinter hidden by the farmer and Sahar in order to destroy the demon master's palace. Schafak lives in the tiniest of rooms, but his heart and imagination are as big as the universe upon which he fixes his gaze every evening. Through a kind of chiastic inversion, cramped space underscores the limitless power and scope of storytelling's reach. From the most restricted of spaces, Schafak's tale allegorically constellates the entire world, encompassed and incarcerated by the evil demon's castle. The splinter literally deconstructs the textual and spatial closure that confines the world's innumerable imprisoned voices. Considering the narrative frame of Mehdi's tale, the palace may even be read as a metaphor for the nationalism that traps the world's populace within its ideological confines; the seemingly insignificant agency of storytelling, symbolized by the splinter, breaks open this prison, reestablishes non(en)closure, and reunites the world's individuals with their stifled voices. In both frame and embedded narrative, the local, particular, and seemingly trivial can be seen to contest the national and open up the universal. The peasant comes into touch with the world *in nuce* in the palace. He uses a fragment to break the chains blocking signification. Anticipating the ultimate liberation of Salim from his speechlessness, the farmer destroys muteness by bringing together the universal and the particular as the subnational/transnational synthesis suggested by Goethean Weltliteratur.

This interpretation of *Erzähler der Nacht* through the dialectical filter of Weltliteratur, a reading that recognizes the novel's structural affinities to the Middle Eastern narrative cycle *A Thousand and One Nights,* allows Schami's novel to be established as a counter-example to Reingard Nethersole's recent argument that the realization of Goethe's Weltliteratur prophecy in the current age is inevitably to be equated with the homogenizing effects of globalization. She argues that postcolonial writing has become in effect too Westernized and too uniform to offer the broad range of structural and rhetorical nuances attractive and inspiring to Goethe and his Romantic contemporaries. She finds that multicultural elements in postcolonial literature nevertheless register a heteroglossic resistance to the current pull toward globalized homogeneousness, and that it should be the role of the literary critic to articulate these traces and point the way to the cultural memory they evoke. Difference and homogenization, are, for Nethersole, the two poles of culture in the age of globalization.[24] However, she strikes a pessimistic note when discussing the eviscerating effects of an internationalized English of the global marketplace, the vocabulary of which is stripped of local, particularized memory. While local registers in postcolonial literature—for Nethersole, transnational literature primarily written in or translated into English—oppose the pull of such linguistic uniformity, this body of works also make us aware of world English's ever more encroaching, homogenizing effects:

> This hybrid new world literature in English at the nexus of center and periphery, while articulating local experience in response to an internationalized culture of literacy, testifies to the widening gulf between the local and the global, to the particular realm of the vernacular, with its unique modes of making contingent historical experience intelligible, and to the general but vacuous vocabulary of commerce.[25]

In *Erzähler der Nacht,* the local and the global can be seen to productively, dialectically interact when the novel is read not as "hybrid new world literature," but as a contemporary work, the discrete multicultural resonances of which are highlighted through recourse to Weltliteratur as a conceptual medium enabling critical discourse. In his previously cited imaginative train ride, Schami notes that literature such as his in Germany "makes a plea for a multicultural society, in which instead of national chauvinism a mutual enrichment of cultures takes place."[26] With its architectonics firmly rooted in the culturally and temporally heterogeneous structure of *A Thousand and One Nights,* Schami's novel elegantly sustains this plea and provides an example of a transnational literature that, contrary to Nethersole's assumptions about the works subsumed by this term, reintroduces the highly variegated "formal and stylistic resources that changed the expressive register of a Goethe and his fellow Romantic writers in Europe."[27]

Schami has written a number of books for children and young adults. *Der geheime Bericht über den Dichter Goethe, der eine Prüfung auf einer arabischen Insel bestand,* co-authored with Uwe-Michael Gutzschhahn, has been marketed and reviewed in Germany as an example of this "Jugendliteratur," literature for the young. As is the case with his other works, including those targeted at a primarily mature audience such as *Erzähler der Nacht*, *Der geheime Bericht* employs a lucid, uncomplicated syntax and a straightforward prose diction. Its appeal for high school-age students is enhanced by an appendix with a table of Goethe's works (including the page numbers of where they are treated in *Der geheime Bericht*) recommended for reading, to which is added a list of well-known theater productions, movies, audio recordings, and musical settings of these works. This is indeed the sort of apparatus one sometimes finds at the conclusion of a work designed for adoption in an American high school or German *Gymnasium*. Nevertheless, the novel possesses the same sort of sophisticated framed narrative/embedded narrative structure, breaks in narrative flow, discrete episodic segmentation, and multiple narrative voices evident in *Erzähler der Nacht*. The architectonic model for *Der geheime Bericht* is probably once again *A Thousand and One Nights*, a work that has appealed throughout the centuries to young and old alike, including Goethe, who read and consulted this work from his early youth to his advanced old age. There are in *Der geheime Bericht*, as in *Erzähler der Nacht*, multiple allusions to *A Thousand and One Nights*, as well as a reference to the "1001 tasks" Goethe was required to fulfill, in spite of which he still found quality time to spend with his grandchildren and other children.[28] Indeed, the mediator of Goethe's works in *Der geheime Bericht* is described as "a pupil of Scheherazade" (*GB*, 127).

A reading of *Der geheime Bericht* is of value because it allows us to reverse the poles of our critical inquiry. While *Erzähler der Nacht* permits Schami's narrative strategy to be examined through the filter of Goethe's Weltliteratur paradigm, *Der geheime Bericht* presents Goethe and his work through the prism of Schami and his collaborator. Indeed, the Weltliteratur concept is central to the novel. It crystallizes the utopian dimension of *Der geheime Bericht*, a dimension rendered all the more powerful by way of contrast with the novel's utterly *dystopian* conclusion, a brief bleak denouement of a sort rarely evident in literature written with a youthful audience in mind.

The opening frame for the novel is fairly straightforward. On the 26th of May in the year 1890, a sailing ship is found drifting off the coast of the island of Bahrain. Its cargo is untouched, but its crew have all been murdered. An investigation is launched by the British imperialists who are coming to dominate the region, but the truth of what happened to the ship is only revealed through the divinations of the German Martha von Suttner. She and her young son, Thomas, were the sole passengers to survive the murderous rampage on board the *Black Prince,* though they were not found on the drifting ship. At Thomas's prompting, they had gone into the ship's cargo hold to inspect it and count its whiskey casks. Martha and Thomas thus remained undetected while the crew was being slaughtered. She realizes that the incursion was an act of revenge against the English by the Raschid tribe, whose rivals, the Saudis, were supported by the English. The ship had been under way to India, where Martha was to have been reunited with her husband, a high-ranking English official in British India's administrative apparatus whom Martha had come to despise. The ship's catastrophe provides her with an opportunity to escape her marriage; after she is sure the marauders have left the ship, she and Thomas climb into a lifeboat and row to the mythical island of Hulm, the sparse vegetation and foreboding coastline of which have allowed it to remain independent from past and present imperial incursions.

As is evident from this brief description, the opening narrative sequence of *Der geheime Bericht* is structured as an adventure story, a pedagogical strategy designed to draw young readers into the body of the text where the novel's central educational mission can be deployed: an introduction to Goethe's works that will ideally inspire *Der geheime Bericht*'s audience to read them. Once on Hulm, mother and son are quickly integrated into court life. Martha, already conversant with Arabic, enters into a loving relationship with the island's most esteemed diplomat and becomes known on the island as Princess Saide. Thomas takes on the Arabic name "Tuma"; reversing the geographic and psychological route his namesake in *Erzähler der Nacht* had taken as a young man, he makes the transition from a Western way of life to that of the Arab world. Tuma becomes the best friend of Crown Prince Hakim, who learns English and German. When his father dies seven years after the arrival of the Europeans, the new Sultan Hakim decides that Hulm will soon no longer remain capable of isolating itself from the rest of the world. In order to acquaint the island's young people with the best literature this outside world has to offer, Hakim sends ten scholarly scouts to Europe's leading nations in order that they may immerse themselves in these lands' poetry and philosophy. Upon their return, they are to try to persuade a commission of scholars to adopt what they believe are the best texts they encountered during their sojourns for Hulm's schools and universities. Using this selection process, Hakim plans to have the island's youth introduced to the West's greatest cultural offerings. Tuma is sent to Berlin, and after a year of study there, he returns to Hulm full of enthusiasm for Goethe's works. With the exception of the brief catastrophic denouement, the remainder of the book, the vast majority of its contents, are devoted to Tuma's report to the commission on Goethe's works, delivered over the course of nine evenings and structurally divided into nine chapters, each of which is devoted to a different work or component of Goethe's life and thought. Tuma's reports are refracted through the pen of Abdullah Alfirdausi, the palace's scribe, whose frequent, often humorous interruptions help lend the novel the discontinuous and recursive narrative ambience characteristic of *A Thousand and One Nights* and other Near and Middle Eastern story cycles.

The discontinuity and breaks in the narrative flow reminiscent of *Erzähler der Nacht* and *A Thousand and One Nights* are not primarily occasioned by Alfirdausi's complaints about the fatigue to hand and mind necessitated by his ceaseless recording of each evening's proceedings, but by the lively discussions that take place among Tuma and the members of the commission charged with selecting the texts to be adopted for the "House of Wisdom," the name of the institution where the books are to be stored and where Hulm's young people are to be schooled in European culture. Tuma's recounting of Goethe's tales and poetry continually inspire these members to engage in the sort of Weltliteratur dialogue Goethe valorized. In the first night, for example, Tuma elucidates *Die Leiden des jungen Werthers* (*The Sorrows of Young Werther*, 1774), which became popular for its unique portrayal of passionate, tragic, unrealizable love. This leads one of the scholars to relate an Arabic tale of tragic love, contoured with details specific to the Middle East. Thus, stories rooted in local particularities but mediated, made globally appealing through their evocation of universal themes, are traded, Arab and German/European frames of reference productively mingle. The value of multicultural exchange mediated through a microcosmic Weltliteratur interchange among nationalities as articulated by Goethe in his paradigm is thereby made evident in a pedagogically appealing manner to *Der geheime Bericht*'s primarily youthful audience. The interrelationship between the highly particular and the global, fundamental to Bakhtin's world literary reading of Goethe, enables the novel's multicultural dialogues. The absolute synthesis of part within whole and whole within part foregrounded by Schami and Gutzschhahn in the novel suggests the architecture of the hermeneutic circle articulated by philosophers from Friedrich Schleiermacher to Hans-Georg Gadamer.[29] This is the case even if the "world" in Weltliteratur and as an idealized multiculturally grounded topos in *Der geheime Bericht* is never truly absolute as a linguistic signifier in Schleiermacher's hermeneutics; the concept "world," in Schleiermacher's view, is only manifest in language in abstract form, through its "schematic construction."[30] Though the "world" in Weltliteratur may be an abstract verbal ideal, it can be drawn upon to expose an even more chimeric affect: the seemingly inviolable homogeneity of the "globe" in "globalization."

When the commission hears Tuma's report on the *West-östlicher Divan*, Goethe's own poetic enactment of a world literary dialogue, a young scholar is moved, after hearing a passage where Goethe claims "Orient and Occident can no longer be separated," to exclaim that "Nothing in our world can still be separated, North and South, East and West." He says that this feeling of global unity occasionally overcomes him when he reads foreign ("fremde") poems and stories (*GB*, 135). Thus, while such a poetically constituted world is informed by *unity*, this unity can only be evoked through the valence of *alterity*, that which is foreign or "fremd." In *Der geheime Bericht,* as in the Goethean Weltliteratur paradigm itself, unity can never be conflated with—or collapse into—homogeneity. To borrow the terms of Jean-Luc Nancy (though Nancy's phrase is inspired by despair at world conflicts in the mid-1990s and the fictitious scholar's view in *Der geheime Bericht* is born of optimism, in still isolated Hulm, generated by a "House of Wisdom" under construction), this "Being of the world" constellated through the Weltliteratur dialogue is "singularly plural and plurally singular."[31] In this "world," unity and multiplicity, multiculturalism and universal brotherhood, are complementary rather than conflicted principles.

In the report delivered in the fourth night, in the course of discussing Goethe's lyric poetry, Tuma and the commission directly thematize the Weltliteratur paradigm.[32] After Tuma recites the poem "Zauberlehrling" ("The Sorcerer's Apprentice," 1797), he notes it was partially derived from Goethe's reading of an episode by the Syrian-Greek poet Lucian. Lucian is described by a member of the commission as, like Goethe, "a divinely gifted wanderer between cultures." She alludes to the circumstance that one of Lucian's books, in turn, was inspired by his reading of the poet Menippus. This realization prompts her to remark that it does no harm to a poetic genius if he allows himself to be inspired by the works of others. Tuma cheerfully adds that this was Goethe's own belief. He thereupon cites Goethe's most famous enunciation of Weltliteratur, his pronouncement to Eckermann in 1827 that he enjoys consulting the works of famous nations, that national literature now has little meaning, the epoch of Weltliteratur has dawned, and all must do their part to accelerate its development. Sultan Hakim is pleased to conclude that "Goethe already pursued in his age an idea [Weltliteratur] which is quite similar to our concept of a House of Wisdom" (*GB*, 70–71). Schami and Gutzschhahn tacitly associate the Weltliteratur paradigm here with the infinitely recursive intertextual web seen as informing all literary texts, a leading principle of structuralist and poststructuralist theory. However, Sultan Hakim's linkage of Weltliteratur to the House of Wisdom he is attempting to establish underscores its pedagogical value, its usefulness in illustrating the historical legitimacy and current powerful agency of multiculturalism in the World Literature classroom or in other academic domains.

The House of Wisdom is configured in *Der geheime Bericht* as the concrete, albeit utopian, embodiment of Weltliteratur. Shortly before the novel's conclusion, it is described not only as Hulm's translation center, but as "an ambassadorial building of all cultures." Europe's languages are soon supplemented by Asian languages, translators and scholars from the entire Arab world flock to Hulm, and it is said that "in the House of Wisdom more experience was collected on translations in one year than in the rest of Arabia in ten years" (*GB*, 160). Translation was absolutely central to Goethe's own Weltliteratur project, but as a recent essay has argued, he recognized that this element tragically undermines Weltliteratur's universal political and cultural ideals: "In its endeavor to transcend international political-cultural hostilities Weltliteratur is inextricably bound up with the tragedy of translation; it is forever potentially undermined by translation's dangerous, dubious, mephistophelian associations."[33] As argued in the introduction, translation's negative associations should be openly discussed in the metatheoretically informed World Literature classroom. Only by doing so can one ameliorate their effects on reading world literature.

Given the contiguity between utopia and tragedy in the domain of translation as an aspect of Weltliteratur, it is appropriate that, immediately after describing the House of Wisdom as a mecca of translation activity, Schami and Gutzschhahn present the brief but powerful account of Hulm's demise. Hulm begins to draw diplomats from Europe and North America who attempt to persuade the sultan to open his island to oil exploration. After their efforts fail, the English circulate the rumor that Hulm intends to ally with Germany in order to conquer Bahrain. The English military uses this accusation as an excuse to annihilate Hulm, though the destruction is presented by the English press as the result of a civil war ended by the Western powers. Tuma and Hakim disappear. Martha (Princess Saide) is injured and loses her husband to the bombardment, but she saves the manuscript of the report and brings it with her into German exile. Hulm is sucked so completely dry of its oil that the entire island sinks into the sea. Thus, the brief economic prosperity oil brings to Hulm is shown to be evanescent, far outweighed by the cultural, political, and ecological destruction it brings in its train. The last line of the novel reveals that Hulm is the Arabic word for "dream" (*GB*, 164). In spite of this dystopian conclusion, designed to draw the attention of *Der geheime Bericht*'s young readers to the desultory realities of petroleum-based imperialist geopolitics past and present,[34] the body of the text articulates the House of Wisdom as a dream of Weltliteratur well worth sustaining.

David Barry has recently noted that "the cosmopolitan spirit of Goethe's Weltliteratur presupposes the useful and productive interplay between identity and difference, between the universal and the particular, the intellectual critical regard for otherness within community."[35] As we have seen, Schami shares these ideals, and this is why his novels are particularly amenable to being read through the dialectical filter of Weltliteratur. Nevertheless, as Seyhan and others have demonstrated, these ideals constitute the broad teleological framework for the many bicultural authors who discursively "cross borders" in contemporary transnational works. In an age of at least superficially homogenizing globalization, employing the critical techniques subsumed by the Weltliteratur paradigm will help unlock the embedded cultural memory, the inassimilable traces of alterity latent in "world literature" today, but will show us how these traces are interwoven with universal themes as well. Discussing contemporary and earlier works under the sign of Weltliteratur will provide added enrichment and inspiration to our students' readings in the World Literature classroom.

Afterword

A Metatheoretical Approach to Teaching World Literature

WRITING AT THE DAWN of the twentieth century, Oscar Wilde was inspired by Goethe's cosmopolitan pronouncements on Weltliteratur to predict that "criticism will annihilate race-prejudices, by insisting upon the unity of the human mind in the variety of its forms."[1] Around a hundred years later, when the twentieth century was coming to a close, Claudio Guillén argued that "we should remember that Goethe," in formulating his Weltliteratur paradigm, "started from the existence of some national literatures—thus making possible a dialogue between the local and the universal, between the one and the many."[2] Wilde composed his lines in 1891, when modernism had not yet begun to introduce a homogenizing cultural practice that, in the perception of some intellectuals, tended to efface national variety in European letters. Guillén originally published *The Challenge of Comparative Literature* in Spanish in 1985,[3] not long before the fall of Soviet Communism and the concomitant rise of globalization, which, in its negative aspect, moves toward a certain homogeneity in all aspects of human existence, political and economic as well as cultural. Perhaps this is why contemporary interpreters of Goethe's paradigm, such as Homi Bhabha, sometimes lose sight of its dialogical dimension and redirect it into such totalizing constants as "hybridity" and "third space," constants that, as Azade Seyhan has noted, forsake "an analysis of actual social spaces where cultures interact and literature as an institution of cultural memory intervenes."[4]

Variety, diversity, particularity, and cultural negotiations in their discrete character have not disappeared from the world literary scene. I believe it can be plausibly argued that contemporary postmodern literature, by renouncing modernist ideals such as a unified, cohesive narration, is thereby freed to focus on local particularities. Nevertheless, I believe that the universalization of American popular culture and the English language creates an enormously inhibiting effect on our students' ability to recognize how the universal and the particular interact not just in contemporary literature, but in almost all literature from all times. Given the tacit current national perception that the spread of English on a global scale makes the study of foreign languages and cultures unnecessary, as well as American mass media representations of the foreign Other as either assimilated, eccentric, impoverished, and/or dangerous, we cannot expect our students to be inherently capable of knowing how to read the "world" in "world literature." Sarah Lawall has noted that in the middle of the twentieth century, when World Literature courses were particularly popular in this country, the traditional questions debated by its instructors with respect to curricular choices, linguistic competence on the part of teaching staff, translation issues, and the study of nonfiction works took place "against the background assumption of similarity or 'one world,'" and she infers that the desire to use World Literature courses in order to transmit canonically stored wisdom and values is still current.[5]

The pedagogical desiderata of teaching ethics and transmitting a storehouse of exemplary universal acumen are best fulfilled, in my view, outside the World Literature classroom, where learning to read outside one's conceptual and geographic borders must be the top priority. Allowing the "background assumption" of which Lawall speaks to dominate the pedagogy of World Literature, that is to say, the attempt to employ world literature primarily to illustrate that, beyond cultural and linguistic differences, we are all children of one universe, must also impair the ability to comprehend the local, the contingent, in literature. Wilde, Guillén, and the many other thinkers who have recognized the balance between the universal and the particular in Goethe's Weltliteratur formulations have led me to believe that teaching Goethe's Weltliteratur concept in introductory World Literature courses helps students to read world literature with an attention to the dialectical nuances scholarship has justifiably underscored in articulating the paradigm. Thus, I used a metatheoretical approach in the "Introduction to Modern World Literature" class I taught in the Fall 2002 and Fall 2003 semesters at Louisiana State University.

Before discussing the metatheoretical methodology of this course, I would like to elaborate a bit on the pedagogical significance of the juxtaposition of the particular and the universal in Goethe's paradigm. In a semiotic analysis of cross-cultural perception as related to the reception of Slavic texts, Jurij Lotman and his colleagues noted the volatile complexity of the parameters governing such perception. The inner sphere of the analyzing culture is (unconsciously) bound by regulative norms in interpreting the outer sphere of the analyzed culture, norms that inevitably distort such analysis. Thus, in the twentieth century, Europeans both exoticized and infantilized Far Eastern and African cultures in the act of appropriating them, wrenching non-Western texts from "their characteristic historical (or psychological) context."[6] According to Lawall, "Lotman's argument suggests that world literature texts must be seen as both alien and familiar: they are certifiably foreign and thus fill the role of an oppositional other, but their foreignness has also been domesticated through being channeled into local recognition-patterns." Furthermore, Lawall argues, unless this channeling is challenged, perception of the world literature text's alterity will not take place, regardless of its canonicity.[7] Too great an emphasis on such a text's universally human elements will surely result in the domestication of which Lawall speaks, but an obsessive focus on its "foreignness" will inevitably bring about the exoticization and estrangement Lotman and his colleagues also isolated as a common pattern in cross-cultural reading and appropriation. Only a dialectical reading, balanced between the poles of the universal and the particular,[8] can possibly obviate such perceptual extremes, and we can capacitate our introductory World Literature students to engage in such reading by familiarizing them with the core principle of Weltliteratur.

It is also worth taking note of Slavoj Žižek's critique of the very principle of a non-socially circumscribed universal, for this critique has pedagogical implications. Žižek argues that we can never comprehend the non-I until we grasp the limits that circumscribe self and Other linguistically and socially. Universals, in his view, are never neutral, but always historical and social constructs. Universals are therefore only comprehensible as a mutual lack borne by both the Other and the self: "In other words, the paradox of the Universal is that its condition of impossibility is its condition of possibility: the dimension of the Universal emerges precisely and only insofar as the Other is not accessible to us in its specificity; or, to put it in Lacanian terms: there is no universality without an *empty signifier*."[9] Certainly, hermeneutic philosophy has consistently demonstrated that our perception of universals is mediated by the particular social-historical constellations that govern our lives. This is a lesson worth communicating to our students, and I frequently do so. One of the most valuable lessons of the World Literature classroom should be that constants of human life experienced at all times and in all places, such as war, love, social conflict, the yearning for beauty, the quest for human rights (Žižek's example), etc., are mediated by our specific individual and collective experiences. Nevertheless, an unqualified embrace of Žižek's position that the universal can only be perceived as a lack binding self and Other would create enormous pedagogical difficulties in a beginning World Literature class, where students need a stronger sense of common humanity linking text and reader as a bridge to understanding the discrete cultural particularities of that text.

I should emphasize that my "Introduction to Modern World Literature" is what the term implies, a course designed for beginning (primarily freshman and sophomore level) students who quite likely have no familiarity with serious literature except for what they studied in middle and high school English courses. Having exposed these students to the broadest chronological, linguistic, and cultural range of modern (mid-seventeenth-century and beyond)[10] literature available in the second volume of *The Norton Anthology of World Masterpieces* at the beginning of their academic career, I believe they are in a position to make informed choices on more in-depth study of particular literatures, cultures, and languages. Given the enormity of the scope of works to be discussed, and the danger of alienating students by throwing too much theory at them, I restricted the exclusively theoretical portion of my course to the first two weeks of a fifteen-week semester, though we subsequently applied the Weltliteratur dialectic to the imaginative works themselves. In giving an introductory overview of the course on the first day of instruction, I asked the students *not* to look at the packet of photocopied materials consisting of a range of discussions on Weltliteratur and World Literature because I devoted the entire second day to a tabula rasa discussion; I wanted to know how students conceptualize the term "world literature" prior to being exposed to published discussions of the paradigm.

In order to facilitate this discussion, I asked my students to imagine that they were teachers of World Literature who had to work without the benefit of an anthology. In order to select texts for inclusion in a World Literature course, it was therefore imperative that they have some purchase on how World Literature should be defined; only on that basis could works be included or excluded. I gave them the following possibilities (making it clear that they need not be thought of as exclusive) but also allowed them to come up with their own category or categories if they so chose: 1. The best works ever written ("great works"); 2. What has been handed down as worth reading by tradition ("canonic works"); 3. Literature that deals with the world at large, not focused on, or rooted in, one nation or culture; 4. Literature *not* written in English (Philo Buck's view); 5. Literature that is *popular* throughout the world; 6. Literature with timeless and universal appeal; 7. Literature *addressed* to the world at large.

I divided the classes into four groups of approximately seven students. Every group believed that categories two and six should be included in any valid conceptualization of World Literature, and one group also favored category five. There was an interesting divergence of views in the Fall 2002 class, however, on what should constitute both "canonic" literature and "timeless" literature. One group of students felt that such choices had to be established on a national or subnational level, and that what was established on those levels should be valid for inclusion in a World Literature classroom. Another group believed that such validity is only established on a *global* scale; truly canonic literature, in this view, is established by a cosmopolitan winnowing process that might well ignore national or subnational proclivities. One student argued that works worthy of inclusion should be imbued by timeless *moral* values, and another argued for the inclusion of the core texts of world religions, such as the Bible and the Koran. The group that believed popularity was an important criterion did not equate popularity with *mass* literature, but with literature rooted in an oral tradition. A group of students in the Fall 2003 class argued that works that impact the course of world *history,* such as Harriet Beecher Stowe's *Uncle Tom's Cabin,* most deserve the appellation "world literature." I set aside this day for group discussions as a way to get students to think about how World Literature theorists and teachers have conceptualized World Literature so that they would be in a better position to comprehend the models and definitions I subsequently presented to them during the theoretical phase of the class.

The next class session consisted of my lecture on the history of the concept, and I discussed at this time the epochally defined cosmopolitan context informing Goethe's initial employment of the term in the late 1820s, the sense that European culture was in the midst of a national-international dialogue allowing Goethe to discern a balance between particular and universal elements within this interchange. In order to convey Goethe's views on Weltliteratur, I read in translation the first three pronouncements on this subject printed in Strich's appendix to his *Goethe and World Literature.*[11] I also read aloud, and clarified, Martin Bollacher's cogent summary of the forward-looking, globalistic essence of Goethe's concept:

> Far from adhering to the—at any rate illusory—boundaries of a German national literature in the domain of aesthetic reflection and poetic production, Goethe points to the integrated character, especially relevant and open in the European context, of the individual literatures and the cosmopolitan-communicative character of the contemporary translation and editorial institutions. This world-literary integration is a paradigm of a literary model obligated to the modern, transnational circulation of thoughts and works.[12]

I also touched on the concept's subsequent history—its general abnegation by German scholars and authors during the nationalistic period between 1848 and 1945, its recuperation by Thomas Mann and Strich as a means to counteract fascistic thought and to infuse Germans with a cosmopolitan spirit, its adaptation as a pedagogical domain in the United States early in the twentieth century, and popular current equations of Weltliteratur with both transnationalism and globalization. The next two class sessions were devoted to discussing texts previously examined in this book by Goethe, Marx/Engels, Hutcheson Macaulay Posnett, Thomas Wentworth Higginson, Richard Moulton, and Guillén, as well as a number of Web sites devoted either to discussions of Weltliteratur or designed for specific World Literature courses at other universities. In our discussion of Goethe, I focused on his optimistic belief that Europe's nations were imbued by a cosmopolitan fellowship in the wake of the Napoleonic Wars, his fear that the French might dominate the world literary dialogue, and how his translation theory fits into his Weltliteratur paradigm.[13] I noted Marx/ Engel's extreme cosmopolitanism, their belief, articulated in the *Communist Manifesto,* that Weltliteratur signified the end of national literatures concomitant to the rise of international capitalism and an internationalized proletariat. By way of comparison and contrast, I discussed Posnett's belief that "world-literature . . . is the severance of literature from defined social groups—the universalising of literature."[14] For Posnett, this is not a recent phenomenon, but quite ancient and *prior to* the advent of discrete national literatures. The educational ideals of Higginson and Moulton were examined in order to show how World Literature began to develop as a pedagogical domain in the United States. The elucidation of these works helped drive home the point that Weltliteratur and World Literature are not self-understood concepts, that they were—and still are—the object of conflicting discursive and pedagogical ideologies. The discussion of Guillén and certain Web sites served as an elaboration of world literature as a truly global—which is to say not exclusively Western—domain of inquiry,[15] and redirected student attention to Weltliteratur as a dialectic of "the local and the universal," to again quote Guillén. I envisioned this discussion as a springboard into the metatheoretically informed analysis of the *belles lettres* constituting the remainder of the semester.

Needless to say, I have little expertise or academic background with respect to most of the world's cultures, and I suspect that this is the case with the vast majority of World Literature teachers. Thus, the challenge of elucidating the local, particular aspect of such cultures as they inform the texts covered in any World Literature classroom would appear to be quite daunting. However, a Weltliteratur-informed reading, in my view, need not dwell at length on subtextual nuances rooted in discrete civilizations as resonant in these works; this is a task for specialist scholars. I view my role in a metatheoretically oriented World Literature classroom as that of enabling students simply to *perceive* patterns of cultural alterity and how they interact with a text's universal elements. In other words, my primary goal is to inculcate the habit of reading texts, particularly foreign texts, using the technique of the Weltliteratur dialectic. This would seem a relatively easy thing to achieve if we overlook the distorting prism of translation and the adroit perception of Lawall, aided by her reading of Lotman and company, that the "foreignness" of such texts tends instinctively to become acclimatized to one's own local frame of reference, and that "access to the cultural polyphony or the 'worlding' of these books is consequently blocked, unless there is some way of disorienting this substitution of self for other."[16] At a time when American-dominated globalization makes such substitution especially facile for our students, the goal of disorientation propounded by Lawall can only be achieved through conscious effort on the part of the World Literature instructor.

Certainly, some background reading is necessary in order to prepare for lectures on culturally unfamiliar works. Using the Internet to show images chronologically and geographically linked to the texts and their authors will also underscore their discrete ambience, their "foreignness," in a vivid manner that words, especially translated words, cannot convey. For example, I used Web images of eighteenth-century Chinese gardens for the first work of imaginative literature we discussed, Cao Xueqin's *The Story of the Stone*. This is a work of eighteenth-century Chinese literature, and the excerpt we examined takes place primarily in a garden. These Web-available garden images illustrate the fluidity between what Westerners would call the natural and supernatural domains, a key, culturally specific, unfamiliar element in Cao Xueqin's work. Even more important with respect to the metatheoretical dimension of the World Literature classroom are the kinds of questions posed in order to direct student reading and discussion, questions for students to ponder as they read the respective assigned works.

In connection with *The Story of the Stone,* I asked students to try to discern what elements reflect a distinctly non-Western world view, but also what makes the story's appeal universal. With respect to cultural specificity, we discussed the Taoist Ying-Yang principle inherent in the tale; Stone is born into the zenith of prosperity, so he must pass into decline during his maturity. The religious polyphony in *The Story of the Stone,* the tale's equation of form with illusion, the motif of reincarnation, intertextual references to other classics of Chinese literature: these elements partially constitute the work's particular dimension, but they are mediated through the universal theme of young love embodied by the relationship between Bao-yu and Dai-yu.

Though a number of works originally written in English were covered in the class, I attempted to make students consciously aware of the fact that we were examining these texts with a different methodology than would be employed in a course taught in an English department. For example, a key focus of our discussion on Jonathan Swift's *Gulliver's Travels* was the manner in which cross-cultural and cross-language encounters of the sort experienced by Englishmen in Swift's day are reflected in Gulliver's engagement with the Houyhnhnms, albeit in the fantastic guise necessitated by Swift's use of satiric inversion, through which horses become creatures endowed with a purified capacity to verbally reason and Gulliver's human cousins, the Yahoos, are the speechless beasts. I pointed out that the circumstance *forcing* Gulliver to learn a foreign tongue in order to survive is unlikely to exist in the present age, when people are conversant with English in all corners of the globe. In foregrounding this culturally exotic (for the present-day American reader) element by way of illustrating that, in an epistemological sense, we are really reading Swift "in translation," I contrasted such a World Literature oriented approach to *Gulliver's Travels* with the way this text would be read in a traditional English literature course, where other concerns, such as Swift's place in the British canon of his period, would undoubtedly receive primary focus. This continuous emphasis on introducing World Literature metatheory into the classroom did result in one unfortunate side effect in this case; on a quiz in the Fall 2002 semester, one confused student discussed what he believed were Swift's direct pronouncements on World Literature!

Though the teacher of introductory World Literature courses cannot assume any knowledge of foreign languages on the part of his or her students, the issue of translation should be in the foreground of a metatheoretically informed World Literature classroom. In addition to discussing Goethe's three levels of translation and how these relate to his Weltliteratur paradigm, I provided the students with a fairly literal translation of Heine's "Die Lorelei," which I printed next to a copy of the German original. We compared this translation with Ernst Feise's more poetic but less terminologically precise rendering of Heine's poem in the *World Masterpieces* anthology[17] in order to explore as fully as possible both the lyric and narrative nuances of the original.

With a bit of research, it is even possible to fruitfully juxtapose literal and poetic translations in the classroom without personal knowledge of the original language. The *World Masterpieces* anthology provides both a highly lyric rendition of eight of Ghalib's Urdu-language *Ghazals* by leading contemporary English-language poets, and some literal translations of individual verses by Aijaz Ahmad. The opening couplet of *Ghazal* XXI is expressed as follows by William Stafford: "Dew on a flower—tears, or something: / hidden spots mark the heart of a cruel woman." A note explains that "flower" in the original Urdu is "lala," an Indian red poppy.[18] In his discussion of this couplet in an edition of the complete *Ghazals* in translation, Ahmad notes that "The Indian poppy is smaller than the Western variety and, with the poetic license which is common in Urdu, one could imply that a dewdrop is sufficient to cover the black that lies at the heart of the flower."[19] Thus, Aijaz's own quite literal rendition of the couplet reads "The dewdrop on the red poppy is not without end/function/ meaning: / The spot on the heart of her who is cruel is a place where shame has come (to pass)."[20] In my classroom elucidation of the verse, I pointed out that Stafford's translation operates at a *universal* level. A flower of no particular variety enacts a metaphoric contrast; dewy, blossomy beauty/a moist eye are juxtaposed with a cold heart. One might see such chiastic inversion in the poetry of any language. Ahmad's translation does not capture the lyric emotion created by Stafford, but does reveal, in conjunction with his commentary, the *particular* nuance of the Urdu verse: the dewdrop is like a mask which completely covers the heart/eye[21] of the indifferent beloved just as it can completely cover the black spots on the tiny Indian red poppy. Images of this poppy available on a variety of Web sites underscored the local, particular nuance of the metaphor.

In addition to using the universal-particular dialectic to guide students between the shoals of domestication and exoticization in their reading of individual texts, I used this fundamental principle of Weltliteratur to help them recognize key features of literary movements. Thus, with respect to Pirandello's *Six Characters in Search of an Author* and Kafka's *The Metamorphosis,* I challenged my students to find any surface elements reflective of national or regional specificity, to find what it is that foregrounds Pirandello's play as Italian and Kafka's story as Czech or Austrian. The fact that such surface elements are completely absent[22] can be used to underscore a certain veracity in the pronouncements of Thomas Mann and Oswald Spengler alluded to in chapter four of this book, namely, that Weltliteratur's cosmopolitan strain was realized through the homogenizing disposition of high modernism.[23] Nevertheless, the polyphonic but locally rooted cultural memories evident in much postcolonial, transnational literature, such as *Damascus Nights,* can also be elucidated through the Weltliteratur dialectic. I condensed the reading advanced in chapter six for our discussion of Schami's novel, highlighting its strong rootedness in 1950s Damascus, its attention to cultural misperceptions between Arabs and, especially, Americans, and the threat that the then-new medium of the transistor radio is shown to pose to both the Syrian capital's ethnic, cultural diversity and its oral storytelling traditions. Thus, with respect to the Weltliteratur dialectic, we discussed how cultural ambiences are highly localized in Schami's novel (as in much transnational literature) but balanced by the universal theme of modernization's destructive impact on traditional ways of life. Of course, a metatheoretically informed World Literature class cannot obviate this impact, but it can lead to greater insight into and appreciation of such traditions, especially traditions foreign to our own.

In an essay originally delivered at a conference on how foreign language and English departments may develop a positive relationship in the future, Roland Greene argues that World Literature is a promising area of intersection. He finds that "at present, *world literature* is a term without a concept, but its latent power in the early twenty-first century is readily imaginable. Not merely an academic slogan for literature read in translation, or for several works out of different national traditions jostling one another without an intellectual program, world literature is properly a renovative concept."[24] In this book, I have tried to demonstrate that Weltliteratur and World Literature have actually been associated with a wide variety of concepts and ideologies, such as canonicity, intercultural commerce, cosmopolitanism, "Great Books," and, more recently, transnationalism and globalization. It is my view that World Literature will only function positively as a "renovative concept," capable both of transcending the vagueness and indefinition Greene associates with it at present and of bringing about a positive interdisciplinarity among departments traditionally associated with one national tradition, if we return to an understanding of Weltliteratur imbued by Goethe's original perception of the paradigm, as the intersection of the local and the universal in literature. When applied to classroom teaching, as my own experience in lecturing, guiding discussions, and evaluating examinations and term papers has demonstrated, such an approach will enable student and instructor alike to engage in readings situated between the extremes of domestication and exoticization. This will help us better understand what unites us as human beings across the globe and across the centuries, but to recognize as well the unique features of the world's diverse cultures and literary movements throughout the ages.

Notes

CHAPTER I. Introduction

1. Hans-J. Weitz, "'Weltliteratur' zuerst bei Wieland," *Arcadia* 22 (1987): 206–8.

2. J. C. Brandt Corstius, "Writing Histories of World Literature," *Yearbook of Comparative and General Literature* 12 (1963): 5–14.

3. Martin Jay, *Marxism and Totality: The Adventures of a Concept from Lukács to Habermas* (Berkeley: Univ. of California Press, 1984).

4. However, at least three cursory treatments have been published: Helmut Bender and Ulrich Melzer, "Zur Geschichte des Begriffes 'Weltliteratur,'" *Saeculum* 9 (1958): 113–23; Arpad Berczik, "Zur Entwicklung des Begriffs 'Weltliteratur' und Anfänge der Vergleichenden Literaturgeschichte," *Acta germanica et romanica* 2 (1967): 3–22; Erwin Koppen, "Weltliteratur," in *Reallexikon der deutschen Literaturgeschichte*, 2nd ed., vol. 4, ed. Klaus Kanzog and Achim Masser (Berlin: Walter de Gruyter, 1984), 815–27. Bender and Melzer cite a very early, somewhat more comprehensive treatment (114 n. 2): Else Beil, *Zur Entwicklung des Begriffes der Weltliteratur* (Leipzig: Voigtländer, 1915). Despite its promising title, this brief book does not examine the Weltliteratur concept beyond early German Romanticism.

5. Michael Thomas Carroll, "Introduction," in *No Small World: Visions and Revisions of World Literature*, ed. Michael Thomas Carroll (Urbana, Ill.: National Council of Teachers of English, 1996), vii.

6. To be sure, not all German scholars employ the term in this self-aware manner. Many critical works in German, particularly comparative and influence studies, simply equate Weltliteratur with the imaginative writing of the world at large. The following two volumes can serve as examples: Edward Jaime, *Stefan George und die Weltliteratur* (Ulm: Aegis, 1949); Bert Nagel, *Kafka und die Weltliteratur: Zusammenhänge und Wechselwirkungen* (Munich: Winkler, 1983). An overview of this critically unreflexive approach to Weltliteratur in Germany is provided by Martin Bollacher, "Goethes Konzeption der Weltliteratur," in *Ironische Propheten: Sprachbewußtsein und Humanität in der Literatur von Herder bis Heine: Studien für Jür-*

gen Brummack zum 65. Geburtstag, ed. Markus Heilmann and Birgit Wägenbaur (Tübingen: Narr, 2001), 170–73.

7. An overview of the progressive transformation of World Literature anthologies from narrowly Western to relatively global in scope, and a perspective on how the current more inclusive approach can be improved in these collections, is provided by David Damrosch, "World Literature Today: From the Old World to the Whole World," *symplokē* 8 (2000): 7–19.

8. Azade Seyhan, *Writing Outside the Nation* (Princeton: Princeton Univ. Press, 2001).

9. To be sure, Americans are frequently exposed to foreign cultures through ethnic cuisine, movies, dance, music concerts, etc. Many Americans enjoy these experiences, and they are led by them to recognize and perhaps even cherish the diversity of such cultures at a superficial level. Stanley Fish sarcastically calls this phenomenon "boutique multiculturalism," and quite rightly asserts that such encounters are little more than "high-profile flirtations with the 'other,'" allowing us little genuine insight into cultural alterity. See his essay "Boutique Multiculturalism," in *Multiculturalism and American Democracy,* ed. Arthur M. Melzer et al. (Lawrence: Univ. Press of Kansas, 1998), 69.

10. The post–Cold War globalization of English and its concomitant homogenizing of the presentation/reception of the world's cultures, particularly through the economics and politics of translation in North America and elsewhere, have been nicely summarized by Timothy Brennan, "The Cuts of Language: The East/West of North/South," *Public Culture* 13 (2001): 39–63, esp. 58–61.

11. William Paulson, *Literary Culture in a World Transformed: A Future for the Humanities* (Ithaca: Cornell Univ. Press, 2001), 2.

12. Lawrence Venuti, *The Scandals of Translation: Towards an Ethics of Difference* (London: Routledge, 1998). See esp. 69–75 and 160–65.

13. Horst Steinmetz, "Weltliteratur—Umriß eines literaturgeschichtlichen Konzepts," *Arcadia* 20 (1985): 15–16.

14. Czeslaw Milosz, *Road-Side Dog,* trans. Czeslaw Milosz and Robert Hass (New York: Farrar, Straus, and Giroux, 1998), 58.

15. This proposal to create a model of Weltliteratur sensitive to such diversity is, of course, absolutely antithetical to the recent notion that world literature should be approached through a "distant reading" that is attuned to uniform global patterns, to adjustments to dominant Western modalities. The articulation of diverse nuances, in this view, is produced through the study of national literatures. See Franco Moretti, "Conjectures on World Literature," *New Left Review,* 2nd ser., 1 (2000): 54–68.

16. Weitz, "'Weltliteratur,'" 208 (Weitz's italics).

17. Johann Wolfgang Goethe, *Gedenkausgabe der Werke, Briefe und Gespräche,* ed. Ernst Beutler, 24 vols. (Zurich: Artemis, 1948–1954). This edition will be cited throughout the book by volume and page number. An abridged translation of Goethe's "Translations" by Sharon Sloan can be found in Rainer Schulte and John Biguenet, eds., *Theories of Translation: An Anthology of Essays from Dryden to Derrida* (Chicago: Univ. of Chicago Press, 1992), 60–63.

18. In consistently using masculine pronouns and possessive adjectives here, I am not engaging in unconscious sexism, but merely translating Goethe's own custom.

19. This is a central tenet of Gadamer's 1960 magnum opus, *Wahrheit und Methode* (*Truth and Method*), first translated in 1975.

20. Goethe's embrace of the ideal literalness of poetic translation strongly influenced Walter Benjamin's views on the link between translation and originary linguistic purity, found in his now widely discussed essay "Die Aufgabe des Übersetzers" ("The Task of the Translator," 1923). See Carrie Asman, "'Der Satz ist die Mauer': Zur Figur des Übersetzers bei Benjamin and Goethe: 'Werther,' 'Faust,' 'Wilhelm Meister,'" *Goethe-Jahrbuch* 111 (1994): 68.

21. Ernst Elster, "World Literature and Comparative Literature (1901)," trans. Eric Metzler, *Yearbook of Comparative and General Literature* 35 (1986): 7–13.

22. Claus Clüver, "The Difference of Eight Decades: World Literature and the Demise of National Literatures," *Yearbook of Comparative and General Literature* 35 (1986): 17.

23. Ibid., 23.

24. Berczik, "Zur Entwicklung des Begriffs 'Weltliteratur,'" 7 n. 9, claims the term "Weltliteratur" was coined by August Ludwig Schlözer in his "Vorstellung der Universaltheorie" (1772).

25. The most significant and cogent of these remarks have been compiled by Fritz Strich and published together at the conclusion to his magnum opus, *Goethe und die Weltliteratur* (Bern: Francke, 1946), 397–400.

26. Steinmetz, "Weltliteratur," 10.

27. Ernst Behler, "Problems of Origin in Modern Literary History," in *Theoretical Issues in Literary History,* ed. David Perkins (Cambridge, Mass.: Harvard Univ. Press, 1991), 12–13.

28. Gerhart Hoffmeister has even argued that the literary universalism of the Brothers Schlegel anticipates the cosmopolitan strain of Goethe's Weltliteratur paradigm, though he recognizes Goethe's rejection of their utopian belief in the exclusive power of art to regenerate society and his refutation of their obsession with the Middle Ages, religion, and a nationalistic patriotism ("Reception in Germany and Abroad," in *The Cambridge Companion to Goethe,* ed. Lesley Sharpe [Cambridge: Cambridge Univ. Press, 2002], 235). John Neubauer maintains, somewhat in contrast to Behler and Hoffmeister, that Friedrich Schlegel was largely responsible for introducing the very principle of national literature and national literary history to academia (see his essay "Writing and Teaching from Limbo," *PMLA* 118 [2003]: 132).

29. Andreas Huyssen, *Die frühromantische Konzeption von Übersetzung und Aneignung: Studien zur frühromantischen Utopie einer deutschen Weltliteratur* (Zurich: Atlantis, 1969).

30. Haskell M. Block, "The Objectives of the Conference," in *The Teaching of World Literature: Proceedings of the Conference at the University of Wisconsin April 24–25, 1959,* ed. Haskell M. Block (Chapel Hill: Univ. of North Carolina Press, 1960), 3.

31. Sarah Lawall, "Introduction: Reading World Literature," in *Reading World Literature: Theory, History, Practice,* ed. Sarah Lawall (Austin: Univ. of Texas Press, 1994), 20–21.

32. Seyhan, *Writing Outside the Nation,* 41–50.

33. Ülker Gökberk, "Understanding Alterity: *Ausländerliteratur* between Relativism and Universalism," in *Theoretical Issues in Literary History,* ed. David Perkins (Cambridge, Mass.: Harvard Univ. Press, 1991), 143–72.

34. In so doing, I had to steer a course between a focus on aesthetics and on the facts of cultural history. On the problems this compromise entails in the World Literature classroom (in an essay that, typical for its time, advocates focusing on the artistic aspect of literature), see Charlton Laird, "World Literature and Teaching," *Yearbook of Comparative and General Literature* 10 (1961): 66–69.

35. René Etiemble, "Faut-il réviser la notion de 'Weltliteratur'?" *Essais de littérature (vraiment) générale*, 3rd ed. (Paris: Gallimard, 1975), 15–36.

CHAPTER 2. The Emergence of *Weltliteratur*

1. Hagen Schulze, *States, Nations and Nationalism: From the Middle Ages to the Present*, trans. William E. Yuill (Oxford: Blackwell, 1996), 198. For Schulze's description of "Turnvater Jahn" in Vienna, see 199.

2. The interdependent antagonism between the poles of globalization and tribalism has been analyzed by Benjamin R. Barber in *Jihad vs. McWorld* (New York: Times Books, 1995).

3. Martin Albrow, "Auf dem Weg zu einer globalen Gesellschaft?" trans. Ilse Utz, in *Perspektiven der Weltgesellschaft*, ed. Ulrich Beck (Frankfurt: Suhrkamp, 1998), 428–32.

4. See Karl S. Guthke, "Destination Goethe: Travelling Englishmen in Weimar," in *Goethe and the English-Speaking World: Essays from the Cambridge Symposium for His 250th Anniversary*, ed. Nicholas Boyle and John Guthrie (Rochester: Camden House, 2002), 111–42, esp. 117–20.

5. Todd Kontje, *German Orientalisms* (Ann Arbor: Univ. of Michigan Press, 2004), 132.

6. Ibid., 123. Kontje exaggerates here; Goethe greatly admired Kalidāsā's celebrated Sanskrit drama *Śākuntala*. See Dorothy Matilda Figueira, *Translating the Orient: The Reception of* Śākuntala *in Nineteenth-Century Europe* (Albany: State Univ. of New York Press, 1991), 12–13.

7. See esp. W. Daniel Wilson, *Das Goethe-Tabu: Protest und Menschenrechte im klassischen Weimar* (Munich: dtv, 1999).

8. See W. Daniel Wilson, "Goethe and the Political World," in *The Cambridge Companion to Goethe*, ed. Lesley Sharpe (Cambridge: Cambridge Univ. Press, 2002), 217.

9. Goethe, cited in Strich, *Goethe und die Weltliteratur*, 398.

10. On Goethe's rejection of this trend, and on its putative spread through the mass media in the present age, see Ulrich Weisstein, *Comparative Literature and Literary Theory: Survey and Introduction*, trans. William Riggan and Ulrich Weisstein (Bloomington: Indiana Univ. Press, 1973), 19.

11. The interconnection between Goethe's Weltliteratur concept and his natural scientific principles is adumbrated by A. R. Hohlfeld, "Goethe's Conception of World Literature," *Fifty Years with Goethe, 1901–1951* (Madison: Univ. of Wisconsin Press, 1953), 343.

12. According to Peter Weber, "Funktionsverständnis in Goethes Auffassung von Weltliteratur," in *Funktion der Literatur: Aspekte, Probleme, Aufgaben*, eds. Dieter Schlenstedt et al. (Berlin: Akademie, 1975), Goethe developed his Weltliteratur concept specifically in *opposition* to a program of national literature. Goethe, in Weber's view, saw national particularities as just a "cover" for the "universally human" ("allgemein Menschliches") configurations he would call forth (133–35).

13. René Wellek, *A History of Modern Criticism: 1750–1950,* vol. 1. (New Haven: Yale Univ. Press, 1955), 221.

14. See Strich, *Goethe und die Weltliteratur,* 46–48.

15. See particularly Martha Woodmansee's chapter "Aesthetic Autonomy as a Weapon in Cultural Politics: Rereading Schiller's *Aesthetic Letters*" in *The Author, Art, and the Market: Rereading the History of Aesthetics* (New York: Columbia Univ. Press, 1994), 57–86. On Goethe's prophetic fear that the age of Weltliteratur presupposed the dawning predominance of "mass culture" on a worldwide scale, see also Bollacher, "Goethes Konzeption der Weltliteratur," 183–85.

16. Gail Finney, "Of Walls and Windows: What German Studies and Comparative Literature Can Offer Each Other," *Comparative Literature* 49 (1997): 261.

17. Fawzi Boubia, "Goethes Theorie der Alterität und die Idee der Weltliteratur: Ein Beitrag zur neueren Kulturdebatte," in *Gegenwart als kulturelles Erbe: Ein Beitrag der Germanistik zur Kulturwissenschaft deutschsprachiger Länder,* ed. Bernd Thum (Munich: iudicium, 1985), 269–82.

18. Ibid., 282, 283–84.

19. Ibid., 290–98.

20. Boubia, "Universal Literature and Otherness," trans. Jeanne Ferguson, *Diogenes* 141 (1988): 81.

21. Ibid., 89–101.

22. Wellek, *A History of Modern Criticism,* 221.

23. Homi K. Bhabha, *The Location of Culture* (London: Routledge, 1994), 7. Bhabha uses this term specifically in connection with the work of Pepon Osorio (7–8).

24. Wellek, *A History of Modern Criticism,* 221.

25. Goethe somewhat contradicted this perspective in one of his conversations with Eckermann (on 31 January 1827) when he expressed the belief that in Chinese novels characters act, think, and feel like those of European authors, except that the Chinese protagonists act in a manner marked by greater clarity, purity, and ethicalness (24:227).

26. Edward Said, *Orientalism* (New York: Vintage Books, 1979), 167–68.

27. Goethe, cited in Strich, *Goethe und die Weltliteratur,* 399.

28. Gerhard R. Kaiser, *Einführung in die vergleichende Literaturwissenschaft: Forschungsstand, Kritik, Aufgaben* (Darmstadt: Wissenschaftliche Buchgesellschaft, 1980), 12.

29. Bhabha, *The Location of Culture,* 147.

30. Ibid., 143.

31. M. M. Bakhtin, "The *Bildungsroman* and Its Significance in the History of Realism (Toward a Historical Typology of the Novel)," in *Speech Genres and Other Late Essays,* ed. Caryl Emerson and Michael Holquist, trans. Vern W. McGee (Austin: Univ. of Texas Press, 1986), 50 (Bakhtin's italics).

32. Bhabha, *The Location of Culture,* 12.

33. Sarah Lawall, "World Literature, Comparative Literature, Teaching Literature," in *Proceedings of the XIIth Congress of the International Comparative Literature Association: Space and Boundaries,* vol. 5, ed. Roger Bauer et al. (Munich: iudicium, 1990), 223.

34. Bakhtin, "The *Bildungsroman,*" 49.

35. Bhabha, *The Location of Culture,* 143.

36. Hartmut Steinecke, "'Weltliteratur'—Zur Diskussion der Goetheschen 'Idee' im Jungen Deutschland," in *Das Junge Deutschland: Kolloquium zum 150. Jahrestag des Verbots vom 10. Dezember 1835,* ed. Joseph A. Kruse and Bernd Kortländer (Hamburg: Hoffmann and Campe, 1987), 162.

37. Bhabha, *The Location of Culture,* 143.

38. Hendrik Birus, "Main Features of Goethe's Concept of World Literature," *Comparative Literature Now: Theories and Practice,* ed. Steven Tötösy de Zepetnek et al. (Paris: Champion, 1999), 38–39.

39. M. M. Bakhtin, "Forms of Time and the Chronotope in the Novel: Notes toward a Historical Poetics," in *The Dialogic Imagination: Four Essays,* ed. Michael Holquist, trans. Caryl Emerson and Michael Holquist (Austin: Univ. of Texas Press, 1981), 84.

40. Bakhtin, "The *Bildungsroman,*" 35.

41. Ibid., 36–37.

42. Bhabha, *The Location of Culture,* 143.

43. Bakhtin, "The *Bildungsroman,*" 37–38.

44. Ibid., 48.

45. Ibid., 49.

46. Birus, "Main Features of Goethe's Concept of World Literature," 38.

47. Seyhan, *Writing Outside the Nation,* 157.

48. Hans Joachim Schrimpf, "Goethes Begriff der Weltliteratur," in *Nationalismus in Germanistik und Dichtung: Dokumentation des Germanistentages in München vom 17.–22. Oktober 1966,* ed. Benno von Wiese and Rudolf Henß (Berlin: Erich Schmidt, 1967), 202–17.

49. Boubia, "Universal Literature and Otherness," 97.

50. Friedrich Schlegel, *Kritische Ausgabe,* vol. 2, ed. Hans Eichner (Paderborn: Schöningh, 1967), 182.

51. Ibid., 147–48.

52. Paul Gordon, *The Critical Double: Figurative Meaning in Aesthetic Discourse* (Tuscaloosa: Univ. of Alabama Press, 1995), 132.

53. Ibid.

54. Huyssen, *Die frühromantische Konzeption von Übersetzung und Aneignung,* 122.

55. Ibid., 162–65.

56. Birus, "Goethe's Concept of World Literature," 32.

57. Huyssen, *Die frühromantische Konzeption von Übersetzung und Aneignung,* 172–73.

58. Goethe, cited in Strich, *Goethe und die Weltliteratur,* 398.

59. George Steiner, "A Footnote to *Weltliteratur,*" *Le Mythe d'Étiemble: Hommages Études et Recherches* (Paris: Didier, 1979), 261–69.

60. Antoine Berman, *The Experience of the Foreign: Culture and Translation in Romantic Germany,* trans. S. Heyvaert (Albany: State Univ. of New York Press, 1992), 56–65.

61. Novalis, *Schriften: Die Werke Friedrich von Hardenbergs,* vol. 3, ed. Richard Samuel et al. (Stuttgart: Kohlhammmer, 1960), 685.

62. Cf. Thomas Bleicher, "Novalis und die Idee der Weltliteratur," *Arcadia* 14 (1979): 254–70. Bleicher posits a direct connection between Novalis's thoughts on the contemporary

cosmopolitan spirit he discerned in the world of commerce and his views on literature, though Novalis never actually used the term Weltliteratur.

63. See the citations and discussion of Novalis and A. W. Schlegel in Huyssen, *Die früh-romantische Konzeption von Übersetzung und Aneignung,* 161.

CHAPTER 3. The Mediation and Contestation of *Weltliteratur*

1. For a description of their encounter, see Jeffrey L. Sammons, *Heinrich Heine: A Modern Biography* (Princeton: Princeton Univ. Press, 1979), 103–4.

2. Bodo Morawe, *Heines "Französische Zustände": Über die Fortschritte des Republikanismus und die anmarschierende Weltliteratur* (Heidelberg: Winter, 1997), 86.

3. Goethe, cited in Strich, *Goethe und die Weltliteratur,* 399.

4. Morawe, *Heines "Französische Zustände,"* 86–88.

5. I am thinking particularly of the essays presented at the 1997 London Heine Conference edited by T. J. Reed and Alexander Stillmark, published under the title *Heine und die Weltliteratur* (Oxford: Legenda, 2000). An exception is Joseph A. Kruse's essay "'In der Literatur wie im Leben hat jeder Sohn einen Vater': Heinrich Heine zwischen Bibel und Homer, Cervantes und Shakespeare" (2–23). Kruse's article takes into account the national-international dialogue at the heart of Goethe's understanding of the Weltliteratur paradigm, and finds that Heine believes this dialogue is achieved primarily through music, which overcomes national boundaries (4–6).

6. Walter Hinck, *Die Wunde Deutschland: Heinrich Heines Dichtung im Widerstreit von Nationalidee, Judentum und Antisemitismus* (Frankfurt: Insel, 1990), 110–11. Hinck claims that the letter was written to Friedrich Merckel, but other Heine scholars dispute this assertion. My thanks to Marianne Tilch of the Heine-Gesellschaft for bringing this controversy to my attention.

7. Bhabha, *The Location of Culture,* 12.

8. In Germany, the most eloquent attempt to envision a new Weltliteratur along the postcolonial lines suggested by Bhabha is provided by Doris Bachmann-Medick, "Multikultur oder kulturelle Differenzen? Neue Konzepte von Weltliteratur und Übersetzung in postkolonialer Perspektive," *Deutsche Vierteljahrsschrift* 68 (1994): 585–612.

9. Hinck, *Die Wunde Deutschland,* 111.

10. Ibid.

11. Goethe, cited in Strich, *Goethe und die Weltliteratur,* 397.

12. Heinrich Heine, *Sämtliche Schriften,* ed. Klaus Briegleb, 6 vols. (Munich: Hanser, 1968–1976). This edition will be cited throughout the chapter by volume (in Roman numerals) and page number.

13. For a discussion of Madame de Staël's salon and her relationship to Rahel Varnhagen, see Lilian R. Furst, "The *Salons* of Germaine de Staël and Rahel Varnhagen," in *Cultural Interactions in the Romantic Age: Critical Essays in Comparative Literature,* ed. Gregory Maertz (Albany: State Univ. of New York Press, 1998), 95–103.

14. Goethe, cited in Strich, *Goethe und die Weltliteratur,* 398–99.

15. Renate Stauf, *Der problematische Europäer: Heinrich Heine im Konflikt zwischen Nationenkritik und gesellschaftlicher Utopie* (Heidelberg: Winter, 1997), 196.

16. See Kruse, "'In der Literatur wie im Leben,'" 9–10.

17. Hendrik Birus, "Goethes Idee der Weltliteratur: Eine historische Vergegenwärtigung," in *Weltliteratur heute: Konzepte und Perspektiven,* ed. Manfred Schmeling (Wurzburg: Königshausen and Neumann, 1995), 23–24.

18. Seyhan, "Cannons Against the Canon: Representations of Tradition and Modernity in Heine's Literary History," *Deutsche Vierteljahrsschrift* 63 (1989): 502.

19. Stauf, *Der problematische Europäer,* 12.

20. Michel Espagne, "Übersetzung und Orientreise: Heines Handschriften zum *Loeve-Veimars-Fragment,*" *Euphorion* 78 (1984): 127–42.

21. Indeed, not all critics agree that Heine's political and cultural views were genuinely cosmopolitan at all. See Jeffrey L. Sammons, "Heine as *Weltbürger?* A Skeptical Inquiry," *Imagination and History: Selected Papers on Nineteenth-Century German Literature* (New York: Peter Lang, 1989), 97–122. As the title of this essay indicates, Sammons finds the view that Heine was fundamentally cosmopolitan in outlook highly dubious. He clearly demonstrates a chauvinist element in the writings of the politically capricious Heine.

22. Benno von Wiese, "Goethe und Heine als Europäer," *Signaturen: Zu Heinrich Heine und seinem Werk* (Berlin: Erich Schmidt, 1976), 209–12. Citation on 212, Wiese's emphasis.

23. See Heinz Hamm, *Goethe und die französische Zeitschrift "Le Globe": Eine Lektüre im Zeichen der "Weltliteratur"* (Weimar: Böhlau, 1998).

24. Sammons, *Heinrich Heine: A Modern Biography,* 160.

25. Hamm, *Goethe und die französische Zeitschrift "Le Globe,"* 11.

26. Wilhelm Gössmann, "Die Herausforderung der Wissenschaft durch die Literatur," in *Heinrich Heine im Spannungsfeld von Literatur und Wissenschaft: Symposium anläßlich der Benennung der Universität Düsseldorf nach Heinrich Heine,* ed. Wilhelm Gössmann and Manfred Windfuhr (Dusseldorf: Hobbing, 1990), 24.

27. Goethe, cited in Strich, *Goethe und die Weltliteratur,* 399.

28. Victor Lange, "Nationalliteratur und Weltliteratur," *Jahrbuch der Goethe-Gesellschaft* 33 (1971): 30.

29. See Wolfgang Theile, "Vermittler französischer Literatur in Deutschland um 1800: Zur Vorgeschichte der Romanischen Philologie," *Germanisch-Romanische Monatsschrift* 73 (1992): 48–66.

30. Though Steinecke is accurate, it should be noted that the *Gespräche* enjoyed neither financial nor critical success when they were first published in 1836; in this year, only 946 copies were sold, and the Young Germans evinced a generally less than enthusiastic response to the work's appearance. The *Gespräche* only began to enjoy decent sales when the copyright limitations that applied to the book expired and when the German middle class began to regard Goethe as a cultural icon after the revolutionary year 1848. See Regine Otto, "Nachwort," in Johann Peter Eckermann, *Gespräche mit Goethe in den letzten Jahren seines Lebens,* 3rd ed., ed. Regine Otto and Peter Wersig (Munich: C. H. Beck, 1988), 694, 698.

31. Steinecke, "'Weltliteratur'—Zur Diskussion der Goetheschen 'Idee' im Jungen Deutschland," 156–58.

32. Ludolf Wienbarg, "Goethe und die Welt-Literatur (1835)," in *Literaturkritik des Jungen Deutschland: Entwicklungen—Tendenzen—Texte,* ed. Hartmut Steinecke (Berlin: Erich Schmidt, 1982), 156–57.

33. Ibid., 164.

34. See Walter Dieze, *Junges Deutschland und deutsche Klassik: Zur Ästhetik und Literaturtheorie des Vormärz* (Berlin: Rütten and Loening, 1957), 21–35.

35. Examples of both tendencies are provided and discussed by René Anglade, "Heinrich Heine: Von der französischen 'Spezialrevoluzion' zur deutschen 'Universalrevoluzion,'" *Heine-Jahrbuch* 38 (1999): 46–73, esp. 65–66.

36. Karl Gutzkow, "Aus: Ueber Göthe im Wendepunkte zweier Jahrhunderte (1836)," in *Literaturkritik des Jungen Deutschland: Entwicklungen—Tendenzen—Texte,* ed. Hartmut Steinecke (Berlin: Erich Schmidt, 1982), 110.

37. Kaiser, *Einführung in die vergleichende Literaturwissenschaft,* 17.

38. Theodor Mundt, *Geschichte der Literatur der Gegenwart,* 2nd ed. (Leipzig: Simion, 1853), 567–68.

39. Steinecke, "'Weltliteratur'—Zur Diskussion der Goetheschen 'Idee' im Jungen Deutschland," 159. Kruse, "'In der Literatur wie im Leben,'" provides a contrasting opinion; he believes Goethe's concept signifies quality as well and emphasizes that "Heine also represents the claim of art and quality in literature" (6).

40. G. G. Gervinus, *Geschichte der deutschen Dichtung,* 4th ed., vol. 5 (Leipzig: Engelmann, 1853), 525–27.

41. Steinecke, "'Weltliteratur'—Zur Diskussion der Goetheschen 'Idee' im Jungen Deutschland," 161–62.

42. See, for example, Kaiser's discussion of Max Koch's 1891 lecture "Nationalität und Nationalitteratur" in *Einführung in die vergleichende Literaturwissenschaft,* 18–19.

43. An exception is Richard M. Meyer's study *Die Weltliteratur im zwanzigsten Jahrhundert: Vom deutschen Standpunkt aus betrachtet* (Stuttgart: Deutsche Verlags-Anstalt, 1913). Meyer felt that Goethe intended his term to signify a division of labor along national lines, leading to a comprehensive harmony. Meyer emphasizes Goethe's belief that the Germans would have an especially significant role in this process, and gives evidence of nationalistic predilections.

44. Steinecke, "'Weltliteratur'—Zur Diskussion der Goetheschen 'Idee' im Jungen Deutschland," 162.

45. See S. S. Prawer, *Karl Marx and World Literature* (Oxford: Clarendon, 1976), 139, 139–40 n. 5.

46. Karl Marx and Friedrich Engels, *Werke,* vol. 4 (Berlin: Dietz, 1959), 466.

CHAPTER 4. Nationalism and Revival

1. Friedrich Meinecke, *Weltbürgertum und Nationalstaat: Studien zur Genesis des deutschen Nationalstaates,* 6th ed. (Munich: R. Oldenburg, 1922), 88–89.

2. Koppen, "Weltliteratur," 821.

3. Kaiser, *Einführung in die vergleichende Literaturwissenschaft,* 18.

4. See Bollacher, "Goethes Konzeption der Weltliteratur," 173.

5. Weisstein, *Comparative Literature and Literary Theory,* has provided a valuable summary of these disputes at the turn of the century in Germany (191–94).

6. Georg Brandes, "Weltlitteratur," *Das litterarische Echo* 2 (1899): 1–2.

7. Ibid., 4.

8. Ernst Elster, "Weltlitteratur und Litteraturvergleichung," *Archiv für das Studium der neueren Sprachen und Literaturen* 107 (1901): 35–36.

9. Ibid., 39.

10. Fritz Strich, "Weltliteratur und vergleichende Literaturgeschichte," in *Philosophie der Literaturwissenschaft*, ed. Emil Ermatinger (Berlin: Junker and Dünnhaupt, 1930), 422.

11. Ibid., 439, 440.

12. Thomas Mann, *Gesammelte Werke in zwölf Bänden* (Frankfurt: Fischer, 1960–1974), 10:870. See also his 1925 essay "Kosmopolitismus" in the same volume (184–91).

13. Ibid., 10:871. Certainly, Mann was not the first European to complain about a breakdown of national distinctions into a cosmopolitan sameness. Rousseau, in his "Considérations sur le gouvernement de Pologne et sur sa réformation projettée" (1772), issued a quite similar lament, though he obviously did not associate this phenomenon with the realization of Weltliteratur. Instead, he complained of universalized selfishness and greed in his age (see *Oeuvres complètes,* vol. 3, ed. Bernard Gagnebin and Marcel Raymond [Paris: Gallimard, 1964], 960). Homogenizing cosmopolitanism is also linked throughout Rousseau's writing to the leveling effect of Enlightenment rationalism in Europe.

14. Oswald Spengler, *Der Untergang des Abendlandes: Umrisse einer Morphologie der Weltgeschichte,* vol. 2, *Welthistorische Perspektiven* (Munich: Beck, 1922), 128.

15. Mann, *Gesammelte Werke,* 9:326. Precisely such works of *Weltliteratur,* Mann claimed in 1942, were of great value in the preparation of his novel cycle *Joseph und seine Brüder* (*Joseph and his Brothers,* 1933–1942). He specifically cites Goethe's *Faust* and Lawrence's Sterne's *Tristram Shandy* (Mann, *Gesammelte Werke,* 11:664).

16. Mann, *Gesammelte Werke,* 9:326–28.

17. Kurt Hildebrandt, *Goethe: Seine Weltweisheit im Gesamtwerk,* 2nd ed. (Leipzig: Philipp Reclam, 1942), 471.

18. Strich, *Goethe und die Weltliteratur,* 27.

19. The equation of Weltliteratur with cultural borderlessness is even more strongly evident in Strich's brief monograph *Goethe und die Schweiz* (Zurich: Artemis, 1949). Strich maintains there that Swiss literature in its multilingual totality can be regarded as a world literary microcosm, and that Switzerland's "indivisible" (transcultural) "unity" had a formative impact on Goethe's thought (14).

20. Anni Carlsson, "Die Entfaltung der Weltliteratur als Prozess," in *Weltliteratur: Festgabe für Fritz Strich zum 70. Geburtstag,* ed. Walter Muschg and Emil Staiger (Bern: Francke, 1952), 51–52.

21. Erich Auerbach, "Philologie der Weltliteratur," in *Weltliteratur: Festgabe für Fritz Strich zum 70. Geburtstag,* ed. Walter Muschg and Emil Staiger (Bern: Francke, 1952), 39.

22. Ibid., 42.

23. Ibid., 40.

24. Hans-Georg Gadamer, *Wahrheit und Methode: Grundzüge einer philosophischen Hermeneutik,* 4th ed. (Tübingen: Mohr, 1975), 154–55.

25. Joel C. Weinsheimer, *Gadamer's Hermeneutics: A Reading of "Truth and Method"* (New Haven: Yale Univ. Press, 1985), 128.

26. Hans Robert Jauß, "Literaturgeschichte als Provokation der Literaturwissenschaft," *Literaturgeschichte als Provokation* (Frankfurt: Suhrkamp, 1970), 203–5.

27. Hans Robert Jauß, "Goethes und Valérys *Faust*: Zur Hermeneutik von Frage und Antwort," *Comparative Literature* 28 (1976): 201–4.

28. Ibid., 202 n. 1.

29. Claus Träger, "Weltgeschichte—Nationalliteratur, Nationalgeschichte—Weltliteratur," *Weimarer Beiträge* 20 (1974): 18–28. For a historical overview of Marxist positions on *Weltliteratur* up to 1982, see Peter Weber, "Goethes Begriff von Weltliteratur: Historische und aktuelle Aspekte," *Weimarer Beiträge* 28 (1982): 90–105. This article also analyzes non- and pre-Marxist views on Weltliteratur from a Communist perspective.

30. Walter Jens, *Nationalliteratur und Weltliteratur—Von Goethe aus Gesehen* (Munich: Kindler, 1988), 36–44. For a discussion of Gide's engagement with Goethe's Weltliteratur paradigm, see Claude Foucart, "André Gides Auffassung des *Connubiums*: Zwischen Klassik und Weltliteratur," in *Weltliteratur heute: Konzepte und Perspektiven,* ed. Manfred Schmeling (Wurzburg: Königshausen and Neumann, 1995), 59–74.

31. Peter Coulmas, *Weltbürger: Geschichte einer Menschheitssehnsucht* (Hamburg: Rowohlt, 1990), 378. A few years later, Kerst Walstra came to the even more dire conclusion that, in the current age of English language–dominated "world fiction," "a German author, if he wishes to belong to Weltliteratur, therefore has only one chance; he must write in English." Walstra also maintains that, outside the academy, Weltliteratur has largely become an empty catchphrase used by publishers to make their wares more attractive to potential customers ("Eine Worthülse der Literaturdebatte? Kritische Anmerkungen zum Begriff *Weltliteratur,*" in *Weltliteratur heute: Konzepte und Perspektiven,* ed. Manfred Schmeling [Wurzburg: Königshausen and Neumann, 1995], 205–7).

32. Hendrik Birus, "Am Schnittpunkt von Komparatistik und Germanistik: Die Idee der Weltliteratur heute," in *Germanistik und Komparatistik: DFG-Symposion 1993,* ed. Hendrik Birus (Stuttgart: Metzler, 1995), 444.

33. Ibid., 457.

34. Manfred Schmeling, "Ist Weltliteratur wünschenswert? Fortschritt und Stillstand im modernen Kulturbewußstein," in *Weltliteratur heute: Konzepte und Perspektiven,* ed. Manfred Schmeling (Wurzburg: Königshausen and Neumann, 1995), 172–73. Schmeling cites the work of Jorge Semprun as an example of such universalized literature.

35. Ibid., 153.

36. Ibid., 166–72.

37. Horst Steinmetz, "Globalisierung und Literatur(geschichte)," *Literatur im Zeitalter der Globalisierung,* ed. Manfred Schmeling et al. (Wurzburg: Königshausen and Neumann, 2000), 189–201.

38. Ibid., 194.

CHAPTER 5. Canonicity/Great Works/Multiculturalism

1. Goethe, cited in Strich, *Goethe und die Weltliteratur,* 398.

2. Hutcheson Macaulay Posnett, *Comparative Literature* (New York: D. Appleton, 1886), 236.

3. José Lambert, "'Weltliteratur' et les études littéraires actuelles: Comment construire des schémas comparatistes?" in *Proceedings of the XIIth Congress of the International Comparative Literature Association: Space and Boundaries of Literature,* vol. 4, ed. Roger Bauer et al. (Munich: iudicium, 1990), 28–35.

4. David Damrosch, *What Is World Literature?* (Princeton: Princeton Univ. Press, 2003), 11–12 (Damrosch's italics).

5. Sarah Lawall, "The Alternate Worlds of World Literature," *ADE Bulletin* 90 (1988): 53, www.mla.org/ade/bulletin/N090/090053.htm (accessed August 2001).

6. See Sigrid Bauschinger, *The Trumpet of Reform: German Literature in Nineteenth-Century New England,* trans. Thomas S. Hansen (Columbia, S.C.: Camden House, 1998), esp. 71–134.

7. These errors and the initial reception of the *Conversations* have been discussed by Russell E. Durning, *Margaret Fuller, Citizen of the World: An Intermediary between European and American Literatures* (Heidelberg: Winter, 1969), 111–13. A more complete translation by the Englishman John Oxenford was published in 1850, and it was more successful than that of Fuller with respect to sales and reprints. See Hans Kohn, "Introduction," J. P. Eckermann, *Conversations with Goethe,* trans. Gisela C. O'Brien (New York: Frederick Ungar, 1964), xiv–xv. Oxenford's translation is still in print today.

8. See Henry A. Pochmann, *German Culture in America: Philosophical and Literary Influences, 1600–1900* (Madison: Univ. of Wisconsin Press, 1957), 444; Margaret Vanderhaar Allen, *The Achievement of Margaret Fuller* (University Park: Pennsylvania State Univ. Press, 1979), 52; Judith Mattson Bean and Joel Myerson, "Introduction," in *Margaret Fuller, Critic: Writings from the New-York Tribune, 1844–1846,* ed. Judith Mattson Bean and Joel Myerson (New York: Columbia Univ. Press, 2000), xxx.

9. Allen, *The Achievement of Margaret Fuller,* 52.

10. See John A. Walz, *German Influence in American Education and Culture* (Philadelphia: Carl Schurz Memorial Foundation, 1936).

11. Thomas Wentworth Higginson, *Margaret Fuller Ossoli* (1890; reprint, New York: Greenwood, 1968), 189.

12. Fuller's translation is provided in Durning, *Margaret Fuller, Citizen of the World,* 112.

13. Thomas Wentworth Higginson, "A World-Literature," *The Century* 39 (1890): 922.

14. Ibid., 923.

15. Ralph P. Rosenberg, "The 'Great Books' in General Education," *Yearbook of Comparative and General Literature* 3 (1954): 20.

16. Higginson complained in "A World-Literature" that the vast majority of Harvard University's more broad-based literature courses were "wholly philological, not in any sense literary" (922).

17. Richard G. Moulton, *World Literature and Its Place in General Culture* (New York: Macmillan, 1911), 13.

18. Sarah Lawall, "Richard Moulton and the Idea of World Literature," in *No Small World: Visions and Revisions of World Literature,* ed. Michael Thomas Carroll (Urbana, Ill.: National Council of Teachers of English, 1996), 11.

19. Moulton, *World Literature and Its Place in General Culture,* 427–28.

20. Ibid., 429–37.

21. Ibid., 179.

22. Ibid., 336–37.

23. Ibid., 287.

24. Lawall, "Richard Moulton and the Idea of World Literature," 16–17.

25. Moulton, *World Literature and Its Place in General Culture,* 449.

26. Ibid., 437.

27. In a paper on university extension published in 1891, Moulton described as slaves those individuals "so entangled in routine duties as never to command leisure" (cited in Lawall, "Richard Moulton and the Idea of World Literature," 16). Lawall criticizes the (probably unintended) racism of this rhetoric (ibid.), but Moulton's description of those enslaved to business seems even more accurate today, when the information age and cutthroat competition create round-the-clock professional obligations.

28. Ibid., 4.

29. Rosenberg, "The 'Great Books' in General Education," 27.

30. Philo M. Buck Jr., "Preface," in *An Anthology of World Literature,* 1st ed., ed. Philo M. Buck Jr. (New York: Macmillan, 1934), v.

31. Philo M. Buck Jr., "Preface to the Third Edition," in *An Anthology of World Literature,* 3rd ed., ed. Philo M. Buck Jr. (New York: Macmillan, 1951), vii.

32. However, it has been argued that editors of contemporary World Literature anthologies continue to resort to an essentialist Oriental/Occidental juxtaposition. See José J. de Vinck, "Anthologizing World Literature," in *No Small World: Visions and Revisions of World Literature,* ed. Michael Thomas Carroll (Urbana, Ill.: National Council of Teachers of English, 1996), 34–40.

33. Buck, "Introduction," *An Anthology of World Literature,* 1st ed., 2. Buck did not revise his introduction in the third edition.

34. In the preface to the first edition, Buck defends the absence of English and American authors by noting that "both of these are abundantly cared for in their own anthologies, and in the many and various courses in high school and college" and by stressing that his anthology brings about "a gathering of foreigners whom one meets less frequently" (vi).

35. Buck, "Introduction," *An Anthology of World Literature,* 1st ed., 1.

36. Philo M. Buck Jr., *The Golden Thread* (New York: Macmillan, 1931), 2.

37. Buck, "Introduction," *An Anthology of World Literature,* 1st ed., 2. This exoticizing is somewhat at odds with the circumstance that Buck grew up in India and studied its history and literature. According to a colleague at Wisconsin, Buck's "deep sympathies and understanding for this early home bred in him a world point of view. In almost every course Indian literature was introduced, then Chinese and later some Japanese" (Hazel S. Alberson, "Non-Western Literature in the World Literature Program," in *The Teaching of World Literature: Proceedings of the Conference at the University of Wisconsin April 24–25, 1959,* ed. Haskell M. Block [Chapel Hill: Univ. of North Carolina Press, 1960], 49–50). Alberson assisted Buck with the anthology.

38. Buck, "Introduction," *An Anthology of World Literature,* 1st ed., 2.

39. Edward W. Said, *Culture and Imperialism* (New York: Knopf, 1993), 46–47. An exception to this early attitude by World Literature and Comparative Literature professionals can be seen in *World Literature: An Anthology of Human Experience,* edited by two other pioneers of World Literature, Arthur E. Christy and Henry W. Wells (1947; reprint, Plainview, N.Y.: Books for Libraries Press, 1971). This anthology groups texts thematically rather than by region

or genre, and includes many works from the Far East. This inclusiveness is perhaps a reflection of Christy's childhood in China and of a lifelong scholarly occupation with Eastern culture.

40. Philo M. Buck Jr., *Literary Criticism: A Study of Values in Literature* (New York: Harper and Brothers, 1930), 143.

41. See Gerald Graff, *Professing Literature: An Institutional History* (Chicago: Univ. of Chicago Press, 1987), 133–34, 162–63.

42. There are certain interesting parallels with respect to chronology, pedagogical priorities, and even founding institutions between the establishment of "Great Books" and "Western Civilization" courses after World War I and the introduction of "World History" and "World Literature" courses after World War II. The evolution of Western Civilization and World History courses is briefly discussed in Ross E. Dunn's introduction to a volume he edited entitled *The New World History: A Teacher's Companion* (Boston: Bedford/St. Martin's, 2000), 1–11. A number of essays in this volume expand on Dunn's overview, highlighting, for example, the seminal role played by Columbia in introducing Western Civilization (labeled "Contemporary Civilization" at Columbia) classes and by the University of Wisconsin in developing World History courses. As regards formal practice, Columbia and Wisconsin were also the founding institutions, respectively, of Great Books and World Literature.

43. Sarah Lawall, "World Literature in Context," in *Global Perspectives on Teaching Literature: Shared Visions and Distinctive Visions,* ed. Sandra Ward Lott et al. (Urbana: National Council of Teachers of English, 1993), 7.

44. See Graff, *Professing Literature,* 136–42, 162–67.

45. See, for example, Jean-Marie Carré, "L'Institut de littérature comparée de l'Université de Paris," *Yearbook of Comparative and General Literature* 1 (1952): 47.

46. Calvin S. Brown, "Debased Standards in World-Literature Courses," *Yearbook of Comparative and General Literature* 2 (1953): 10–11.

47. See Graff, *Professing Literature,* 173–79.

48. Brown, "Debased Standards in World-Literature Courses," 12–14.

49. Ibid., 12.

50. Graff, *Professing Literature,* 134. Graff cites Trilling here in establishing Erskine as the popularizer of General Education in the humanities.

51. Lionel Trilling, "English Literature and American Education," *Sewanee Review* 66 (1958): 372–73.

52. Graff, *Professing Literature,* 134.

53. These contrasts are delineated by Weldon M. Williams, "Intensive and Extensive Approaches in the Teaching of World Literature," in *The Teaching of World Literature: Proceedings of the Conference at the University of Wisconsin April 24–25, 1959,* ed. Haskell M. Block (Chapel Hill: Univ. of North Carolina Press, 1960), 73–81. Williams notes that he modeled his own Great Books courses on Erskine's approach, but confined them to his upper division students at Kent State University.

54. Finney, "Of Walls and Windows," 261.

55. Lawall, "World Literature in Context," 7.

56. Trilling, "English Literature and American Education," 373–74.

57. Ibid., 379, 380 (Trilling's italics); Block, "The Objectives of the Conference," 3.

58. Williams, "Intensive and Extensive Approaches in the Teaching of World Literature," 81.

59. Liselotte Dieckmann and Leon A. Gottfried, "General Literature at Washington University," in *The Teaching of World Literature: Proceedings of the Conference at the University of Wisconsin April 24–25, 1959,* ed. Haskell M. Block (Chapel Hill: Univ. of North Carolina Press, 1960), 101–2.

60. Werner P. Friederich, "On the Integrity of Our Planning," in *The Teaching of World Literature: Proceedings of the Conference at the University of Wisconsin April 24–25, 1959,* ed. Haskell M. Block (Chapel Hill: Univ. of North Carolina Press, 1960), 11–16.

61. Ibid., 22.

62. Ibid., 9.

63. Harry Levin et al., "The Levin Report, 1965," in *Comparative Literature in the Age of Multiculturalism,* ed. Charles Bernheimer (Baltimore: Johns Hopkins Univ. Press, 1995), 23.

64. Albert Guérard, *Preface to World Literature* (New York: Henry Holt, 1940), 3–4.

65. Ibid., 16.

66. François Jost, "Littérature comparée et littérature universelle," *Orbis Litterarum* 27 (1972): 20.

67. Robert J. Clements, *Comparative Literature as Academic Discipline: A Statement of Principles, Praxis, Standards* (New York: Modern Language Association of America, 1978), 7.

68. Ibid., 28.

69. Thomas Greene et al., "The Greene Report, 1975," in *Comparative Literature in the Age of Multiculturalism,* ed. Charles Bernheimer (Baltimore: Johns Hopkins Univ. Press, 1995), 36. It should be noted, however, that this report tacitly assumes that the "equation" of World Literature and Comparative Literature is unfortunate (30).

70. Clements, *Comparative Literature as Academic Discipline,* 26.

71. Ibid., 26–28.

72. Ibid., 26.

73. Nevertheless, the goal of educating students about domestic multiculturalism should not be conflated with the aims of the World Literature classroom. The prominent comparatist Dorothy Figueira of the University of Georgia has complained that multicultural requirements at that institution pressure the World Literature teacher to include a large measure of American ethnic literature within the class curriculum. Global culture thus tends to be distorted by being forced into the constricting frame of American ethnicity. Such an approach clearly makes the perception of the foreign particular a near impossibility. See Figueira's essay "Comparative Literature and the Illusion of Multiculturalism," *Literary Research* 17, no. 34 (2000): 249–54.

74. A. Owen Aldridge, *The Reemergence of World Literature: A Study of Asia and the West* (Newark: Univ. of Delaware Press, 1986), 9.

75. Ibid., 55 (Aldridge's italics).

76. Fredric Jameson, "World Literature in an Age of Multinational Capitalism," in *The Current in Criticism: Essays on the Present and Future of Literary Theory,* ed. Clayton Koelb and Virgil Lokke (West Lafayette: Purdue Univ. Press, 1987), 139.

77. Aijaz Ahmad, "Jameson's Rhetoric of Otherness and the 'National Allegory,'" *In Theory: Classes, Nations, Literatures* (London: Verso, 1992), 95–122.

78. For a historical overview of the Santa Cruz program and the ideology behind its inception, see Kristin Ross, "The World Literature and Cultural Studies Program," *Critical Inquiry* 19 (1993): 666–76. Ross was one of its founders. The program was bitterly opposed by another former professor at UC Santa Cruz, John M. Ellis. In *Literature Lost: Social Agendas and the Corruption of the Humanities* (New Haven: Yale Univ. Press, 1997), he claims that "World Literature" as understood by the program's founders is only the "technical term" for "the literature of the downtrodden" (254 n. 8). Based on Ross's description of exemplary courses taught in the program, it would seem that Ellis's description, while somewhat sardonic, is not incorrect.

79. William J. Bennett, *To Reclaim a Legacy: A Report on the Humanities in Higher Education* (Washington, D.C.: National Endowment for the Humanities, 1984), 30.

80. Lynne V. Cheney, *50 Hours: A Core Curriculum for College Students* (Washington, D.C.: National Endowment for the Humanities, 1989), 17.

81. Mary Louise Pratt, "Humanities for the Future: Reflections on the Western Culture Debate at Stanford," *South Atlantic Quarterly* 89 (1990): 8.

82. Ibid., 21 (Pratt's italics).

83. Lawall, "World Literature in Context," esp. 3, 10–12.

84. "Report on World Literature," *ACLA Newsletter* 19, no. 2 (1988): 1–3.

85. Lawall, "Introduction: Reading World Literature," 12–20.

86. The very title of this journal reflects the dissensus produced by the paradigm with which we are dealing. The journal began publication in 1927 as *Books Abroad,* and focused exclusively on contemporary foreign language literature. The title was changed in 1977 in order to reflect the *inclusion* of U.S. literature among the oeuvres reviewed by the journal. See Ivar Ivask, "World Literature Today, or Books Abroad II and Geography III," *World Literature Today* 51 (1977): 5. "World Literature" in this sense is antithetical to the practice of its first pedagogical practitioner, Philo Buck, whose World Literature anthology *excluded* English language works.

87. J. Hillis Miller, "'World Literature' in the Age of Telecommunications," *World Literature Today* 74 (2000): 559–61.

88. The productivity of a team-taught World Literature class can be gleaned from Vilashini Cooppan's summary of her experiences at Yale University, where a focus on the interaction between the global and the local was clearly an imperative for those who taught the World Literature sequence. The Yale team created "polychronic encounters" between thematically related texts, such as Near Eastern "Just Sufferer" literature on the one hand, and the story of Job and the Proverbs from the Bible, on the other. See Cooppan's essay "World Literature and Global Theory: Comparative Literature for the New Millenium," *symplokē* 9 (2001): 15–43.

89. Gayatri Chakravorty Spivak, *Death of a Discipline* (New York: Columbia Univ. Press, 2003), xii.

90. Ibid., 39.

91. Ibid., 73.

92. Ibid., 87.

93. Damrosch and Lawall are good examples of distinguished comparatists who serve as general editors of World Literature anthologies. Damrosch edited the recently published

Longman Anthology of World Literature (2004), and Lawall is the general editor of the most recent editions of the *Norton Anthology of World Literature.*

94. David Damrosch, *We Scholars: Changing the Culture of the University* (Cambridge, Mass.: Harvard Univ. Press, 1995), 119.

95. For a contrasting view, which eschews not only liberal diversity models but regards "World Literature" as an obsolete concept because of its putative abnegation of politics and economics, see Amitava Kumar, ed., *World Bank Literature* (Minneapolis: Univ. of Minnesota Press, 2003). Kumar and other contributors to this volume believe "World Bank Literature" should replace "World Literature" as a dominant pedagogical model because they believe students must become aware of how global capitalist institutions such as the World Bank are both entwined with and contested by the globe's diverse cultures. In addition to generally misrepresenting Weltliteratur as inscribed by a traditional nation-state paradigm, these essays ignore the simple fact that a model such as "World Bank Literature" can, at best, be applied to postcolonial works, and is irrelevant as a category for literature created prior to the second half of the twentieth century. Ignoring the need to inculcate an appreciation for diverse cultures in students creates the danger that very few of them will be inspired to pursue an in-depth study of one or more particular literatures, though a "World Bank Literature" approach may move some students to become politically active.

CHAPTER 6. The Dialectical Filter of *Weltliteratur*

1. Harald Weinrich, "Chamisso, Chamisso Authors, and Globalization," intro. Marshall Brown, trans. Marshall Brown and Jane K. Brown, *PMLA* 119 (2004): 1346.

2. See James J. Sheehan, *German History, 1770–1866* (Oxford: Clarendon Press, 1989), 551.

3. Jim Bergman, cartoon, *The Advocate* (Baton Rouge), 16 August 2001, 8B.

4. Steinmetz, "Globalisierung und Literatur(geschichte)," 196.

5. Robert Eric Livingston, "Glocal Knowledges: Agency and Place in Literary Studies," *PMLA* 116 (2001): 145–57.

6. Ibid., 151.

7. In German-language literature, this vitality is underscored by the ongoing renewal of regionally/provincially rooted postmodern "Heimat" (homeland) literature. See Jürgen Bolten, "Heimat im Aufwind: Anmerkungen zur Sozialgeschichte eines Bedeutungswandels," in *Literatur und Provinz: Das Konzept "Heimat" in der neueren Literatur,* ed. Hans-Georg Pott (Paderborn: Ferdinand Schöningh, 1986), 23–38.

8. Theodor Adorno, "Reconciliation under Duress," trans. Rodney Livingstone, *Aesthetics and Politics* (London: NLB, 1977), 151–76.

9. Said, *Culture and Imperialism,* xxv–xxvi.

10. Bhabha, *The Location of Culture,* 12.

11. During his childhood, Schami experienced Damascus as a site of tolerance and respect for religious and ethnic diversity. He admits to stylizing Damascus in his reminiscences into a domain where utopian humanitarian dreams become reality, and this is reflected in his literature. In the 1960s and 1970s, with the rise of Western-backed Islamic fundamentalism, Damascus as a place marked by multicultural harmony ceased to exist, and this circumstance prompted Schami, a Christian, to emigrate to Germany. See Rafik Schami, *Damals dort und heute hier: Über Fremdsein,* ed. Erich Jooß (Freiburg: Herder, 1998), 29–36.

12. On the centrality of multiculturalism in Schami's oeuvre, see esp. Iman Osman Khalil, "Zum Konzept der Multikulturalität im Werk Rafik Schamis," *Monatshefte* 86 (1994): 201–17.

13. Seyhan, *Writing Outside the Nation*, 44.

14. Hans Joachim Schrimpf, *Goethes Begriff der Weltliteratur* (Stuttgart: Metzler, 1968), 33.

15. Bhabha, *The Location of Culture*, 12.

16. Rafik Schami, *Erzähler der Nacht* (Weinheim: Beltz and Gelberg, 1989; Munich: dtv, 2001), 26. Hereafter cited in the text as *EN*, followed by the page number.

17. Seyhan, *Writing Outside the Nation*, 43.

18. See Katharina Mommsen, *Goethe und 1001 Nacht* (Frankfurt: Suhrkamp, 1981).

19. Rafik Schami, *Vom Zauber der Zunge: Reden gegen das Verstummen,* 2nd ed. (Frauenfeld: Im Waldgut, 1991), 16–17.

20. Gökberk, "Understanding Alterity," 143–72.

21. Ibid., 166.

22. Iman Osman Khalil, "From the Margins to the Center: Arab-German Authors and Issues," in *Transforming the Center, Eroding the Margins: Essays on Ethnic and Cultural Boundaries in German-Speaking Countries,* ed. Dagmar C. G. Lorenz and Renate S. Posthofen (Columbia, S.C.: Camden House, 1998), 228, 229.

23. See Mommsen, *Goethe und 1001 Nacht,* 57–64.

24. Reingard Nethersole, "Models of Globalization," *PMLA* 116 (2001): 638–49. Nethersole's perspective here is related to that of Leo Kreutzer, who argues that current "Welt*literatur*" (he uses italics to differentiate the term from the German for "world economy," "world communication," etc.) is not simply subjected to current tendencies toward assimilation, but critically reflects on, and thus resists, this homogenizing process. See his essay "'WELTLITERATUR!' Weltliteratur? Zur kulturpolitischen Diskussion eines verfänglichen Begriffs," *Welfengarten: Jahrbuch für Essayismus* 6 (1996): 222.

25. Nethersole, "Models of Globalization," 640, 646–47 n. 4.

26. Schami, *Vom Zauber der Zunge,* 12.

27. Nethersole, "Models of Globalization," 639–40.

28. Rafik Schami and Uwe-Michael Gutzschhahn, *Der geheime Bericht über den Dichter Goethe, der eine Prüfung auf einer arabischen Insel bestand* (Munich: Carl Hanser, 1999), 149. Hereafter cited in the text as *GB,* followed by the page number.

29. See David Couzens Hoy, *The Critical Circle: Literature, History, and Philosophical Hermeneutics* (Berkeley: Univ. of California Press, 1978).

30. This element in Schleiermacher's hermeneutics is elucidated by Manfred Frank, *Das individuelle Allgemeine: Textstrukturierung und -interpretation nach Schleiermacher* (Frankfurt: Suhrkamp, 1977), 196.

31. Jean-Luc Nancy, *Being Singular Plural,* trans. Robert D. Richardson and Anne E. O'Byrne (Stanford: Stanford Univ. Press, 2000), xiv.

32. It is also mentioned in a brief biographical appendix to *Der geheime Bericht,* where the year of its Goethean coinage is incorrectly said to be 1830 (*GB,* 180).

33. David Barry, "Faustian Pursuits: The Political-Cultural Dimensions of Goethe's *Weltliteratur* and the Tragedy of Translation," *German Quarterly* 74 (2001): 182.

34. The disastrous effects of oil-driven economics and politics, abetted by neo-imperialism,

on culture and democracy in the Arab world today are also underscored by Said, *Culture and Imperialism,* 299–301.

35. Barry, "Faustian Pursuits," 167.

CHAPTER 7. Afterword

1. Oscar Wilde, "*Intentions* (1891): The Critic as Artist," *The Artist as Critic: Critical Writings of Oscar Wilde,* ed. Richard Ellmann (New York: Random House, 1969), 405.

2. Claudio Guillén, *The Challenge of Comparative Literature,* trans. Cola Franzen (Cambridge, Mass.: Harvard Univ. Press, 1993), 39–40.

3. The first half of the book's original Spanish title, *Entre lo uno et lo diverso,* seems to reflect Goethe's Weltliteratur paradigm as well.

4. Seyhan, *Writing Outside the Nation,* 5.

5. Lawall, "Introduction," *Reading World Literature,* 10, 20–21.

6. Jurij Lotman et al., "Theses on the Semiotic Study of Cultures (as Applied to Slavic Texts)," in *The Tell-Tale Sign: A Survey of Semiotics,* ed. Thomas A. Sebeok (Lisse, Netherlands: Peter de Ridder, 1975), 57–61.

7. Lawall, "Introduction," *Reading World Literature,* 11–12.

8. As Damrosch and Wai Chee Dimock have argued, however, neither the universal nor the particular are static concepts, but fluid and, even in the case of "universality," sometimes "culturally situated." See Damrosch, *What Is World Literature?* 135.

9. Slavoj Žižek and F. W. J. von Schelling, *The Abyss of Freedom/Ages of the World: An Essay by Slavoj Žižek with the Text of Schelling's* "Die Weltalter" *(Second Draft, 1813) in English Translation by Judith Norman* (Ann Arbor: Univ. of Michigan Press, 1997), 50–51 (Žižek's italics).

10. LSU now offers annually a one-year sequence of Early and Modern World Literature courses. The home department for this sequence is the Comparative Literature program, but it is cross-listed with English.

11. Fritz Strich, *Goethe and World Literature,* trans. C. A. M. SYM (London: Routledge and Kegan Paul, 1949), 349.

12. Bollacher, "Goethes Konzeption der Weltliteratur," 175–76.

13. The photocopied materials of Goethe's works were: "Some Passages Pertaining to the Concept of World Literature," in *Comparative Literature: The Early Years. An Anthology of Essays,* ed. Hans-Joachim Schulz and Phillip H. Rhein (Chapel Hill: Univ. of North Carolina Press, 1973), 3–11, as well as an English-language version of the translation theory in *West-East Divan*: "Translations," trans. Sharon Sloan, in *Theories of Translation: An Anthology of Essays from Dryden to Derrida,* ed. Rainer Schulte and John Biguenet (Chicago: Univ. of Chicago Press, 1992), 60–63.

14. Posnett, *Comparative Literature,* 236.

15. Particularly valuable here is Lawall's essay "The Alternate Worlds of World Literature," which is available online at www.mla.org/ade/bulletin/N090/090053.htm (accessed August 2001).

16. Lawall, "Introduction," *Reading World Literature,* 12.

17. Heinrich Heine, "Loreley," trans. Ernst Feise, in *The Norton Anthology of World*

Masterpieces, Expanded Edition, vol. 2, ed. Maynard Mack et al. (New York: Norton, 1995), 828–29.

18. Ghalib, *Ghazals,* XXI, trans. William Stafford, in *The Norton Anthology of World Masterpieces, Expanded Edition,* vol. 2, ed. Maynard Mack et al. (New York: Norton, 1995), 1058.

19. Aijaz Ahmad, ed., *Ghazals of Ghalib* (New York: Columbia Univ. Press, 1971), 98.

20. Ibid., 97.

21. This ambiguity is inherent in the original, for, as Ahmad notes, nineteenth-century Urdu verse uses the red poppy "as a metaphor for the heart, or for the eye. If the heart, it is a bleeding heart, like Shelley's. If the eye, always that of a woman who has been crying (eyes are therefore red). Thus, dewdrop on a red poppy could be tears in the bloodshot eyes of a woman" (ibid., 98).

22. Of course, the influence of national and regional backgrounds on even modernists should not be ignored in the classroom. For example, the unique mediatory position of Prague's German-speaking Jewish writers in the early twentieth century between that city's German-Christian and Czech nationalists, who sought political hegemony through culturally oriented ideological polemics, and these "Prague Circle" Jewish writers' own conflicted territorial perceptions, were critical in shaping Kafka's writing, as Scott Spector has shown in his *Prague Territories: National Conflict and Cultural Innovation in Franz Kafka's Fin de Siècle* (Berkeley: Univ. of California Press, 2000). This work proved particularly useful for my classroom elucidation of Kafka's complex multicultural frame of reference. Damrosch provides a good overview of polarized scholarly attempts, reflected in both editorial debates in Germany and in translation debates in the English-speaking world, to situate Kafka as either a cosmopolitan modernist or as a highly localized Czech/Jewish/German writer. See *What Is World Literature?* 187–205.

23. There are exceptions, of course. I taught Aimé Césaire's "Notebook of a Return to the Native Land" as modernist in its impulse to poetically transcend the fragmented status he perceived among the world's blacks in the 1930s and thereby to bring about unity through a literature rooted in this overarching "negritude," but I noted that this universal impulse receives its vitality, indeed its sense of agency, from a firm anchoring in the space and time of the poet's native land, Martinique. My approach here represents another variation on the use of Goethe's universal-particular Weltliteratur dialectic.

24. Roland Greene, "The Post-English English," *PMLA* 117 (2002): 1244 (Greene's italics).

Works Cited

Adorno, Theodor. "Reconciliation under Duress." Translated by Rodney Living-stone. *Aesthetics and Politics.* London: NLB, 1977. 151–76.

Ahmad, Aijaz, ed. *Ghazals of Ghalib.* New York: Columbia Univ. Press, 1971.

———. "Jameson's Rhetoric of Otherness and the 'National Allegory.'" In *Theory: Classes, Nations, Literatures.* London: Verso, 1992. 95–122.

Alberson, Hazel S. "Non-Western Literature in the World Literature Program." In *The Teaching of World Literature: Proceedings of the Conference at the University of Wisconsin April 24–25, 1959,* edited by Haskell M. Block. Chapel Hill: Univ. of North Carolina Press, 1960. 45–52.

Albrow, Martin. "Auf dem Weg zu einer globalen Gesellschaft?" Translated by Ilse Utz. In *Perspektiven der Weltgesellschaft,* edited by Ulrich Beck. Frankfurt: Suhrkamp, 1998. 411–34.

Aldridge, A. Owen. *The Reemergence of World Literature: A Study of Asia and the West.* Newark: Univ. of Delaware Press, 1986.

Allen, Margaret Vanderhaar. *The Achievement of Margaret Fuller.* University Park: Pennsylvania State Univ. Press, 1979.

Anglade, René. "Heinrich Heine: Von der französischen 'Spezialrevoluzion' zur deutschen 'Universalrevoluzion.'" *Heine-Jahrbuch* 38 (1999): 46–73.

Asman, Carrie. "'Der Satz ist die Mauer': Zur Figur des Übersetzers bei Benjamin und Goethe: 'Werther,' 'Faust,' 'Wilhelm Meister.'" *Goethe-Jahrbuch* III (1994): 61–79.

Auerbach, Erich. "Philologie der Weltliteratur." In *Weltliteratur: Festgabe für Fritz Strich zum 70. Geburtstag,* edited by Walter Muschg and Emil Staiger. Bern: Francke, 1952. 39–50.

Bachmann-Medick, Doris. "Multikultur oder kulturelle Differenzen? Neue Konzepte von Weltliteratur und Übersetzung in postkolonialer Perspektive." *Deutsche Vierteljahrsschrift* 68 (1994): 585–612.

Bakhtin, M. M. "The *Bildungsroman* and Its Significance in the History of Realism (Toward a Historical Typology of the Novel)." In *Speech Genres and Other Late Essays,* edited by Caryl Emerson and Michael Holquist, translated by Vern W. McGee. Austin: Univ. of Texas Press, 1986. 10–59.

———. "Forms of Time and of the Chronotope in the Novel: Notes toward a Historical Poetics." In *The Dialogic Imagination: Four Essays,* edited by Michael Holquist, translated by Caryl Emerson and Michael Holquist. Austin: Univ. of Texas Press, 1981. 84–258.

Barber, Benjamin R. *Jihad vs. McWorld.* New York: Times Books, 1995.

Barry, David. "Faustian Pursuits: The Political-Cultural Dimension of Goethe's *Weltliteratur* and the Tragedy of Translation." *German Quarterly* 74 (2001): 164–85.

Bauschinger, Sigrid. *The Trumpet of Reform: German Literature in Nineteenth-Century New England.* Translated by Thomas S. Hansen. Columbia, S.C.: Camden House, 1998.

Bean, Judith Mattson, and Joel Myerson. "Introduction." In *Margaret Fuller, Critic: Writings from the New-York Tribune, 1844–1846,* edited by Judith Mattson Bean and Joel Myerson. New York: Columbia Univ. Press, 2000. xv–xl.

Behler, Ernst. "Problems of Origin in Modern Literary History." In *Theoretical Issues in Literary History,* edited by David Perkins. Cambridge, Mass.: Harvard Univ. Press, 1991. 9–34.

Beil, Else. *Zur Entwicklung des Begriffes der Weltliteratur.* Leipzig: Voigtländer, 1915.

Bender, Helmut, and Ulrich Melzer. "Zur Geschichte des Begriffs 'Weltliteratur.'" *Saeculum* 9 (1958): 113–23.

Bennett, William J. *To Reclaim a Legacy: A Report on the Humanities in Higher Education.* Washington, D.C.: National Endowment for the Humanities, 1984.

Berczik, Arpad. "Zur Entwicklung des Begriffs 'Weltliteratur' und Anfänge der Vergleichenden Literaturgeschichte." *Acta germanica et romanica* 2 (1967): 3–22.

Bergman, Jim. Cartoon. *The Advocate* (Baton Rouge), 16 August 2001, 8B.

Berman, Antoine. *The Experience of the Foreign: Culture and Translation in Romantic Germany.* Translated by S. Heyvaert. Albany: State Univ. of New York Press, 1992.

Bernheimer, Charles, ed. *Comparative Literature in the Age of Multiculturalism.* Baltimore: Johns Hopkins Univ. Press, 1995.

Bhabha, Homi K. *The Location of Culture.* London: Routledge, 1994.

Birus, Hendrik. "Am Schnittpunkt von Komparatistik und Germanistik: Die Idee der Weltliteratur heute." In *Germanistik und Komparatistik: DFG-Symposion 1993*, edited by Hendrik Birus. Stuttgart: Metzler, 1995. 439–57.

———. "Goethes Idee der Weltliteratur: Eine historische Vergegenwärtigung." In *Weltliteratur heute: Konzepte und Perspektiven*, edited by Manfred Schmeling. Wurzburg: Königshausen and Neumann, 1995. 5–28.

———. "Main Features of Goethe's Concept of World Literature." In *Comparative Literature Now: Theories and Practice*, edited by Steven Tötösy de Zepetnek et al. Paris: Champion, 1999. 31–41.

Bleicher, Thomas. "Novalis und die Idee der Weltliteratur." *Arcadia* 14 (1979): 254–70.

Block, Haskell M. "The Objectives of the Conference." In *The Teaching of World Literature: Proceedings of the Conference at the University of Wisconsin April 24– 25, 1959*, edited by Haskell M. Block. Chapel Hill: Univ. of North Carolina Press, 1960. 2–7.

———, ed. *The Teaching of World Literature: Proceedings of the Conference at the University of Wisconsin April 24–25, 1959*. Chapel Hill: Univ. of North Carolina Press, 1960.

Bollacher, Martin. "Goethes Konzeption der Weltliteratur." In *Ironische Propheten: Sprachbewußtsein und Humanität in der Literatur von Herder bis Heine: Studien für Jürgen Brummack zum 65. Geburtstag*, edited by Markus Heilmann and Birgit Wägenbaur. Tübingen: Narr, 2001. 169–85.

Bolten, Jürgen. "Heimat im Aufwind: Anmerkungen zur Sozialgeschichte eines Bedeutungswandels." In *Literatur und Provinz: Das Konzept "Heimat" in der neueren Literatur*, edited by Hans-Georg Pott. Paderborn: Ferdinand Schöningh, 1986. 23–38.

Boubia, Fawzi. "Goethes Theorie der Alterität und die Idee der Weltliteratur: Ein Beitrag zur neueren Kulturdebatte." In *Gegenwart als kulturelles Erbe: Ein Beitrag der Germanistik zur Kulturwissenschaft deutschsprachiger Länder*, edited by Bernd Thum. Munich: iudicium, 1985. 269–301.

———. "Universal Literature and Otherness." Translated by Jeanne Ferguson. *Diogenes* 141 (1988): 76–101.

Brandes, Georg. "Weltlitteratur." *Das litterarische Echo* 2 (1899): 1–5.

Brandt Corstius, J. C. "Writing Histories of World Literature." *Yearbook of Comparative and General Literature* 12 (1963): 5–14.

Brennan, Timothy. "The Cuts of Language: The East/West of North/South." *Public Culture* 13 (2001): 39–63.

Brown, Calvin S. "Debased Standards in World-Literature Courses." *Yearbook of Comparative and General Literature* 2 (1953): 10–14.

Buck, Philo M., Jr., ed. *An Anthology of World Literature*. 1st ed. New York: Macmillan, 1934.

————, ed. *An Anthology of World Literature*. 3rd ed. New York: Macmillan, 1951.

————. *The Golden Thread*. New York: Macmillan, 1931.

————. *Literary Criticism: A Study of Values in Literature*. New York: Harper and Brothers, 1930.

Carlsson, Anni. "Die Entfaltung der Weltliteratur als Prozess." In *Weltliteratur: Festgabe für Fritz Strich zum 70. Geburtstag,* edited by Walter Muschg and Emil Staiger. Bern: Francke, 1952. 51–65.

Carré, Jean-Marie. "L'Institut de littérature comparée de l'Université de Paris." *Yearbook of Comparative and General Literature* 1 (1952): 46–48.

Carroll, Michael Thomas, ed. *No Small World: Visions and Revisions of World Literature*. Urbana, Ill.: National Council of Teachers of English, 1996.

Cheney, Lynne V. *50 Hours: A Core Curriculum for College Students*. Washington, D.C.: National Endowment for the Humanities, 1989.

Christy, Arthur E., and Henry W. Wells, eds. *World Literature: An Anthology of Human Experience*. 1947. Reprint, Plainview, N.Y.: Books for Libraries Press, 1971.

Clements, Robert J. *Comparative Literature as Academic Discipline: A Statement of Principles, Praxis, Standards*. New York: Modern Language Association of America, 1978.

Clüver, Claus. "The Difference of Eight Decades: World Literature and the Demise of National Literatures." *Yearbook of Comparative and General Literature* 35 (1986): 14–24.

Cooppan, Vilashini. "World Literature and Global Theory: Comparative Literature for the New Millenium." *symplokē* 9 (2001): 15–43.

Coulmas, Peter. *Weltbürger: Geschichte einer Menschheitssehnsucht*. Hamburg: Rowohlt, 1990.

Damrosch, David. *We Scholars: Changing the Culture of the University*. Cambridge, Mass.: Harvard Univ. Press, 1995.

————. *What Is World Literature?* Princeton: Princeton Univ. Press, 2003.

————. "World Literature Today: From the Old World to the Whole World." *symplokē* 8 (2000): 7–19.

Dieckmann, Liselotte, and Leon A. Gottfried. "General Literature at Washington University." In *The Teaching of World Literature: Proceedings of the Conference at the University of Wisconsin April 24–25, 1959,* edited by Haskell M. Block. Chapel Hill: Univ. of North Carolina Press, 1960. 101–7.

Dieze, Walter. *Junges Deutschland und deutsche Klassik: Zur Ästhetik und Literaturtheorie des Vormärz*. Berlin: Rütten and Loening, 1957.

Dunn, Ross E., ed. *The New World History: A Teacher's Companion*. Boston: Bedford/St. Martin's, 2000.

Durning, Russell E. *Margaret Fuller, Citizen of the World: An Intermediary between European and American Literatures.* Heidelberg: Winter, 1969.

Ellis, John M. *Literature Lost: Social Agendas and the Corruption of the Humanities.* New Haven: Yale Univ. Press, 1997.

Elster, Ernst. "Weltlitteratur und Litteraturvergleichung." *Archiv für das Studium der neueren Sprachen und Literaturen* 107 (1901): 33–47.

———. "World Literature and Comparative Literature (1901)." Translated by Eric Metzler. *Yearbook of Comparative and General Literature* 35 (1986): 7–13.

Espagne, Michel. "Übersetzung und Orientreise: Heines Handschriften zum *Loeve-Veimars-Fragment.*" *Euphorion* 78 (1984): 127–42.

Etiemble, René. "Faut-il réviser la notion de *Weltliteratur?*" *Essais de littérature (vraiement) générale.* 3rd ed. Paris: Gallimard, 1975. 15–36.

Figueira, Dorothy. "Comparative Literature and the Illusion of Multiculturalism." *Literary Research* 17, no. 34 (2000): 249–54.

———. *Translating the Orient: The Reception of* Śākuntala *in Nineteenth-Century Europe.* Albany: State Univ. of New York Press, 1991.

Finney, Gail. "Of Walls and Windows: What German Studies and Comparative Literature Can Offer Each Other." *Comparative Literature* 49 (1997): 259–66.

Fish, Stanley. "Boutique Multiculturalism." In *Multiculturalism and American Democracy,* edited by Arthur M. Melzer et al. Lawrence: Univ. Press of Kansas, 1998. 69–88.

Foucart, Claude. "André Gides Auffassung des *Connubiums:* Zwischen Klassik und Weltliteratur." In *Weltliteratur heute: Konzepte und Perspektiven,* edited by Manfred Schmeling. Wurzburg: Königshausen and Neumann, 1995. 59–74.

Frank, Manfred. *Das individuelle Allgemeine: Textstrukturierung und -interpretation nach Schleiermacher.* Frankfurt: Suhrkamp, 1977.

Friedrich, Werner P. "On the Integrity of Our Planning." In *The Teaching of World Literature: Proceedings of the Conference at the University of Wisconsin April 24–25, 1959,* edited by Haskell M. Block. Chapel Hill: Univ. of North Carolina Press, 1960. 9–22.

Furst, Lilian R. "The *Salons* of Germaine de Staël and Rahel Varnhagen." In *Cultural Interactions in the Romantic Age: Critical Essays in Comparative Literature,* edited by Gregory Maertz. Albany: State Univ. of New York Press, 1998. 95–103.

Gadamer, Hans-Georg. *Wahrheit und Methode: Grundzüge einer philosophischen Hermeneutik.* 4th ed. Tübingen: Mohr, 1975.

Gervinus, G. G. *Geschichte der deutschen Dichtung.* 4th ed. Vol. 5. Leipzig: Engelmann, 1853.

Ghalib. *Ghazals.* XXI. Translated by William Stafford. In *The Norton Anthology of World Masterpieces, Expanded Edition.* Vol. 2, edited by Maynard Mack et al. New York: Norton, 1995. 1058.

Goethe, Johann Wolfgang. *Gedenkausgabe der Werke, Briefe und Gespräche.* Edited by Ernst Beutler. 24 vols. Zurich: Artemis, 1948–1954.

———. "Some Passages Pertaining to the Concept of World Literature." In *Comparative Literature: The Early Years. An Anthology of Essays,* edited by Hans-Joachim Schulz and Phillip H. Rhein. Chapel Hill: Univ. of North Carolina Press, 1973. 3–11.

———. "Translations." Translated by Sharon Sloan. In *Theories of Translation: An Anthology of Essays from Dryden to Derrida,* edited by Rainer Schulte and John Biguenet. Chicago: Univ. of Chicago Press, 1992. 60–63.

Gökberk, Ülker. "Understanding Alterity: *Ausländerliteratur* between Relativism and Universalism." In *Theoretical Issues in Literary History,* edited by David Perkins. Cambridge, Mass.: Harvard Univ. Press, 1991. 143–72.

Gordon, Paul. *The Critical Double: Figurative Meaning in Aesthetic Discourse.* Tuscaloosa: Univ. of Alabama Press, 1995.

Gössmann, Wilhelm. "Die Herausforderung der Wissenschaft durch die Literatur." In *Heinrich Heine im Spannungsfeld von Literatur und Wissenschaft: Symposium anläßlich der Benennung der Universität Düsseldorf nach Heinrich Heine,* edited by Wilhelm Gössmann and Manfred Windfuhr. Dusseldorf: Hobbing, 1990. 11–24.

Graff, Gerald. *Professing Literature: An Institutional History.* Chicago: Univ. of Chicago Press, 1987.

Greene, Roland. "The Post-English English." *PMLA* 117 (2002): 1241–44.

Greene, Thomas, et al. "The Greene Report, 1975." In *Comparative Literature in the Age of Multiculturalism,* edited by Charles Bernheimer. Baltimore: Johns Hopkins Univ. Press, 1995. 28–38.

Guérard, Albert. *Preface to World Literature.* New York: Henry Holt, 1940.

Guillén, Claudio. *The Challenge of Comparative Literature.* Translated by Cola Franzen. Cambridge, Mass.: Harvard Univ. Press, 1993.

Guthke, Karl S. "Destination Goethe: Travelling Englishmen in Weimar." In *Goethe and the English-Speaking World: Essays from the Cambridge Symposium for His 250th Anniversary,* edited by Nicholas Boyle and John Guthrie. Rochester: Camden House, 2002. 111–42.

Gutzkow, Karl. "Aus: Ueber Göthe im Wendepunkte zweier Jahrhunderte (1836)." In *Literaturkritik des Jungen Deutschland: Entwicklungen—Tendenzen—Texte,* edited by Hartmut Steinecke. Berlin: Erich Schmidt, 1982. 110–13.

Hamm, Heinz. *Goethe und die französische Zeitschrift "Le Globe": Eine Lektüre im Zeichen der "Weltliteratur."* Weimar: Böhlau, 1998.

Heine, Heinrich. "Loreley." Translated by Ernst Feise. In *The Norton Anthology of World Masterpieces, Expanded Edition.* Vol. 2, ed. Maynard Mack et al. New York: Norton, 1995. 828–29.

————. *Sämtliche Schriften.* Edited by Klaus Briegleb. 6 vols. Munich: Hanser, 1968–1976.

Higginson, Thomas Wentworth. *Margaret Fuller Ossoli.* 1890. Reprint, New York: Greenwood, 1968.

————. "A World-Literature." *The Century* 39 (1890): 922–23.

Hildebrandt, Kurt. *Goethe: Seine Weltweisheit im Gesamtwerk.* 2nd ed. Leipzig: Philipp Reclam, 1942.

Hinck, Walter. *Die Wunde Deutschland: Heinrich Heines Dichtung im Widerstreit von Nationalidee, Judentum und Antisemetismus.* Frankfurt: Insel, 1990.

Hoffmeister, Gerhart. "Reception in Germany and Abroad." In *The Cambridge Companion to Goethe,* edited by Lesley Sharpe. Cambridge: Cambridge Univ. Press, 2002. 232–55.

Hohlfeld, A. R. "Goethe's Conception of World Literature." *Fifty Years with Goethe, 1901–1951.* Madison: Univ. of Wisconsin Press, 1953. 339–50.

Hoy, David Couzens. *The Critical Circle: Literature, History, and Philosophical Hermeneutics.* Berkeley: Univ. of California Press, 1978.

Huyssen, Andreas. *Die frühromantische Konzeption von Übersetzung und Aneignung: Studien zur frühromantischen Utopie einer deutschen Weltliteratur.* Zurich: Atlantis, 1969.

Ivask, Ivar. "World Literature Today, or Books Abroad II and Geography III." *World Literature Today* 51 (1977): 5–6.

Jaime, Edward. *Stefan George und die Weltliteratur.* Ulm: Aegis, 1949.

Jameson, Fredric. "World Literature in an Age of Multinational Capitalism." In *The Current in Criticism: Essays on the Present and Future of Literary Theory,* edited by Clayton Koelb and Virgil Lokke. West Lafayette, Ind.: Purdue Univ. Press, 1987. 139–58.

Jauß, Hans Robert. "Goethes und Valérys *Faust*: Zur Hermeneutik von Frage und Antwort." *Comparative Literature* 28 (1976): 201–32.

————. "Literaturgeschichte als Provokation der Literaturwissenschaft." *Literaturgeschichte als Provokation.* Frankfurt: Suhrkamp, 1970. 144–207.

Jay, Martin. *Marxism and Totality: The Adventures of a Concept from Lukács to Habermas.* Berkeley: Univ. of California Press, 1984.

Jens, Walter. *Nationalliteratur und Weltliteratur—Von Goethe aus Gesehen.* Munich: Kindler, 1988.

Jost, François. "Littérature comparée et littérature universelle." *Orbis Litterarum* 27 (1972): 13–27.

Kaiser, Gerhard R. *Einführung in die vergleichende Literaturwissenschaft: Forschungsstand, Kritik, Aufgaben.* Darmstadt: Wissenschaftliche Buchgesellschaft, 1980.

Khalil, Iman Osman. "From the Margins to the Center: Arab-German Authors and Issues." In *Transforming the Center, Eroding the Margins: Essays on Ethnic and Cultural Boundaries in German-Speaking Countries,* edited by Dagmar C. G. Lorenz and Renate S. Posthofen. Columbia, S.C.: Camden House, 1998. 227–37.

————. "Zum Konzept der Multikulturalität im Werk Rafik Schamis." *Monatshefte* 86 (1994): 201–17.

Kohn, Hans. "Introduction." In J. P. Eckermann, *Conversations with Goethe,* translated by Gisela C. O'Brien. New York: Frederick Ungar, 1964. v–xvi.

Kontje, Todd. *German Orientalisms.* Ann Arbor: Univ. of Michigan Press, 2004.

Koppen, Erwin. "Weltliteratur." In *Reallexikon der deutschen Literaturgeschichte.* 2nd ed. Vol. 4, edited by Klaus Kanzog and Achim Masser. Berlin: Walter de Gruyter, 1984. 815–27.

Kreutzer, Leo. "'WELTLITERATUR!' Weltliteratur? Zur kulturpolitischen Diskussion eines verfänglichen Begriffs." *Welfengarten: Jahrbuch für Essayismus* 6 (1996): 213–30.

Kruse, Joseph A. "'In der Literatur wie im Leben hat jeder Sohn einen Vater': Heinrich Heine zwischen Bibel und Homer, Cervantes und Shakespeare." In *Heine und die Weltliteratur,* edited by T. J. Reed and Alexander Stillmark. Oxford: Legenda, 2000. 2–23.

Kumar, Amitava, ed. *World Bank Literature.* Minneapolis: Univ. of Minnesota Press, 2003.

Laird, Charlton. "World Literature and Teaching." *Yearbook of Comparative and General Literature* 10 (1961): 66–69.

Lambert, José. "'Weltliteratur' et les études littéraires actuelles: Comment construire des schémas comparatistes?" In *Proceedings of the XIIth Congress of the International Comparative Literature Association: Space and Boundaries of Literature,* vol. 4., edited by Roger Bauer et al. Munich: iudicium, 1990. 28–35.

Lange, Victor. "Nationalliteratur und Weltliteratur." *Jahrbuch der Goethe-Gesellschaft* 33 (1971): 15–30.

Lawall, Sarah. "The Alternate Worlds of World Literature." *ADE Bulletin* 90 (1988): 53–58. www.mla.org/ade/bulletin/N090/090053.htm (accessed August 2001).

————. "Introduction: Reading World Literature." In *Reading World Literature: Theory, History, Practice,* edited by Sarah Lawall. Austin: Univ. of Texas Press, 1994. 1–64.

————. "Richard Moulton and the Idea of World Literature." In *No Small World: Visions and Revisions of World Literature,* edited by Michael Thomas Carroll. Urbana, Ill.: National Council of Teachers of English, 1996. 3–19.

————. "World Literature, Comparative Literature, Teaching Literature." In *Proceedings of the XIIth Congress of the International Comparative Literature Asso-*

ciation: Space and Boundaries of Literature, vol. 5, edited by Roger Bauer et al. Munich: iudicium, 1990. 219–24.

———. "World Literature in Context." In *Global Perspectives on Teaching Literature: Shared Visions and Distinctive Visions,* edited by Sandra Ward Lott et al. Urbana: National Council of Teachers of English, 1993. 3–18.

Levin, Harry, et al. "The Levin Report, 1965." In *Comparative Literature in the Age of Multiculturalism,* edited by Charles Bernheimer. Baltimore: Johns Hopkins Univ. Press, 1995. 21–27.

Livingston, Robert Eric. "Glocal Knowledges: Agency and Place in Literary Studies." *PMLA* 116 (2001): 145–57.

Lotman, Jurij, et al. "Theses on the Semiotic Study of Cultures (as Applied to Slavic Texts)." In *The Tell-Tale Sign: A Survey of Semiotics,* edited by Thomas A. Sebeok. Lisse, Netherlands: Peter de Ridder, 1975. 57–83.

Mack, Maynard, et al., eds. *The Norton Anthology of World Masterpieces: Expanded Edition.* Vol. 2. New York: Norton, 1995.

Mann, Thomas. *Gesammelte Werke in zwölf Bänden.* 12 vols. Frankfurt: Fischer, 1960–1974.

Marx, Karl, and Friedrich Engels. *Werke.* Vol. 4. Berlin: Dietz, 1959.

Meinecke, Friedrich. *Weltbürgertum und Nationalstaat: Studien zur Genesis des deutschen Nationalstaates.* 6th ed. Munich: R. Oldenbourg, 1922.

Meyer, Richard M. *Die Weltliteratur im zwanzigsten Jahrhundert: Vom deutschen Standpunkt aus betrachtet.* Stuttgart: Deutsche Verlags-Anstalt, 1913.

Miller, J. Hillis. "'World Literature' in the Age of Telecommunications." *World Literature Today* 74 (2000): 559–61.

Milosz, Czeslaw. *Road-Side Dog.* Translated by Czeslaw Milosz and Robert Hass. New York: Farrar, Straus, and Giroux, 1998.

Mommsen, Katharina. *Goethe und 1001 Nacht.* Frankfurt: Suhrkamp, 1981.

Morawe, Bodo. *Heines "Französische Zustände": Über die Fortschritte des Republikanismus und die anmarschierende Weltliteratur.* Heidelberg: Winter, 1997.

Moretti, Franco. "Conjectures on World Literature." *New Left Review.* 2nd ser., 1 (2000): 54–68.

Moulton, Richard G. *World Literature and Its Place in General Culture.* New York: Macmillan, 1911.

Mundt, Theodor. *Geschichte der Literatur der Gegenwart.* 2nd ed. Leipzig: Simion, 1853.

Muschg, Walter, and Emil Staiger, eds. *Weltliteratur: Festgabe für Fritz Strich zum 70. Geburtstag.* Bern: Francke, 1952.

Nagel, Bert. *Kafka und die Weltliteratur: Zusammenhänge und Wechselwirkungen.* Munich: Winkler, 1983.

Nancy, Jean-Luc. *Being Singular Plural*. Translated by Robert D. Richardson and Anne E. O'Byrne. Stanford: Stanford Univ. Press, 2000.

Nethersole, Reingard. "Models of Globalization." *PMLA* 116 (2001): 638–49.

Neubauer, John. "Writing and Teaching from Limbo." *PMLA* 118 (2003): 131–33.

Novalis. *Schriften: Die Werke Friedrich von Hardenbergs*. Vol. 3, edited by Richard Samuel et al. Stuttgart: Kohlhammer, 1960.

Otto, Regine. "Nachwort." In Johann Peter Eckermann, *Gespräche mit Goethe in den letzten Jahren seines Lebens,* 3rd ed., edited by Regine Otto and Peter Wersig. Munich: C. H. Beck, 1988. 679–703.

Paulson, William. *Literary Culture in a World Transformed: A Future for the Humanities*. Ithaca: Cornell Univ. Press, 2001.

Perkins, David, ed. *Theoretical Issues in Literary History*. Cambridge, Mass.: Harvard Univ. Press, 1991.

Pochmann, Henry A. *German Culture in America: Philosophical and Literary Influences, 1600–1900*. Madison: Univ. of Wisconsin Press, 1957.

Posnett, Hutcheson Macaulay. *Comparative Literature*. New York: D. Appleton, 1886.

Pratt, Mary Louise. "Humanities for the Future: Reflections on the Western Culture Debate at Stanford." *South Atlantic Quarterly* 89 (1990): 7–25.

Prawer, S. S. *Karl Marx and World Literature*. Oxford: Clarendon, 1976.

Reed, T. J., and Alexander Stillmark, eds. *Heine und die Weltliteratur*. Oxford: Legenda, 2000.

"Report on World Literature." *ACLA Newsletter* 19, no. 2 (1988): 1–3. Summary statement of the NEH Institute in the Theory and Teaching of World Literature (directed by Sarah Lawall), summer 1987, at the University of Massachusetts at Amherst.

Rosenberg, Ralph P. "The 'Great Books' in General Education." *Yearbook of Comparative and General Literature* 3 (1954): 20–35.

Ross, Kristin. "The World Literature and Cultural Studies Program." *Critical Inquiry* 19 (1993): 666–76.

Rousseau, Jean-Jacques. *Oeuvres complètes*. Vol. 3, edited by Bernard Gagnebin and Marcel Raymond. Paris: Gallimard, 1964.

Said, Edward W. *Culture and Imperialism*. New York: Knopf, 1993.

———. *Orientalism*. New York: Vintage Books, 1979.

Sammons, Jeffrey L. "Heine as *Weltbürger*? A Skeptical Inquiry." *Imagination and History: Selected Papers on Nineteenth-Century German Literature*. New York: Peter Lang, 1989. 97–122.

———. *Heinrich Heine: A Modern Biography*. Princeton: Princeton Univ. Press, 1979.

Schami, Rafik. *Damals dort und heute hier: Über Fremdsein*. Edited by Erich Jooß. Freiburg: Herder, 1998.

———. *Erzähler der Nacht*. Weinheim: Beltz and Gelberg, 1989; Munich: dtv, 2001.

———. *Vom Zauber der Zunge: Reden gegen das Verstummen*. 2nd ed. Frauenfeld: Im Waldgut, 1991.

Schami, Rafik, and Uwe-Michael Gutzschhahn. *Der geheime Bericht über den Dichter Goethe, der eine Prüfung auf einer arabischen Insel bestand*. Munich: Carl Hanser, 1999.

Schlegel, Friedrich. *Kritische Ausgabe*. Vol. 2., edited by Hans Eichner. Paderborn: Schöningh, 1967.

Schmeling, Manfred. "Ist Weltliteratur wünschenswert? Fortschritt und Stillstand im modernen Kulturbewußtsein." In *Weltliteratur heute: Konzepte und Perspektiven*, edited by Manfred Schmeling. Wurzburg: Königshausen and Neumann, 1995. 153–77.

———, ed. *Weltliteratur heute: Konzepte und Perspektiven*. Wurzburg: Königshausen and Neumann, 1995.

Schrimpf, Hans Joachim. "Goethes Begriff der Weltliteratur." In *Nationalismus in Germanistik und Dichtung: Dokumentation des Germanistentages in München vom 17.–22. Oktober 1966*, edited by Benno von Wiese and Rudolf Henß. Berlin: Erich Schmidt, 1967. 202–17.

———. *Goethes Begriff der Weltliteratur*. Stuttgart: Metzler, 1968.

Schulze, Hagen. *States, Nations and Nationalism: From the Middle Ages to the Present*. Translated by William E. Yuill. Oxford: Blackwell, 1996.

Seyhan, Azade. "Canons Against the Canon: Representations of Tradition and Modernity in Heine's Literary History." *Deutsche Vierteljahrsschrift* 63 (1989): 494–520.

———. *Writing Outside the Nation*. Princeton: Princeton Univ. Press, 2001.

Sharpe, Lesley, ed. *The Cambridge Companion to Goethe*. Cambridge: Cambridge Univ. Press, 2002.

Sheehan, James J. *German History, 1770–1866*. Oxford: Clarendon Press, 1989.

Spector, Scott. *Prague Territories: National Conflict and Cultural Innovation in Franz Kafka's Fin de Siècle*. Berkeley: Univ. of California Press, 2000.

Spengler, Oswald. *Der Untergang des Abendlandes: Umrisse einer Morphologie der Weltgeschichte*. Vol. 2, *Welthistorische Perspektiven*. Munich: Beck, 1922.

Spivak, Gayatri Chakravorty. *Death of a Discipline*. New York: Columbia Univ. Press, 2003.

Stauf, Renate. *Der problematische Europäer: Heinrich Heine im Konflikt zwischen Nationenkritik und gesellschaftlicher Utopie*. Heidelberg: Winter, 1997.

Steinecke, Hartmut, ed. *Literaturkritik des Jungen Deutschland: Entwicklungen— Tendenzen—Texte*. Berlin: Erich Schmidt, 1982.

———. "'Weltliteratur'—Zur Diskussion der Goetheschen 'Idee' im Jungen Deutschland." In *Das Junge Deutschland: Kolloquium zum 150. Jahrestag des Verbots vom 10. Dezember 1835,* edited be Joseph A. Kruse and Bernd Kortländer. Hamburg: Hoffmann and Campe, 1987. 155–72.

Steiner, George. "A Footnote to *Weltliteratur.*" *Le Mythe d'Étiemble: Hommages Études et Recherches.* Paris: Didier, 1979. 261–69.

Steinmetz, Horst. "Globalisierung und Literatur(geschichte)." In *Literatur im Zeitalter der Globalisierung,* edited by Manfred Schmeling et al. Wurzburg: Königshausen and Neumann, 2000. 189–201.

———. "Weltliteratur—Umriß eines literaturgeschichtlichen Konzepts." *Arcadia* 20 (1985): 2–19.

Strich, Fritz. *Goethe and World Literature.* Translated by C. A. M. SYM. London: Routledge and Kegan Paul, 1949.

———. *Goethe und die Schweiz.* Zurich: Artemis, 1949.

———. *Goethe und die Weltliteratur.* Bern: Francke, 1946.

———. "Weltliteratur und vergleichende Literaturgeschichte." In *Philosophie der Literaturwissenschaft,* edited by Emil Ermatinger. Berlin: Junker and Dünnhaupt, 1930. 422–41.

Theile, Wolfgang. "Vermittler französischer Literatur in Deutschland um 1800: Zur Vorgeschichte der Romanischen Philologie." *Germanisch-Romanische Monatsschrift* 73 (1992): 48–66.

Träger, Claus. "Weltgeschichte—Nationalliteratur, Nationalgeschichte—Weltliteratur." *Weimarer Beiträge* 20 (1974): 18–28.

Trilling, Lionel. "English Literature and American Education." *Sewanee Review* 66 (1958): 364–81.

Venuti, Lawrence. *The Scandals of Translation: Towards an Ethics of Difference.* London: Routledge, 1998.

Vinck, José J. de. "Anthologizing World Literature." In *No Small World: Visions and Revisions of World Literature,* edited by Michael Thomas Carroll. Urbana, Ill.: National Council of Teachers of English, 1996. 34–40.

Walstra, Kerst. "Eine Worthülse der Literaturdebatte? Kritische Anmerkungen zum Begriff *Weltliteratur.*" In *Weltliteratur heute: Konzepte und Perspektiven,* edited by Manfred Schmeling. Wurzburg: Königshausen and Neumann, 1995. 179–208.

Walz, John A. *German Influence in American Education and Culture.* Philadelphia: Carl Schurz Memorial Foundation, 1936.

Weber, Peter. "Funktionsverständnis in Goethes Auffassung von Weltliteratur." In *Funktion der Literatur: Aspekte, Probleme, Aufgaben,* edited by Dieter Schlenstedt et al. Berlin: Akademie, 1975. 133–39.

———. "Goethes Begriff von Weltliteratur: Historische und aktuelle Aspekte." *Weimarer Beiträge* 28 (1982): 90–105.

Weinrich, Harald. "Chamisso, Chamisso Authors, and Globalization." Introduced by Marshall Brown. Translated by Marshall Brown and Jane K. Brown. *PMLA* 119 (2004): 1336–46.

Weinsheimer, Joel C. *Gadamer's Hermeneutics: A Reading of "Truth and Method."* New Haven: Yale Univ. Press, 1985.

Weisstein, Ulrich. *Comparative Literature and Literary Theory: Survey and Introduction.* Translated by William Riggan and Ulrich Weisstein. Bloomington: Indiana Univ. Press, 1973.

Weitz, Hans-J. "'Weltliteratur' zuerst bei Wieland." *Arcadia* 22 (1987): 206–8.

Wellek, René. *A History of Modern Criticism: 1750–1950.* Vol. 1. New Haven: Yale Univ. Press, 1955.

Wienbarg, Ludolf. "Goethe und die Welt-Literatur (1835)." In *Literaturkritik des Jungen Deutschland: Entwicklungen—Tendenzen—Texte,* edited by Hartmut Steinecke. Berlin: Erich Schmidt, 1982. 155–64.

Wiese, Benno von. "Goethe und Heine als Europäer." *Signaturen: Zu Heinrich Heine und seinem Werk.* Berlin: Erich Schmidt, 1976. 196–220.

Wilde, Oscar. "*Intentions* (1891): The Critic as Artist." *The Artist as Critic: Critical Writings of Oscar Wilde.* Edited by Richard Ellmann. New York: Random House, 1969. 340–408.

Williams, Weldon M. "Intensive and Extensive Approaches in the Teaching of World Literature." In *The Teaching of World Literature: Proceedings of the Conference at the University of Wisconsin April 24–25, 1959,* edited by Haskell M. Block. Chapel Hill: Univ. of North Carolina Press, 1960. 73–81.

Wilson, W. Daniel. *Das Goethe-Tabu: Protest und Menschenrechte im klassischen Weimar.* Munich: dtv, 1999.

———. "Goethe and the Political World." In *The Cambridge Companion to Goethe,* edited by Lesley Sharpe. Cambridge: Cambridge Univ. Press, 2002. 207–18.

Woodmansee, Martha. *The Author, Art, and the Market: Rereading the History of Aesthetics.* New York: Columbia Univ. Press, 1994.

Žižek Slavoj, and F. W. J. von Schelling. *The Abyss of Freedom/Ages of the World: An Essay by Slavoj Žižek with the Text of Schelling's "Die Weltalter" (Second Draft, 1813) in English Translation by Judith Norman.* Ann Arbor: Univ. of Michigan Press, 1997.

Index

Adorno, Theodor, 118

Ahmad, Aijaz, 107, 147–48, 170n21

Alberson, Hazel S., 163n37

Albrow, Martin, 20

Aldridge, A. Owen, 107

Allen, Margaret Vanderhaar, 86, 162n8

alterity (otherness), 5, 7, 14, 15, 16, 17,
   25–28, 41, 42, 45, 46, 56, 80, 81, 82, 110,
   112–14, 116, 117, 125, 126, 137, 139, 140,
   141, 145, 149, 152n9, 152n15

American Comparative Literature Association. *See* Comparative Literature:
   and American Comparative Literature
   Association

Andersen, Hans Christian, 69

Anglade, René, 159n35

anthologies. *See* World Literature anthologies

area studies, 112

Arnim, Achim von, 38

Asman, Carrie, 153n30

Auerbach, Erich, 5–6, 14, 73, 116

August, Duke Carl, 22

Ausländerliteratur (literature of foreigners),
   124–25

Austen, Jane, 87

Bachmann-Medick, Doris, 157n8

Bakhtin, Mikhail, 7, 12, 15, 31–33, 34–35,
   36–37, 38, 39, 40, 79, 82, 125, 134

Barber, Benjamin R., 154n2

Barry, David, 136–37

Bauschinger, Sigrid, 162n6

Bean, Judith Mattson, 162n8

Beckett, Samuel, 81

Behler, Ernst, 12, 153n28

Beil, Else, 151n4

Bender, Helmut, 151n4

Benjamin, Walter, 36, 153n20

Bennett, William, 107, 108

Berczik, Arpad, 151n4, 153n24

Bergman, Jim, 117

Berman, Antoine, 41, 44–45

Bhabha, Homi K., 2, 29, 31, 32, 33, 34–35,
   39, 51, 119, 122, 138, 155n23, 157n8

Bible, the, 91, 143, 166n88

Birus, Hendrik, 36, 38, 43, 54–55, 80

Bleicher, Thomas, 156n62

Block, Haskell, 14, 103

Boisserée, Sulpiz, 22

Bollacher, Martin, 143, 151n6, 155n15, 159n4

Bolten, Jürgen, 167n7

Borges, Jorge Luis, 123